C. Wright Mills and the
Cuban Revolution

C. WRIGHT MILLS, PHOTO BY YAROSLAVA MILLS.

ENVISIONING CUBA

Louis A. Pérez Jr., editor

Envisioning Cuba publishes outstanding, innovative works in Cuban studies, drawn from diverse subjects and disciplines in the humanities and social sciences, from the colonial period through the post–Cold War era. Featuring innovative scholarship engaged with theoretical approaches and interpretive frameworks informed by social, cultural, and intellectual perspectives, the series highlights the exploration of historical and cultural circumstances and conditions related to the development of Cuban self-definition and national identity.

C. Wright Mills and the Cuban Revolution

An Exercise in the Art of Sociological Imagination

A. Javier Treviño

The University of North Carolina Press CHAPEL HILL

© 2017 The University of North Carolina Press
All rights reserved
Set in Espinosa Nova by Westchester Publishing Services
Manufactured in the United States of America

The University of North Carolina Press has been a member of the Green Press Initiative since 2003.

Library of Congress Cataloging-in-Publication Data
Names: Treviño, A. Javier, 1958– author.
Title: C. Wright Mills and the Cuban Revolution : an exercise in the art of sociological imagination / A. Javier Treviño.
Other titles: Envisioning Cuba.
Description: Chapel Hill : University of North Carolina Press, [2017] | Series: Envisioning Cuba | Includes bibliographical references and index.
Identifiers: LCCN 2016047327 | ISBN 9781469633091 (cloth : alk. paper) | ISBN 9781469633107 (pbk : alk. paper) | ISBN 9781469633114 (ebook)
Subjects: LCSH: Mills, C. Wright (Charles Wright), 1916–1962. Listen, Yankee. | Mills, C. Wright (Charles Wright), 1916–1962. | Cuba—History—Revolution, 1959—Interviews. | Sociologists—United States—History—20th century.
Classification: LCC HN203.5 .T74 2017 | DDC 306.097291—dc23 LC record available at https://lccn.loc.gov/2016047327

Cover illustrations: Photographs by C. Wright Mills. © 2017 Nikolas Mills. All rights reserved.

Contents

Chronology of Events vii

Introduction 1

CHAPTER ONE
The Cuban Summer of C. Wright Mills 6

CHAPTER TWO
Insurrection, Revolution, Invasion 18

CHAPTER THREE
Mills on Individuals, Intellectuals, and Interviewing 35

CHAPTER FOUR
Recorded Interviews with Cuban Officials 53

CHAPTER FIVE
Recorded Interviews with Cuban Citizens 76

CHAPTER SIX
Fellow-Traveling with Fidel 109

CHAPTER SEVEN
The Book That Sold Half a Million Copies 131

CHAPTER EIGHT
Confronting the Enemy 159

Acknowledgments 177
Appendix 1 179
Appendix 2 181
A Note on the Interviews 183

Biographical Notes 185
Notes 191
Bibliography 221
Index 227

A gallery of images follows page 108

Chronology of Events

1948	Publication of *The New Men of Power: America's Labor Leaders*
1950	Publication of *Puerto Rican Journey: New York's Newest Migrants* by Mills, Clarence Senior, and Rose Kohn Goldsen
September 1951	Publication of *White Collar: The American Middle Classes*
March 9, 1952	Fulgencio Batista seizes power in Cuba
July 26, 1953	Students led by Fidel Castro attack the Moncada barracks in Santiago de Cuba in an attempt to spark a revolt against the Batista dictatorship
September 1953	Publication of *Character and Social Structure: The Psychology of Social Institutions* by Gerth and Mills
October 16, 1953	Fidel Castro makes "History Will Absolve Me" defense speech. Castro and thirty-one Moncadistas are sentenced to the Presidio Modelo prison on the Isle of Pines.
April 1956	Publication of *The Power Elite*
December 2, 1956	Fidel Castro, Ernesto "Ché" Guevara, and eighty other guerrilla fighters disembark from the yacht *Granma* in Oriente province.
May 19, 1957	Robert Taber's documentary *Rebels of the Sierra Maestra: The Story of Cuba's Jungle Fighters* airs on CBS
1958	Publication of *The Causes of World War Three*
1959	Publication of *The Sociological Imagination*
January 1, 1959	Batista flees Cuba, and the 26th of July Movement, led by Fidel Castro, assumes power
May 17, 1959	The Revolutionary government implements the Agrarian Reform Law limiting the size of farms to 3,333 acres and real estate to 1,000 acres

January 1960	Robert Taber and Alan Sager found the Fair Play for Cuba Committee
January–February 1960	Planes from Florida engage in bombing and sabotage missions to Cuba
January–March 1960	Mills teaches a seminar on Marxism at the National University of Mexico
February 4–13, 1960	Soviet Deputy Premier Anastas Mikoyan visits Cuba to negotiate economic and trade agreements with Castro
February 22–March 20, 1960	Jean-Paul Sartre and Simone de Beauvoir visit Cuba
March 4, 1960	French munitions freighter *La Coubre* explodes while being unloaded in Havana harbor
March 17, 1960	Eisenhower approves plan for the invasion of Cuba by exiles
April 20–May 20, 1960	Mills travels to the Soviet Union for the first time
July 9, 1960	Soviet Premier Nikita Khrushchev announces that the Soviet Union will provide Cuba with military aid in case of U.S. attack
Summer 1960	Mills meets with Ian Ballantine about publishing *Listen, Yankee*
August 8–24, 1960	Mills visits Cuba and interviews Cuban revolutionaries
September 9, 1960	Confidential informant "T1" tells the FBI that Mills had been to Cuba and conducted interviews with Cuban officials
September 1960	Castro addresses the UN General Assembly. Stays at Theresa Hotel in Harlem and meets with Mills and others at a reception at the hotel.
October 19, 1960	The United States imposes an embargo on exports to Cuba (except for food and medicine)
October 26, 1960	FBI Director J. Edgar Hoover reviews manuscript of *Listen, Yankee*

November 1960	Publication of *Listen, Yankee: The Revolution in Cuba*. John F. Kennedy is elected president. Mills delivers talk, "How to Improve Relations with Cuba and South America," to an audience of Americans for Democratic Action in New York City.
December 1960	Excerpts from *Listen, Yankee* appear in *Harper's* magazine. Mills suffers a major heart attack. The New York FBI office begins a discreet preliminary investigation of Mills.
January 1961	Lawsuit against Mills and Ballantine Books, publisher of *Listen, Yankee*, is filed. The Eisenhower administration severs all diplomatic relations with Cuba and bans travel to the island. Cuban government launches Literacy Campaign.
April 17, 1961	Invasion of Cuba at the Bay of Pigs
April 24, 1961	Mills and family leave for Europe and the Soviet Union
April 27, 1961	First and second editions of the Spanish translation of *Listen, Yankee—Escucha, yanqui*—are issued in Mexico by the publishing house Fondo de Cultura Económica
June 1961	Mills meets with Jean-Paul Sartre and Simone de Beauvoir in Paris
July 1961	Publication of the third edition of *Escucha, yanqui* with the update, "Escucha otra vez, yanqui"
December 2, 1961	Castro declares, "I am a Marxist-Leninist"
Late March / early April 1962	Publication of *The Marxists*
January 27, 1962	Mills and family return to the United States
March 20, 1962	Mills dies of heart failure

April 16, 1962	The New York FBI office submits its closing report on Mills
December 17, 2014	President Barack Obama announces the restoration of full diplomatic relations with Cuba, after fifty-five years of antagonism

C. Wright Mills and the
Cuban Revolution

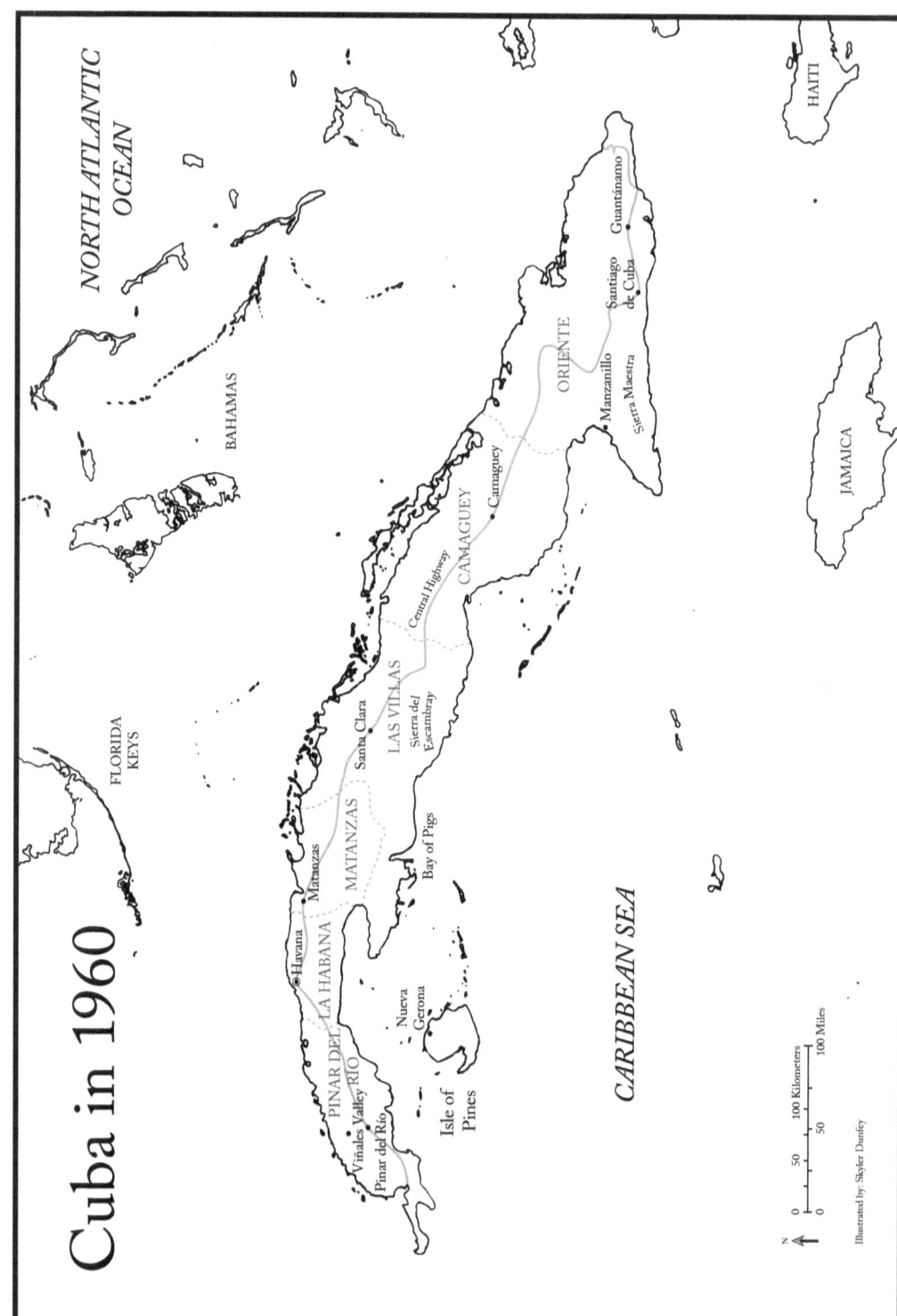

Introduction

The North American sociologist C. Wright Mills traveled to Cuba, once, to experience firsthand that island's transition to a new sovereign state, some eighteen months after the triumph of its Revolution. Upon returning to the United States, Mills wrote a small paperback on much of what he had heard and seen, which he titled *Listen, Yankee: The Revolution in Cuba*.[1] As he explains in the opening sentence, "This book reflects the mood as well as the contents of discussions and interviews with rebel soldiers and intellectuals, officials, journalists and professors in Cuba, during August, 1960."

On first reading *Listen, Yankee* as a graduate student and shortly before undertaking my first trip to Cuba in 1987 I wondered if I would be seeing some of the same places that Mills had visited on his trek through the island over a quarter century before. There were those out-of-the-way cities like Manzanillo and Santiago de Cuba, but also the more well-known locations of Havana and the Sierra Maestra, and the exotically named Isle of Pines. I knew from the book's foreword—the "Note to the Reader, I"— that Mills had spoken with many "Cubans close to events." This included discussions with most of the leaders of the Revolutionary government like Fidel Castro and Ernesto "Ché" Guevara. I later learned that he had gone there with a wire recorder in hand and speculated on what those interviews had revealed to him. Who exactly were the Cubans "close to events" with whom he spoke, other than disembodied names that he lists in the note thanking them for their generosity, patience, and time? What *in particular* did they tell him about their lives—their moods and wishes, their aspirations and discontents? And what about the Revolution—an event that was still very much in the making during Mills's sojourn to the Caribbean island?

Then there was the enigmatic best-selling paperback itself—presented from the perspective of the Cuban revolutionary—that Mills wrote within a matter of weeks. Was *Listen, Yankee* a work in sociology? It certainly didn't read like his previous analytical studies, *White Collar* and *The Power Elite*. Was it a polemical academic treatise like his famous volume *The Sociological Imagination*? Perhaps it was a manifesto of sorts, or a piece of journalism (in the pejorative sense of the term), or a political "pamphlet" as he liked to call it, in the tradition of *The Causes of World War Three*, which Mills had published a couple of years before and for which he was judged by some to be a *touche-à-tout*. And that audacious title; it seemed to intentionally mock North American—*Yankee*—readers, demanding their attention with the imperative, *Listen!*

Many years passed, during which time I reread *Listen, Yankee* in preparation for a book I was writing on Mills's social thought. Then one pleasant Sunday afternoon in 2014, as my wife and I, over coffee and cookies with Kathryn—Mills's younger daughter—and her husband, poured over photographs that Kathryn had taken on her recent visit to Cuba, I wondered aloud about those long-ago interviews and their recordings. A week or so later I was delighted to receive in the mail CD copies of the original audiotapes. (Later, Kathryn provided several sheets of contact strip proofs of photographs taken by Mills in Cuba, which supplied an additional wealth of information.) If there are other audio recordings of their kind, I am not aware of them. I here make them available—transcribed and translated—for the first time, with extensive annotations to explain and contextualize their content.

It is impossible to say exactly how many people Mills spoke with during the course of his two-week research expedition in Cuba. He audiotaped at least eight interviews. Though Mills spoke with many people on the island, and took copious notes on what they said, he did not record them all. This is likely the case with the highest-ranking Cuban officials. For example, Saul Landau points out that as Mills was leaving to interview Ché Guevara he took with him a notebook and a couple of cameras, but Landau does not mention the wire recorder.[2]

Mills interviewed and recorded people from different walks of life and social statuses, those who worked for the Revolutionary government and those who did not, the educated and the uneducated, six men and three women.

One purpose of this book is to present the opinions, perspectives, and comments of the Cubans who spoke with Mills in the summer of 1960. As such it is also important to "hear" Mills as an expert interviewer and ascertain how he used what he learned from his informants to write *Listen, Yankee*. Indeed, the interviews themselves are a study in methodology that give a glimpse into Mills's own techniques (conscious or otherwise) of investigation: whom he interviewed, which lines of inquiry he pursued, how he managed and timed the interviews, and how he interacted with the respondents.

I have organized the book as follows. The first three chapters provide the historical and theoretical background in which to situate all of the aforementioned. Chapter 1 places Mills's experiences in Cuba in the larger sociohistorical contemporaneous context. It not only depicts the major social and political transformations in the revolutionary process that were transpiring at the time Mills was on the island, it also considers wider global events of that summer, against the backdrop of Cold War tensions, of pertinence to Castro's Cuba. In addition, it describes the effervescent mood that permeated the island during his visit.

Chapter 2 furnishes a sociohistorical account of those main events and turning points of the armed struggle against the tyranny of Fulgencio Batista, beginning with Fidel Castro's first assault on the dictator's troops in 1953. It also examines how the Revolution was being made at the time that Mills visited Cuba in 1960 as well as how the revolutionary project was threatened by the U.S.-sponsored military invasion at the Bay of Pigs in 1961. Thus, the main period in Cuban history analyzed here is roughly between 1953 and 1961.

Chapter 3 examines the conceptual and empirical methods Mills applied in understanding the Cuban revolutionaries, whose thoughts and sentiments he so eloquently and passionately expressed in *Listen, Yankee*. These have to do with his view of individuals as seekers of freedom, of intellectuals as agents of social change, and of interviewing as a way of discerning people's character structure—their symbols, their self-images, their personalities.

Chapters 4 and 5, where those particular Cuban testimonies are presented, form the book's core. They are intended to show that the Cubans Mills spoke with, and whom he presents in *Listen, Yankee* in composite portrait, are not anonymous, disembodied revolutionaries, but real people with particular hopes, dreams, and fears. In all cases I have reproduced the interviews either in full, or nearly in full, for two main reasons. First, they constitute the primary data on which Mills relied to compose the unique narrative—the "voice" of the Cuban revolutionary—which he used to great effect. Indeed, in the notes and acknowledgments to *Listen, Yankee* Mills makes it clear that while he relied on various materials to write the book—memoranda and statistical collections compiled from various Cuban sources, scholarly articles and books on Latin America, books on the Cuban Revolution, and historical accounts of U.S.-Cuban relations—"my fundamental sources, however, are my own interviews and observations in Cuba." Additionally, since the voice of the Cuban revolutionary is an ideal type of sorts—and many passages in *Listen, Yankee* are, in fact, composite interviews—it is important to know what exactly Mills's respondents said to him. All of his interviewees' responses form a conglomerate, and Mills (with only one brief exception) does not quote them in the book. He explains in the foreword that, "having been given the privilege of seeing whatever I asked to see and candid answers to all the questions I asked, I do not feel direct quotation is permissible."[3] Thus, identifying the interviewees and presenting their specific words, the tone and quality of their arguments, addresses the question of who said what and how.

Similarly, Chapter 6 consists of two transcriptions of recordings that Mills made detailing his experiences and conversations with Fidel Castro. These are important not only because they offer a firsthand account of Mills's conference with the prime minister, but because they also reveal Mills's impressions of Castro and the revolution he was leading. Mills, who did not speak Spanish, spent three-and-a-half eighteen-hour days traveling and conversing with Castro and Juan Arcocha, who served as his translator. On at least one occasion Mills took meticulous notes of such a conversation, but did not record it; later that day he made an audio recording of those notes as he dictated them onto the recorder. I have transcribed these verbatim in Chapter 6. In addition, in that same chapter is another recording that Mills made of interactions Castro had with military men on the Isle of Pines.

Because this book is also very much "a book about a book," the last two chapters tell the story of *Listen, Yankee*—its contents, but also its production and reception. Chapter 7 examines how the information conveyed and topics covered in the interviews led Mills to construct *Listen, Yankee*'s full-throated message of revolutionary cry. As a technical extension of this, and as a way of verifying the authenticity of the message Mills articulates in *Listen, Yankee*, in Appendix 1 selected passages from the interviews are compared with parallel passages from *Listen, Yankee*. Also included in Chapter 7 is a transcription of a recording Mills made of a meeting he had with the publisher, Ian Ballantine, laying out his vision of, and production plans for, *Listen, Yankee*. Chapter 8, the final chapter, looks at the considerable consequences this mass-market paperback had on Mills, personally and professionally. That chapter includes a transcription of a telephone conversation, tape-recorded by Mills, with a mysterious "Mr. Hadley," who was likely an FBI agent assigned to investigate Mills and his ties to the Cuban revolutionaries.

Finally, as a kind of subtext, this book also recounts the experiences of four central figures whose lives became inextricably intertwined during that fateful summer of 1960. First and foremost, of course, is C. Wright Mills, the irascible, larger-than-life sociologist from Columbia University, who, until his death in 1962, garnered a surprising notoriety for writing about the early Cuban Revolution. Absolutely central to any account of the Revolution—including this one—is one of the most influential orators and leaders in the Americas, the indefatigable Fidel Castro, who made the Revolution and continued as its active guide until his retirement in 2008. There is also the indispensable and revealing Juan Arcocha, the young Cuban journalist who served as interpreter to both Mills and Castro during their discussions and Mills's peregrinations through the island and who, in 1971, went into self-imposed exile. But there is another figure—largely in the background, but very pertinent to this record: the French existentialist philosopher and one of the twentieth century's most emblematic intellectuals, Jean-Paul Sartre. All four of them—Mills, Castro, Arcocha, and Sartre—had different and complicated relationships with each other. But the singular event that compelled their biographies to intersect at a decisive moment in the history of Cold War geopolitics—with its attendant animosities and intrigues—was the Cuban Revolution.

Setting aside the detailed richness of Mills's Cuba interviews, we may ask: Isn't it the case that no matter how much notoriety *Listen, Yankee* garnered at the time of its publication, no matter how much of a bestseller it was and how informative it may have been to the North American public, it nonetheless lacks the conceptual substance and sociological sophistication of Mills's earlier works and holds, in fact, "only historical interest today"?[4] This is indeed the case, and so a third aim of this book is to tell the story behind the story; that is, to hear the voices and know the inner lives of the human variety that contributed to the making and the attempted unmaking of *Listen, Yankee*. These include the voices and inner lives of the Cuban revolutionaries, to be sure, but also of the critics, reviewers, publishers, politicians, federal agents, exiles, defectors, intellectuals, journalists, novelists, friends and foes, and of course, Mills himself.[5] This then is a study in historical sociology, but one that quite consciously considers biography in the context of social structure. Put another way, the topic of C. Wright Mills and the Cuban Revolution provides the opportunity for engaging in an exercise in the art of sociological imagination.

CHAPTER ONE

The Cuban Summer of C. Wright Mills

On encountering the numerous writings and communications by C. Wright Mills on the Cuban Revolution, the unwary reader could be forgiven for thinking that Mills had spent many long years immersed in its study. Quite the contrary; from the time Cuba first came to Mills's political awareness—when he began clipping newspaper articles about the situation on the island—until his death—by which time he had published *Listen, Yankee* and delivered many talks on the subject—was only a two-year period. Shortly after the victory of the Revolution, Mills had frequently been questioned in Latin America about his and his country's stand on the new government of Fidel Castro: "Until the summer of 1960, I had never been in Cuba, or even thought about it much. In fact, the previous fall, when I was in Brazil, and in the spring of 1960, when I was in Mexico for several months, I was embarrassed not to have any firm attitude towards the Cuban revolution. For in both Rio de Janeiro and Mexico City, Cuba was of course a major topic of discussion. But I did not know what was happening there, much less what I might think about it, and I was then busy with other studies."[1]

The impassioned interest of Latin American intellectuals and journalists on the subject, which seemed fundamental in Latin American life, kindled Mills's desire to go to the Caribbean island and write about its revolution in the making. Indeed, of the three Western revolutions of the twentieth century, the Mexican (1910), the Russian (1917), and the Cuban (1959), only the latter was temporally accessible to Mills. And while Mills was not a political journalist in the manner of John Reed, he nonetheless wanted to report on—wanted to *understand*—the social forces that had produced the Cuban Revolution, and that were still in operation. And so after intensive preparation, he journeyed to the Caribbean that summer of 1960 to be an authentic witness to the incipient Cuban experiment.

Preparing for Cuba

Prior to his Cuban sojourn, Mills's two principal Latin American concerns had been Mexico, where he had spent several months in early 1960 teaching a seminar in Marxism at the National University of Mexico, and before that, Puerto Rico, where he had visited in the late 1940s when researching his study on Puerto Rican migrants.[2] Indeed, according to historian Rafael Rojas, the central referent of Spanish and U.S. colonialism in *Listen, Yankee* had its origins, in large part, in the Puerto Rican project.[3] But, in truth, Mills's first foray into the Latino/Latin American cultural scene was not with Puerto Ricans but with Mexican Americans. Mills, whose parents had lived in South Texas during the 1930s, believed he had a grasp on the character structure of Mexican American youth and based this understanding on three or four years of experience he had with the nightlife of Mexican Americans in San Antonio, Texas.[4]

In any event, Mills now read deliberately all he could on one small island in Latin America—Cuba—and began to discover that something very interesting was happening there. Because, at the time, there were only a few books he could consult for information on the Cuban revolutionary project and to guide his investigations, it is worth briefly considering the three volumes that Mills read in preparation for his trip.

The first of these, *Castro, Cuba, and Justice*, by the renowned *Chicago Sun-Times* correspondent Ray Brennan, who devoted four months to researching the book, is a journalistic account sympathetic to the 26th of July Movement's insurgence against Batista. Brennan spent many weeks with Castro in Havana, in Santiago, in the Sierra Maestra, and later in New York. Highly adulatory of the rebel leader, Brennan praises his "courage, deep loyalty to friends, almost limitless endurance of hardships and sacrifices, his love of freedom, and his revolutionary spirit." Written somewhat like a factual novel, with liberal use of contemporaneous American colloquialisms, Brennan creates dialogue that very likely happened, but probably not in the exact words in which he presents it. The book gives highly readable accounts of various participants in the armed struggle—both Fidelistas and Batistianos—with whom Brennan spoke. A graphic, lurid chapter on the various tortures and atrocities perpetrated by the Batista regime against insurgents and ordinary citizens was likely included to justify the relentless firing-squad shootings of Batista war criminals that followed the victory of the Revolution and to underscore the notion of "justice" in the book's title—a notion that was quickly beginning to take on an ominous overtone to many North Americans as the summary trials and mass executions continued. Perhaps of most help to Mills were those questions of immediate relevance that Brennan posed about the bourgeoning revolution: What kind of man is Castro, really? Is there a danger of his becoming another Batista? How much communistic influence, if any, is he up against? How much did the

Communists contribute to winning the war? What is going to happen to American business interests in Cuba? Will it ever be possible to build a stable Cuban economy on the foundation of ruination left by the Batista administration?

Another book that Mills consulted was *Fidel Castro: Rebel-Liberator or Dictator?* Written by Latin America correspondent Jules Dubois, who covered the civil war for the *Chicago Tribune*, it chronicles the insurrection and revolutionary events on the Cuban island up to March 1959. Perhaps more than any other journalist writing about the Revolution, Dubois (who may have been an asset for the Central Intelligence Agency) had the most impeccable credentials, coupled with a fearlessness that allowed him access to central actors and events denied other correspondents. For example, in 1957 he interviewed, in their hideouts, first, Armando Hart, the most hunted urban guerrilla in Havana at the time, and later, Vilma Espín, organizer of the women's underground resistance movement. Dubois had spoken with many of the top guerrilla fighters, including several times with Raúl Castro, and was the reporter to be granted the first exclusive postvictory interview with Fidel Castro. He also interviewed Fulgencio Batista, was eyewitness to many of the historical events in the making of the Revolution, and was presumably well acquainted with Ché Guevara's father in Argentina. Dubois's book, which may be regarded as a sort of biography of Fidel Castro, reads much like a war correspondent's dispatches from the front. It was assembled fast, in twenty days, and published fast, a few days thereafter. Though the book was largely sympathetic to Castro and the early Revolution, shortly after its publication Dubois became fiercely anti-Castro, and by November 1960 he was writing editorials highly disparaging of Mills and *Listen, Yankee*.

But the volume that Mills judged to the best of the lot, and that provided him with the most recent account of events (it reports on developments up to May 1960), was Leo Huberman and Paul M. Sweezy's *Cuba: The Anatomy of a Revolution*. In a preliminary draft of *Listen, Yankee* Mills wrote of the Huberman and Sweezy work: "It is a good book, and I have drawn upon it for details as well as for more general viewpoints."[5]

Contrary to Brennan and Dubois—who as journalists embedded with the insurrectionists and rebels reported on the actions of *individuals*—Huberman and Sweezy, as economic analysts, scrutinized more closely the nascent revolutionary *society*. By further contrast, Mills, as sociologist, considered both the *character structure* (the conduct patterns, self-images, and aspirations) of the individuals with whom he had discussions, as well as the *social structure* (the norms, values, and institutions) of the new Cuban society.

In any event, Huberman and Sweezy, coeditors of the important socialist magazine *Monthly Review*, which they cofounded in 1949, were both acclaimed socialists and readily admit that "we ourselves, as veterans of the left-wing movement, felt thoroughly at home in the intellectual and moral atmosphere of the Cuban Revolution, much more so than we do in that of the 'affluent society.'"[6] Moreover, they characterize the new regime as *socialist* and speculate that it would remain so, given the government's increasing nationalization of various industries.

Of particular relevance to Mills's pre-arrival preparation is that Huberman and Sweezy raise several questions that he may have been inspired to further pursue with his interviewees: Are the Communists working themselves into a position from which they can take over control of the revolutionary regime? As the momentum of the Revolution dies down, will there be a need for a cohesive political apparatus as an intermediary between leadership and masses? Will the 26th of July Movement become a genuine political party? In addition, the authors also provided an agenda of sorts that could have inspired Mills in his research: interviewing top government officials such as Armando Hart, Enrique Oltuski, and Ché Guevara, and visiting the Camilo Cienfuegos School City.

Huberman and Sweezy had previously met the Cuban Ambassador to the UN, Raúl Roa Kourí, at the *Monthly Review* bookshop in New York City. Impressed by their sincere interest in the Revolution's progress, Roa Kourí urged Ché Guevara to invite the economists to Cuba.[7] The pair spent several weeks on the island during the spring of 1960 researching their book. Later, in the autumn, they returned to the Caribbean nation for several weeks in order to prepare a second edition that included an updated epilogue. Thus, they were in Cuba just shortly *before* and then shortly *after* Mills's arrival in the summer. They were compelled to return to the island, given that the stages and phases of the revolutionary process were morphing quickly, too quickly, to properly do justice to any attempt at characterizing it: "In fact, hardly anything about it is the same—its personnel, its organization, its aims, even the personality of its leaders have all undergone more or less radical changes. Fidel Castro has learned much and changed accordingly in the brief period of less than a year and a half."[8] This situation of social events moving at astonishing speed was one that Mills, qua sociologist, could hardly resist: he needed to analyze the Revolution's dynamic course of syncopated evolution, to comprehend the improvisational qualities of a going revolution.[9]

Revolutionary Transformations and Cold War Events

Irving Louis Horowitz is correct in stating that "Mills was reacting to the first years of a revolution whose structure had not yet crystallized."[10] But what exactly were those major transformations, those pivotal social and economic reforms in the revolutionary process that were taking place *at the time Mills was on the island* that would solidify Cuba's social structure? Working from Huberman and Sweezy's before-and-after comparative impressions, two interrelated developments are salient.

The first is that the process of *nationalization*—of expropriating foreign and domestic enterprises and putting them in the hands of the Revolutionary government—was speeding up, entering its advanced stages. Indeed, just a few days before Mills arrived in the country, the new regime had suddenly seized a large part of U.S. corporate holdings on the island, notably, the electric power company, the telephone company, the oil refineries, and all of the sugar mills. The great nationalization wave crested in late October, when Castro expropriated all foreign enterprises operating in Cuba, including 166 U.S.-owned companies. All this was in reprisal against U.S. economic aggression intended to cripple the island's economy; first by having U.S.-owned Cuban oil companies—namely, Esso, Texaco, and Shell—refuse to refine oil imported into Cuba and then by drastically reducing the sugar quota, the amount of sugar the United States would import from Cuba. In an escalating series of moves and countermoves between Havana and Washington, the Eisenhower administration had placed an embargo on exports to the Cuban island except for medicines, medical supplies, and foodstuffs. The following year the petulant tug-of-war that led to the severing of all relations between the two countries could be assessed as follows: "If the United States is now alarmed by the 'radicalization' of the Cuban Revolution, it has itself to thank; for most of the radical measures of the Castro regime have been taken in direct reaction to threats from Washington."[11]

The other defining change, stemming in no small measure from the process of nationalization, was the formation of a significant and identifiable *counterrevolutionary sentiment* expressed by the landlords whose income had been cut, the landowners whose estates had been expropriated, the bankers and business owners whose profits had been curtailed, and the professional and civic leaders who had lost their political clout. They amounted to a considerable and growing number of dissidents and defectors. Inside Cuba, this counterrevolutionary drift was not a coordinated movement and therefore of no real threat to the regime. Outside the country, however, it was a different matter; indeed, the Cuban exile community in Miami was already plotting a comeback. They were being incited and abetted by the U.S. government to attack and encroach on the island. Thus, at least as indicated by the audiotapes, Mills spent more time discussing counterrevolutionary plots with his interviewees—of an impending invasion of Cuba by the United States—than he did the expropriation of U.S.-owned properties. But he and his interviewees had justifiable cause for concern, and apparently so did Soviet Premier Nikita Khrushchev, who, only a few weeks before, in a speech made in Moscow, had warned the United States that "Soviet artillerymen can support the Cuban people with their rocket fire, should the aggressive forces in the Pentagon dare to start intervention against Cuba." What is more, Mills well understood the dynamics of counterrevolution, which he and Hans Gerth had defined as "the organized and successful endeavor of previous ruling groups to re-establish themselves in power in the name of the old or newly wrought legitimations."[12] The Cubans who had defected and who had taken the path of exile were indeed being organized in Florida—politically and militarily by the Central Intelligence Agency—but their endeavors to regain power in Cuba would ultimately be wholly unsuccessful and, indeed, nothing short of humiliating.

Other significant developments during the summer of 1960 of pertinence to Castro's Cuba include the following: On May 17 the CIA established Radio Swan, a radio station broadcasting to Cuba that was a part of the Eisenhower-approved plan for covert operations to undermine the Revolutionary regime. In June the Frente Revolucionario Democrático was formed by Cuban exiles in the United States intending to establish an invasion force to overthrow Castro. Also that month, U.S. embassy legal attachés Edwin L. Sweet and William G. Friedman were arrested at a meeting of counterrevolutionary conspirators and charged with encouraging terrorist acts, granting asylum, financing subversive publications, and smuggling weapons. They were immediately expelled from Cuba. On July 8 the Soviet Union announced that it would purchase 700,000 tons of sugar—Cuba's biggest export crop—to cover the deficit created by the U.S. quota system. And in what is doubtless one of the most bizarre and harebrained schemes perpetrated by the CIA, around the time Mills was making his trek through Cuba, the CIA's Office of Security initiated a plot to hire mafiosi, who had

had their syndicate interests driven out of their Havana gambling casinos by the Castro government, to "eliminate" the Cuban leader.

Global events of that summer—of secondary significance to the situation in Cuba but of supreme importance in the context of Cold War tensions—included the shooting down, over Soviet airspace, of a U-2 spy plane flown by CIA pilot Francis Gary Powers; the Congo declaring its independence from Belgium and aligning itself with Moscow; and tens of thousands of leftist Japanese students holding massive street demonstrations in Tokyo in protest of U.S. military bases in that country.

In broader view, the Cold War period between 1953 and 1961 was largely defined by the looming threat of nuclear war: the annihilation of the two world superpowers, the United States and the Soviet Union, and, for that matter, of most of the planet. Eisenhower's main foreign policy in this regard was the "containment" of Soviet expansion through "brinksmanship." This meant that, given its superior nuclear arsenal, the United States would push the Soviet Union to the threshold of war in order to exact concessions. In addition, there was the idea—or more accurately, the *hope*—that the USSR's inefficient economy would collapse in its attempt to keep up with the "arms race." Thus, during this period the Eisenhower administration increased the number of nuclear warheads from 1,000 to 18,000, and in 1961 deployed fifteen Jupiter ballistic missiles in Turkey, aimed at the USSR's cities, including Moscow. For all this, Eisenhower, in his January 17, 1961, farewell presidential address to the nation, warned against the bourgeoning "military-industrial complex"—the insidious power of the economic military alliance, the power-profit relationship between the U.S. munitions makers and the Pentagon—which Mills had been decrying for years.[13] Indeed, Mills, and many other American and European intellectuals, called for a politics of responsibility in order to avoid a total and absurd nuclear war. In *The Causes of World War Three*, Mills urgently informs his readers that the United States and the Soviet Union shared too closely the "military metaphysic," a view through which all global issues are seen in terms of national security and defense.[14] As such, he calls upon the clergy, scientists, and the intellectual community to take a responsible and moral stand on the issue of peace and nuclear disarmament. Mills endeavors to persuade American and Soviet intellectuals to prevail over the high immorality and crackpot realism of their respective countries' power elites—in Washington and in the Kremlin—and to, by their own efforts, sue for a separate peace. Only in this way, Mills argued, could the drift toward mass destruction be reversed. Mills's clarion call had a significant impact in galvanizing the antinuclear peace movement in the United States and abroad. But a mere four years after the publication of the *Causes* and two years after the appearance of *Listen, Yankee*, the two superpowers, and the world, came closest to the brink of nuclear Armageddon than at any other moment in history. It was over the installation of nuclear-armed Soviet missiles on the island of Cuba.

Witnessing the New Cuba

These events and potentialities notwithstanding, Mills's objective in going to Cuba, as he declares it in *Listen, Yankee*, was a relatively simple one: to find out the truth about what is really happening in Cuba and tell it to the North American people. He traveled through the island during the sixteen days of August 8–24, 1960, on a tour organized by Robert Taber, who was a founding member of a group of intellectuals and activists in solidarity with Cuba, the Fair Play for Cuba Committee (FPCC), and by Raúl Roa Kourí, who was the high-raking Cuban official in charge of relations with the FPCC. Taber, a CBS journalist, had achieved some notoriety for having interviewed, in 1957, Fidel Castro in his hideout, deep in the mountains of the Sierra Maestra. Roa Kourí, a diplomat, was attached to Cuba's permanent mission at the United Nations, where he served as representative of the Economic and Finance Committee. In July 1960, Roa Kourí, through the good offices of Taber, contacted Mills. Over lunch in Manhattan, the three men discussed the possibility of Mills making a tour of Cuba similar to the one previously made by Huberman and Sweezy, which had been arranged by Roa Kourí. Mills became enthused with the notion and agreed to again meet with Taber and Roa Kourí after he had a better sense of when he could travel. After putting in order matters pertaining to his classes at Columbia University, Mills contacted Roa Kourí, who then arranged his trip and contacts in Havana.[15]

But Mills was far from unique in traveling to the "Pearl of the Antilles." Indeed, shortly after the success of the Revolution, thousands of young people from around the globe flocked to the island, wanting to become directly involved in revolutionary work,[16] and Taber, under the auspices of the FPCC, was organizing many of these trips. Indeed, Cuba, at the time, offered what Rafael Rojas calls "a spectacle of ideas" and, as such, became a place of pilgrimage for students and intellectuals of various types of socialist thought.[17] But these trips were not mere junkets for hedonistic undergraduates on spring break seeking bacchanalian pleasure, nor for holidaymakers wanting to sun themselves on Varadero Beach. In fact, when in September 1960 a Columbia University student asked Fidel Castro whether Cuba intended to establish a student-exchange program, the prime minister replied: "Yes, we are setting up a special institute to handle student visitors, an institute to promote friendship between peoples. Special prices and facilities are already available to visiting students. We welcome all visitors, especially students who are interested in studying our social problems, and have not come to Cuba just to have a good time."[18]

In addition to Mills, a host of renowned, politically progressive artists, writers, and thinkers made the pilgrimage to the Caribbean nation over the course of the first five or so years of its Revolution. These included Leroi Jones (later Amiri Baraka), Lawrence Ferlinghetti, Pablo Neruda, Octavio Paz, Mario Vargas Llosa, Allen Ginsberg, Oscar Lewis, Gabriel García Márquez, Graham Greene, Carlos Fuentes, and no less a personage than Jean-Paul Sartre, who was personally invited to visit the new Cuba by the editor of the newspaper *Revolución*, Carlos Franqui. The desire to have Sartre, and also Mills, come to the Cuban island was rooted in the realization that it was necessary to invite famous intellectuals with the goal that they would experience the Revolution, appraise it, and be influenced by it, and refer to it with greater legitimacy than could other observers. Sartre, who was received as an intellectual superstar in Cuba, was invited there not only because of his fame and his prominence as a man of the Left, but, most significantly, because he had publically declared in France his solidarity with the Revolution.[19] In any event, these and other literary lights "came not to peer at Cuba from behind their hotel curtains," as scores of journalists before them had done, "but rather to make their observation an active participation."[20] It was, however, Sartre and Mills, both of whom visited the island in 1960—during the Revolution's afterglow—who were largely responsible for the initial excitement among Europeans and North Americans concerning Cuba.[21]

In 1960 this excitement—this exuberant mass enthusiasm—which the early stage of a successful revolution always generates, captivated and drew scores of revolutionary tourists who came to the island armed, not with guns and revolvers, but with cameras and audio recorders. What, we may ask, was the character of this transfiguring emotional experience that the Cuban people sensed deeply, that confronted visitors immediately upon arriving in Havana, and that the U.S. government was wholly incapable of comprehending? "It was the release of pent-up feelings of frustration, it was an overwhelming welling up of pride, it was a dizzying sense of participation in building a new nation and a new epoch. It was zeal, dedication, excitement. And it was a raw-nerve feeling of sensitivity about the whole undertaking."[22]

Three and a half decades later, Juan Arcocha could still recall vividly those sensations of exultation and hope that permeated the island during that intoxicating time: "How distant those days in mid-1960 now seem! In Cuba we lived in moments of constant frenzy. The revolutionary fervor was at its peak and in it participated the great majority of the population."[23] Carlos Franqui lyrically describes the revolutionary ferment at the time that Jean-Paul Sartre, accompanied by Simone de Beauvoir, was in Cuba in the spring of 1960 as follows: "There was a party atmosphere throughout the island, a collective joy that manifested itself in singing and playing bongo drums. It was a Cuban way of changing life: voluntary labor, militia duty, rumba, all at the same time."[24] During these early halcyon days, large crowds of *habaneros* (residents of Havana) could be found—on the streets, plazas, and other public places—animatedly discussing the Revolution into the wee hours of the morning.[25]

Upon arriving in Havana, Mills met, quite by accident, another FPCC member, Saul Landau, who shared with the sociologist his experiences of life on the island. Landau, who would later become Mills's research assistant, tells of Mills's awkwardness on first meeting with Armando Hart, who was then minister of education, and his wife, Haydée Santamaría, who was directing the cultural center, Casa de las Américas, which she had founded in Havana. One evening, they, along with interpreter Juan Arcocha, were preparing to go to dinner with Mills, who was looking a bit like Hemingway—bearded, puffing on his pipe, and wearing a sweat-stained bush jacket. Hart was in his most conservative blue suit, Haydée in an evening dress, and Arcocha in expensive Havana evening clothes. "I should've worn a tie," the unconventional Mills ruefully confided to Landau. Hart, in particular, was shy and embarrassed, and the formal introductions were painful.[26]

While Mills was still in Havana, Fidel Castro paid him a personal visit at the relatively new Hotel Riviera, located on the Malecón oceanfront boulevard, where Mills was lodged.[27] Even before setting out on his islandwide expedition, Mills saw, in the hotel's vast lobby, about 400 volunteers in their weather-stained uniforms who had just arrived from the Sierra Maestra, where they had been working alongside and teaching literacy—but also basic hygiene—to children and adults among the *guajiro* (peasant) families. Tilting his camera lens down from his room, Mills photographed a platoon of militiamen who were also employees of the hotel, drilling—marching back-and-forth across the parking lot beyond the hexagon-shaped swimming pool, as they enthusiastically shouted in military cadence, "*Uno, dos, tres, cuatro!*" Within a few months, in preparation for a military invasion by the United States, those same militiamen would begin digging trenches outside the Riviera where 340 North American members of the Fair Play for Cuba Committee would be sojourning.

This then was Mills's introduction to Cuba. And it is doubtless the case that, at the very start of his journey, Mills had, as his friend K. S. Karol put it, "breathed fresh air" in Havana; "he had met revolutionaries of a new type, imbued with all the best ideas of the Left. He had been profoundly moved."[28]

Clearly Fidel Castro wanted the Columbia University sociologist to see, up close, as much of the new Cuba as possible, and so he provided Mills with a guide and a motor vehicle to tour freely, view the economic situation, and witness the improvements that the Revolutionary government was making.[29] Mills and Taber drove southwest on the two-lane Carretera Central, the Central Highway, from Havana to the province of Oriente at the eastern tip of the island, where Mills interviewed Franz Stettmeier and his wife, Elvira Escobar. About one-third of the way on their approximately 1,000-kilometer trip, they picked up a hitchhiking rebel soldier in Las Villas who had been building houses for the *campesinos* (peasant farmers). Mills and Taber then got off the Central Highway at Bayamo and headed west to Manzanillo.[30]

In addition to Taber, throughout much of his time in Cuba, Mills was accompanied by René C. Vallejo, who was Castro's aide-de-camp and personal physician. Mills spent several days with Vallejo, who spoke fluent English, and at least on one occasion traveled with him on a small aircraft. He also spent many hours with Fidel Castro, first in the province of Pinar del Río, initially having dinner with him in the lush Viñales Valley, and then accompanying him, as part of his official entourage, on a rain-soaked excursion of the Isle of Pines (these events are chronicled in Chapter 6).

At one point, along with the Cuban Revolution's two most visible leaders, Castro and Ché Guevara, Mills reviewed troops in drill. But he also spoke with many other Cubans who were not part of the revolutionary inner circle. Most of those interviews were conducted in Oriente, primarily in and around the Spanish-colonial city of Santiago de Cuba. The interview with the highest-ranking military official that he recorded, Comandante Dermidio Escalona, was likely held at the opposite end of the island, in Pinar del Río.

Everywhere Mills went he witnessed the Cuban people rehabilitating and transforming—they were *constructing*—a new society. On billboards everywhere was the slogan, "Revolution is to Build." In the Manzanillo district he saw a newly constructed road stretching for thirty kilometers along a shore where previously even horses had been unable to travel during the rainy season. Mills visited what had been a private ranch of 30,000 acres that had been converted into a dairy center where he interviewed Elba Luisa Batista Benitez and her husband, Lauro Fiallo Barrero. Nearby, Mills visited a chicken hatchery that was producing 75,000 chicks every three weeks. South of Manzanillo along the coastal plain, in Media Luna, he observed workmen outfitting recently constructed concrete block houses with new refrigerators, ceramic toilets and sinks, and gas stoves.[31] Mills, Taber, and Arcocha then proceeded to the tiny fishing village of Puerto de Belic in Oriente's southern shore, near the mangrove swamp where Fidel Castro and his expeditionary force made their historic landing in the most famous boat in Cuba, the *Granma*, in 1956.

Continuing on to the Sierra Maestra, Mills hiked the physically demanding trail up to the Pico Turquino, at almost 7,000 feet, the highest peak in Cuba, to La Plata where Castro had based his command headquarters during the insurrection. On the way, he snapped pictures of a crudely lettered sign that read, *Aquí Nació La Liberta de Cuba* (Here was born Cuba's freedom). He, Taber, and Arcocha spent time at the Camilo Cienfuegos School City, where they saw children at work and play and attending classes. At the School City, Mills interviewed Captain Isabel Rielo, who had been a soldier in the Rebel Army's female platoon at the time of the rebellion.

It must have been a grueling and exhausting sixteen days for the middle-aged Mills as he traversed the length and breadth of the Pennsylvania-sized country and spoke with countless of people of all ages and social stations. But all that Mills saw and heard during that summer in 1960 was part of his "Cuba-present"—a time of *revolutionary transition* that can only be properly understood in relation to "Cuba-past" and "Cuba-future." In this case, Cuba-past had its beginning point on July 26, 1953, the start of the *insurrection* against the Batista tyranny. Cuba-future, in terms relevant and relative to Mills's arrival in the Caribbean nation, is set on April 17, 1961, the first day of the U.S.-sponsored *invasion* at the Bay of Pigs.

CHAPTER TWO

Insurrection, Revolution, Invasion

A proper sociology, Mills explains in *The Sociological Imagination*, must consider three coordinate points: biography, history, and society. Particularly important in apprehending the structural changes being brought about by the Cuban Revolution—that is to say, in addressing the question, Where is Cuban society going?—is understanding the historical transformation of its social institutions. For Mills, anticipating revolutionary trends—and countertrends—however rapidly they may be occurring, requires knowledge of the transition from one historical period to another.[1] In other words, a true understanding of the future of Revolutionary Cuba and of the Cuban revolutionaries demands full and adroit use of a historical analysis of three events in Cuban twentieth-century history: insurrection, revolution, and invasion.[2]

Insurrection

It was a long line of ruthless and corrupt dictators, dating back to the early twentieth century, which ultimately instigated the insurrection that exploded into violent revolution. This brief account of that complex and turbulent political history begins with one of the worst of these tyrants, the bloody dictator Gerardo "The Butcher" Machado, who came to power in 1924. Led by politically conscious students at the University of Havana who formed the Directorio Estudiante Universitario (DEU), the Cuban people were finally able to overthrow Machado's repressive regime in the summer of 1933. Later that year, an unscrupulously ambitious thirty-two-year-old sergeant, Fulgencio Batista, seized control of the army and took over Cuba. A one-time physician, Ramón Grau, was elected president, but Batista, ruling behind the scenes as the strong man, imposed censorship on all media and jailed and tortured his opponents. In 1940, after helping the Communists gain control of the Cuban Confederation of Workers (CTC), Batista stole the election and became president of the Republic.

After pressure by the U.S. State Department to hold honest elections, Grau again took office in 1944 and governed until 1948. Though Grau had run as a reform candidate, he was as corrupt as Machado and Batista had been. One of Grau's cabinet members, Carlos Prío, who in his youth had been a member of the DEU and had participated in the overthrow of Machado, became president in 1948. Four years later, Batista entered the presidential race, and running for Congress with the recently formed Ortodoxo (or Liberal Democratic) Party was the young lawyer, Fidel Castro, who called for responsible government and an end to corruption. The elections were scheduled for early summer, but were never held because Batista had launched a coup d'état against Prío, taking over the armed forces as he had in 1933, and again assumed power in Cuba. Soon thereafter, Batista's government was formally recognized by U.S. president Dwight D. Eisenhower.

Fidel Castro filed a legal brief before the Court of Constitutional Guarantees in Havana in which he demanded that Batista's seizure of power be declared unconstitutional and that, for all his various crimes, Batista be sentenced to a term of no less than 100 years in prison. The court ruled that the revolution was the source of law, and therefore Batista, being in office as a result of the revolution, could not be regarded as the illegitimate president of the country.

Given this outcome, Castro determined that he would launch a military operation against the dictatorship and rid Cuba of Batista. He organized a poorly trained and poorly armed group of about 160 men and two women to carry out what was basically a suicide mission. This was to be an assault on the Moncada army barracks, on the outskirts of Santiago de Cuba, where hundreds of soldiers who were supporting the dictatorship were quartered. Jean-Paul Sartre fittingly articulated the desperate circumstances that confronted Castro and his insurgents at the time: "You need an intolerable evil before a people will launch an assault against barracks, before they will battle with bare hands against armed men."[3]

The object was to seize the garrison and radio station, broadcast an appeal to the people to support the rebel forces against the dictator, and establish a revolutionary government, with Santiago as its capital.

On July 26, 1953, Castro ordered a squad to take the Palace of Justice, a three-story building housing the offices of the adjutant general, which was located adjacent to the barracks. Another group, led by Abel Santamaría, and that included his sister, Haydée Santamaría, was to occupy the Civil Hospital located in front of the main entrance of the fortress, in the event there were casualties. Fidel Castro, with several men, would launch the main attack on the Moncada Barracks. But things went quickly awry. A sentry alerted the fort, and rifle and machine-gun fire met the attackers, who were poorly armed and greatly outnumbered. Realizing they had failed their objective, Castro ordered an immediate withdrawal. Some of the revolutionaries dispersed into the city, where they received refuge and help by some of the residents of Santiago. One of those who helped them escape was Mills's interviewee, Elvira Escobar, about which he writes in the Cuban revolutionary's voice: "She wasn't really in [the insurrection], then, but she and some other women helped those boys get out of the city. She just got filled up with sentiment for what she called 'those poor lost boys.' But we told her they weren't lost and they weren't boys. They were revolutionaries and they were men and they were going to win. They had already won—they had torn the mask off Batista in the raid. . . . It was the turning point."[4]

More than half of the men and the two women who participated in the assault were taken prisoner, including Fidel Castro.

Total rebel casualties at Moncada came to sixty-one dead, while Army losses totaled eighteen. The large majority of the insurrectionists killed were victims of the Army's inhumanity and cruelty—they were tortured and massacred *after* the fighting had ended. Batista then ordered that for each soldier who fell in the attack, ten prisoners were to be killed in reprisal. An indiscriminate slaughter took place over three days, and many of those who were summarily executed were innocent youths of the city. Indeed, every person under thirty was suspected of being a rebel or sympathizer.

Though the Moncada attack was a military failure for the rebels, it nonetheless served to arouse the spirit of resistance to the Batista tyranny among the people of Oriente. The assault of July 26, 1953, gave birth, and a name, to an insurrectionary organization—the 26th of July Movement—that was to wage and eventually win a civil war.

One hundred and twenty-two defendants, including townspeople who had aided the rebels, were brought to trial. Castro was charged with conspiracy to raise an insurrection and incite rebellion against the constitutional powers of the state. Acting as his own lawyer, he addressed the court in his defense. The essence of his argument was that, with Batista's military coup of 1952, the powers of the state had been usurped, and therefore the charges made against Castro failed to fit legal specifications. His oral defense, which was an indictment of the Batista regime, was to become the revolutionary manifesto of the insurrection. Fidel Castro ended with the words that would become immortalized throughout the island and beyond: "Condemn me. It doesn't matter. History will absolve me."

Along with the other Moncada fighters, the Moncadistas, the judges convicted and sentenced the defendants. Castro was condemned to fifteen years' confinement in the military penitentiary, the Presidio Modelo, on the Isle of Pines. The young revolutionary had become a hero to the people who had lost faith in the old-line politicians like Grau and Prío. His views were sought by those who saw in him some hope for regeneration in the country.

On February 24, 1955, Batista went to the polls, unopposed, and was inaugurated for another four-year term. But public pressure was building up for him to grant a general amnesty to all political prisoners, and in May Castro was released from prison, along with his brother Raúl and all other Moncadistas still alive and who had not already been freed.

Early in July Castro departed for Mexico to gather arms and men to invade his homeland and depose Batista. In Mexico he announced the formal organization of the 26th of July Movement as an independent revolutionary organization and began training an expeditionary force in the tactics of guerrilla warfare. He and his men purchased a sixty-foot wooden yacht, the *Granma*, which had been designed to accommodate only about a dozen passengers, but which, in fact, carried eighty-two expeditionaries, including weapons, ammunition, and provisions. The landing of the *Granma* in Cuba was timed to coincide with an uprising in Santiago, conducted by rebel sympathizers led by Frank País, but the *Granma* had been delayed by rough waters, mechanical problems, and other mishaps. The Santiago fighters, who attacked government and military installations on schedule, were alone in their battle, and the revolt was violently crushed.

After seven days of sailing, the overloaded vessel made landfall on December 2, 1956, in a mangrove swamp near the village of Belic on the remote southern shore of Oriente. It had been sighted while still far offshore and aircraft began to indiscriminately strafe the area where the expeditionary force had disembarked. Batista's propaganda machine falsely reported that all the invaders aboard the *Granma*, including Fidel Castro, had been killed.

As they made their way inland, the rebels were involved in several skirmishes with Batista's army. In the end only eleven of the original eighty-two who sailed from Mexico survived, which included Fidel Castro, Raúl Castro, Ché Guevara, and Camilo Cienfuegos. Ragged, hungry, and exhausted, they ascended the steep, jagged slopes of the mountains to begin the military campaign in the dense subtropical forest of the Sierra Maestra.

Aware of the need to publicize the activities of the guerrilla movement, Castro invited Herbert Matthews of the *New York Times* to interview him. On February 17, 1957, Matthews traveled deep into the Sierra Maestra and spent several hours with the *barbudos*, the bearded guerrilla fighters, and their leader. A week later he published the first of three front-page articles to appear in the *Times*. This was definitive proof that Castro had not been killed, as government communiqués had claimed. The following month CBS sent Robert Taber and Wendell Hoffman to interview and film the rebel commander, who spoke to the television cameras in English, making an appeal for the United States to stop shipping arms to Batista. A hunted fugitive with a price on his head, Castro confidently told Taber, "We have struck the spark of the Revolution.... The last battle will be fought in the capital." The product of that effort was the prime-time news special *Rebels of the Sierra Maestra: The Story of Cuba's Jungle Fighters*, which was broadcast on a Sunday evening in May 1957. The film had the effect, as Van Gosse puts it, of bringing "directly into stateside living rooms the guerillas, Fidel himself, and most important, the three [U.S. Navy] servicemen's sons from the base at Guantánamo who had joined the tiny *Ejercito Rebelde*."[5] Indeed, other spirited North American volunteers would soon take up arms on the side of the rebels and against the tyranny of Fulgencio Batista.[6]

The publicity attracted more recruits, many of them *campesinos*, to join the fighting forces in large numbers. The Rebel Army took part in several decisive battles against Batista's soldiers—first at La Plata, at the foothills of Pico Turquino, and later at El Uvero, El Jigüe, Santa Clara, Yaguajay—all resulting in victories for them. This was because the rebels were implementing the classic pattern of guerrilla warfare for which the Cuban Army was completely unprepared. Castro's strategy was to make quick hit-and-run forays against arms depots or on small detachments of troops on the move.

The accelerated pace of the guerrilla campaign in the mountains was matched, and indeed preceded, by the efforts of the underground resistance in the towns and cities. On July 30, 1957, the Santiago police ambushed and shot down the leading urban guerilla at the time, the twenty-three-year-old Frank País. Castro learned of the killing and ordered that País be buried with full honors as a colonel of the Rebel Army, a rank higher than Castro's. At País's funeral there was a long procession to the cemetery as thousands of protesters, including a group of middle-class women who carried signs saying STOP KILLING OUR SONS, filled the streets of Santiago. These protests started a general strike that spread throughout the country and signaled the beginning of an organized civil resistance on a broad scale.

The leader of the 26th of July underground in Havana, Armando Hart, organized acts of agitation, sabotage, and other subversive operations against the dictatorship. He was arrested three times in less than two years, once having made a sensational escape from a courtroom. Hart's last arrest occurred as he was returning from consultations with Castro in the Sierra. He was sent to the penitentiary in the Isle of Pines, where he remained until Batista's defeat.

Other underground rebels were involved in terrorist activities designed to maintain a constant state of alarm. Highway bridges, public buildings, and the homes and businesses of Batistianos, Batista officials and supporters, were blown up or burned. Rebel activities were answered by the government with tenfold reprisals. It was not unusual to find the bodies of boys and men hanging from trees or lampposts. The jails were filled with sympathizers of the 26th of July Movement.

Castro's rebels, the Fidelistas, regularly came down from the Sierra Maestra to attack transport and electric-power facilities, disrupt highway and railway traffic, and cut telephone and telegraph lines. However, instead of seeking to neutralize the insurrection through moderate means, the Batista regime exacerbated it by meeting sabotage with a murderous repression that was, in the end, self-defeating, because it drove thousands of Cubans into the legions of rebel sympathizers.

In May 1958 Batista launched an all-out campaign to crush the Rebel Army once and for all. This was a major offensive of over 10,000 soldiers against approximately 300 rebels in the Sierra Maestra. After three months the result was a disastrous defeat for the dictator, with about 10 percent of his forces lost—through death, wounding, capture, or desertion. In a desperate attempt to hold on to power, he turned to his fellow tyrants, Somoza of Nicaragua and Trujillo of the Dominican Republic, to supply him with arms and ammunition against the insurrectional forces.

U.S. Embassy personnel were forbidden by Ambassador Earl E. T. Smith from communicating in any way with members of the 26th of July Movement. Personnel from the U.S. Military Mission, which included the Army, Navy, and Air Force, continued training Batista's troops, one side of the civil war. In August 1958, the coordinator of the Cuban Revolutionary Civilian Front, José Miró Cardona, wrote to President Eisenhower requesting that the U.S. military missions be withdrawn from Cuba, arguing that their involvement constituted a form of intervention in the country's internal affairs during an ongoing civil war. The U.S. State Department replied that the military mission would not be withdrawn under any circumstances. This compelled the journalist Jules Dubois, who had personally experienced many of these events, to inform his U.S. readers: "The generation that was fighting Batista was going to rule Cuba and we were festering sores in their hearts, building up resentments in their minds and fanning the enmity of their relatives and the entire Cuban people by insisting on the continued training of an army by our mission—an army headed for inevitable defeat."[7]

That defeat finally came on New Year's Eve, 1958. By that time, five of the six provinces were aflame, with rebels overrunning cities and towns, sugar mills, and cattle ranches. The Fidelistas would be in the Cuban capital within hours. At exactly midnight, Batista, dressed in his tuxedo, announced that he would resign and leave the island permanently. He summoned his closest cronies, those whose torture and execution of political prisoners and innocent civilians he had rewarded with promotions and gifts. At one thirty in the morning Batista took a Cadillac to the military airport and forty minutes later boarded a DC-4 airliner. Along with his wife and about 180 of his henchmen, Batista fled to the Dominican Republic, reputedly taking seven suitcases filled with 300 to 400 million dollars. The *guerrilleros* had defeated a standing army of 30,000 men that the United States had trained and equipped with the finest modern weapons—tanks, guns, warplanes, and bombs—used to kill 20,000 Cubans during seven years of bloody dictatorship.

The dictator had fled in disgrace; the twenty-five-month insurrection was now over. Year One of the Revolution, dubbed the "Year of Liberation," had begun.

Revolution

Fidel Castro was having coffee at a sugar plantation in Oriente when at nine o'clock the following morning, January 1, he heard the news of Batista's flight. He immediately took to the airwaves of Radio Rebelde and broadcast to the nation the following proclamation that he would repeat, later that day, from the balcony of City Hall in Santiago de Cuba:

> Instructions of the General headquarters to all commanders of the Rebel Army and to the people:
> Whatever news from the capital may be, our troops should not cease fire at any time.
> Our forces should continue their operations against the enemy on all battlefronts....
> Apparently, there has been a coup d'état in the capital. The conditions in which the coup was produced are not known by the Rebel Army....

The dictatorship has collapsed as a consequence of the crushing defeats suffered in the last weeks, but that does not mean to say that the Revolution has already triumphed.

Revolution *yes*! Military coup, *no*!

It was crucial to Castro that the Cuban people understand that this was not a "palace revolution" in which, to quote Gerth and Mills, "usurpers—often from within the ruling stratum—displace the ruler ... without changing the master symbols."[8] The Cuban Revolution had to be a complete and absolute triumph in order to prevent any possibility of a civilian or military junta. As the influential journalist Walter Lippmann accurately put it: "What is going on in Cuba today is no mere palace revolution at the top, in which one oligarchy has ousted another. This is a social revolution involving the masses of the Cuban people, and its aim is not to install a new set of rulers but to work out a new social order."[9]

Lippmann was correct in his depiction of the Rebel victory producing a *social* revolution, but it was always also a *radical* one—aimed at altering the basic structure of Cuban society. It was, moreover, what Gerth and Mills had previously identified as a *total* revolution, characterized by a sudden and violent transformation of all institutional orders (kinship, religious, political, military, and economic) that brought about a change of values as well as a restructuring of a system of domination and authority. And it was, specifically, very much a *political and economic* revolution, again, according to Gerth and Mills, given that changes in the legal order of private property rights were instigated in the political order, which in turn created qualitatively new institutions—most notably, in the case of Cuba, the *agrarian cooperative*—that came to predominance in the economic order.[10] Indeed, so critical was the collectivization of agricultural production to revolutionary transformation that Huberman and Sweezy regarded it as "Cuba's most distinctive contribution to the storehouse of institutional inventions from which future revolutions can draw their inspiration and examples."[11]

But a revolution, as Huberman and Sweezy point out, "is a process, not an event. It unfolds through many stages and phases. It never stands still."[12] And neither did Fidel Castro, the Revolution's master symbol, stand still as, on January 2, he began his triumphal march, on the Central Highway from Santiago to Havana, with 1,500 of his rebel troops in a victory caravan that consisted of Sherman tanks, armored cars, buses, army trucks, and jeeps. It seemed that everyone on this 1,000-kilometer trek across the island wanted to see the rebel leader—to hear him speak in person, to touch him, to shake his hand, or to kiss him.

Three days later Castro was in Camagüey, in central Cuba, where he issued orders to his commanders to begin summary courts-martial and try war criminals, officers, noncommissioned officers, privates, policemen, and civilians for having killed unarmed civilians or torturing and killing members of the rebel forces.

On January 8, Castro and his cavalcade finally reached the Cuban capital, where they made their triumphal entry and were welcomed by nearly 1 million enthusiastic *habaneros* carrying placards, waving the flags of Cuba and the 26th of July Movement, and shouting *Viva Fidel!* The crowds cheered and showered the rebels and their young charismatic leader with confetti and serpentines. Ruby Hart Phillips, who witnessed many of these events on that historic day, describes Fidel Castro and the Cuban people, their present and impending experiences, as follows: "He stood there before them, proof that the power of the Cuban army had been broken by the people themselves. He stood there before them, unentangled and uncompromised, free of all the factious political parties. The revolution was won. Now Fidel Castro was ready to begin the program of reforms which was designed to change the political, economic, and social structure of the Republic."[13]

The reforms came in quick succession. Only one month into the Revolution, the U.S. military missions were withdrawn at the request of the Cuban government. Castro felt that U.S. officers who trained Batista's army, which he had defeated, could not teach him anything about warfare in his country.

There were also far-reaching educational reforms in a country where the illiteracy rate was conservatively estimated at 37.5 percent. In rural areas, up to one-third of the country's schoolage children never attended school at all. Thousands of previously unemployed teachers volunteered to serve in improvised schools, without pay. There was also further expansion, with the building of new schools and the training of new teachers. Various educational experiments were taking place; a case in point was the Camilo Cienfuegos School City that was being built in the foothills of the Sierra Maestra that Mills visited on the way to La Plata. The campus was, in effect, an immense boarding school where peasant children could get a complete education, from first grade through high school. It was also to be an agricultural and manufacturing center in which the students themselves would produce enough to make the city economically self-sustainable.

Other social transformations implemented that first year, also quite progressive and extensive, were in the area of housing. Cuba, a country with 6 million inhabitants, had a perpetual shortage of decent housing. In 1958, two-thirds of the rural habitations still consisted of the scattered *bohíos*, those huts of palm and wood, with earth floors, found in conditions of open sewers, squalor, and filth. Over half of the rural dwellings lacked all lavatory arrangements; only 15 percent of town houses and 1 percent of country houses had baths. The Revolutionary government instituted a housing program and began wide-scale construction of homes for families throughout the island. These were largely cinder-block units built in attractive, hygenic environments, each equipped with all the modern conveniences: indoor plumbing, sinks, refrigerators. By the end of 1959, some 10,000 such units had been completed. The goal for 1960—when Mills observed the houses being built in the town of Media Luna—was to assemble 20,000 units, at a cost of about $2,000 each, by year's end.

In Havana, rents had long been excessively high. And so, as part of the 1960 Urban Reform Law, the cost of home and apartment rentals was reduced by up to 50 percent (which was considered just by the tenants but unreasonable by owners of the properties) in order to eliminate the rent gouging that had taken as much as one-third of the income of urban workers. Private owners were required to sell sites at low uniform prices to anyone willing to start construction. This measure made it so that half of urban tenants became homeowners.

But by far the most sweeping—and overtly radical—socioeconomic transformation undertaken by the Revolutionary government was instigated by the passage, on May 17, 1959, of the Agrarian Reform Law. Indeed, 1960 was known as the "Year of Agrarian Reform," and Mills came to the island in the middle of that massive agricultural campaign. His friend and traveling companion, Comandante René Vallejo, had been chief of the Agrarian Reform in Manzanillo and then served as provincial delegate, first in Camagüey, and later, at the time that Mills met him, in Oriente.

At the time of the Revolution the economic situation in rural Cuba was as follows. Seventy-five percent of the agricultural land was owned by 8 percent of the property holders. One hundred and forty thousand peasants either owned, rented, or squatted on less than 33 acres of land each, barely enough to be self-sustaining. In addition, there were about 300,000 rural workers and cane-cutters living in conditions of abject misery in marginal lands, swamps, and the trackless mountains. With agrarian reform, the Castro regime distributed government-owned land, expropriated farm lands over 1,000 acres, and banned land ownership by foreigners. Land holdings expropriated by the Cuban political regime were distributed among 700,000 landless peasants, with priority given to any tenants, sharecroppers, or squatters who might be living on the expropriated property in question.

But the reform law involved more than just the equitable distribution of land ownership through the "intervention"[14] and the expropriation of large landed estates that had previously belonged to Batista henchmen and *latifundistas*.[15] It was, in fact, intended to produce diversified farming, develop industry, and eliminate the dependence on the one-crop system of agriculture. It was to make the economy more efficient and improve the standard of living for the Cuban people through collective cultivation. This led to what became the basic Cuban agricultural enterprise in the reform: the cooperative farm—of which there were 881 in existence in August 1960 when Mills was on the island. Even though the new regime issued twenty-year government bonds bearing 4.5 percent interest annually in payment for the expropriated property, opponents of the agrarian reform nonetheless denounced it as confiscatory, illegal, and communistic. When the outlines of the agrarian reform program became known to the popular press in the United States, there was speculation that the U.S. government might have to intervene to save the Cuban island from communism.

Given that the agrarian reform was by far the biggest revolutionary undertaking, the Castro government created the National Institute of Agrarian Reform (INRA), the economic agency with extensive powers to apply and enforce the Agrarian Reform Law in all sectors of the economy. INRA's broader goal was to make the island more nearly self-sustainable and to relieve the still critical unemployment problem. Many of its key personnel, particularly its provincial officials, were rebel soldiers.

By the time Mills arrived in Cuba, INRA had appropriated over 8 million acres and had plowed and planted about 250,000 acres of previously uncultivated land, which was being devoted to growing rice, corn, peanuts, cotton, and beans—crops that Cuba had traditionally imported.

During the first year of the Revolution, while Cuba's social structure was undergoing these major changes, its ideological dynamic was also experiencing a kind of metamorphosis. Thus, with the execution by firing squad of approximately 500 war criminals; the appointment of Osvaldo Dorticós, who had connections to the Cuban Communist Party, as president of the Republic; Comandante Huber Matos's public concern with the growing influence of Communists in the revolutionary government and his subsequent arrest on charges of treason, Cuba was, by early 1959, being labeled by the U.S. government as a communist country—the only one in the Western Hemisphere. It was therefore inevitable that tensions between Washington and Havana would increase, and not at all surprising that Castro would get the cold shoulder treatment on his first visit to the United States as prime minster in April 1959. President Eisenhower refused to greet the Cuban leader, who made it clear to everyone that he was not in the country to beg for economic assistance. The American president instead headed to a golf course to avoid any chance of meeting the bearded revolutionary. The two heads of state were as far away from a meeting of the minds as they could possibly be. Indeed, in October, when a reporter asked Eisenhower what he supposed was aggravating Castro's invectives against the United States, the president responded, as historian Jim Rasenberger puts it, "with bafflement, if not a touch of obtuseness," saying, "Here is a country that you would believe, on the basis of our history, would be one of our real friends. The whole history . . . would seem to make it a puzzling matter to figure out just exactly why the Cubans and the Cuban government would be so unhappy."[16]

By Year Two of the Revolution, diplomatic relations between the two countries were deteriorating rapidly, and U.S. suspicions of the Castro regime being communist were heightened. Matters were aggravated further when, on February 4, 1960, Anastas Mikoyan, the first deputy premier of the Kremlin and one of the most powerful members of the Soviet Presidium, arrived in Havana from Moscow. Mikoyan and Castro signed a trade agreement in which the Soviets pledged to purchase 1 million tons of sugar from Cuba, with payment to be partly in petroleum, machinery, trucks, tractors, and manufactured products—all of which Cuba desperately needed for industrializing.

But the most dramatic tragedy that befell the early Revolution happened in the spring of 1960, when a disastrous explosion occurred as the French freighter *La Coubre*, which was laden with small-arms munitions that had been purchased by the Cubans in Belgium, was being unloaded in Havana harbor. More than 100 longshoremen, soldiers, and rescue workers were killed, and 300 more were injured. Something, or somebody, had ignited the ship, which set off a series of blasts that had caused the waterfront carnage.

The following day at a memorial service for those who had been killed by the explosion, which Sartre and Simone de Beauvoir attended, Castro indignantly denounced the disaster as sabotage and blamed the United States for the plot. For Castro, the *La Coubre* terrorist attack had a twofold purpose: it was the way the CIA could ensure that the munitions were not delivered, and, more ominously, it was a harbinger for a U.S.-led invasion of his country.

Invasion

It was, in a word, counterrevolution that led to the Cuban invasion. At the time that Castro and the Moncadistas were instigating the insurrection, and long before the triumph of the Revolution, Mills (with Hans Gerth) was already involved in a sociological analysis of counterrevolution—an analysis that precisely explained the events that ended, with disastrous consequences, at the remote marshy inlet on the southern coast of Cuba known as the Bay of Pigs:

> New theories are developed which dispute the legitimacy of the revolutionary regime and debunk, psychologically, theoretically, and politically, its new measures and styles of life. So after the first revolutionary shocks have been overcome, fatalism and defeatism tend to wane and give way to political plotting, inspired by the observation of incipient cracks and points of strain in the new structure. Out of informal gatherings grow nuclei of political and perhaps eventually military organizations. Their leaders play on the sentiments of the disappointed, woo the good will of foreign governments who may hesitate to grant recognition to the revolutionary regime.[17]

From its infelicitous inception to its tragic end, the U.S.-sponsored invasion of Cuba at the Bay of Pigs was an astonishingly irresponsible and reckless scheme perpetrated by the CIA under two Washington administrations.

The story begins at the start of 1960, when the CIA's official position was that Castro had to go because he was allegedly falling into the communist embrace of the Soviet Union. This meant removing the Cuban prime minister without revealing direct involvement by the CIA, the Pentagon, the State Department, and the president of the United States. And so the intelligence agency began to surreptitiously establish working arrangements with Cuban exiles and defectors who had been flooding into Florida since 1959. It began cobbling together a coalition from among numerous anti-Castro groups that included moderates who had some disagreements with the Revolution's trajectory, but that also included Batistianos eager to return Cuba to its pre-Revolution status quo. In March, President Eisenhower gave the CIA permission to organize the Cuban exiles into an armed force.

A couple of months later, during the May Day celebrations in Havana, Castro told a crowd of 500,000 that the United States was preparing a military offensive against Cuba through Guatemala. On that day, his supporters for the first time burst out publicly in the chant of *Cuba, sí, Yanqui no*.

Though the Eisenhower administration loudly and indignantly denied any planned aggression against the Revolutionary regime, Castro wasn't buying it and began mobilizing his entire military establishment to defend against an imminent attack by the United States on Cuba's national sovereignty.

In July the first recruits of the counterrevolutionary invasion force began to arrive in a remote corner of southwestern Guatemala for training. The CIA began building an airstrip to serve as home base to the invading brigade's air force. Thus, by the time C. Wright Mills set foot on the island in August, there were already some 400 Cuban exiles—mercenaries, as Castro was now referring to them—being trained in Guatemala.

A few days after being elected president in November, John F. Kennedy was briefed on the CIA's plan to assemble a strike force intended to topple the Castro regime. At the same time, the Cubans went before the United Nations, formally charging that a U.S.-backed attack on Cuba was imminent, and Castro began a propaganda counteroffensive. He spoke frequently, and accurately, of the training camps in Guatemala. By that time, the invasion brigade of exiles had become the best-known "secret" in the world; Castro mobilized all army units, including a civilian militia of more than 600,000 strong, and placed them on emergency alert.

On January 4, 1961, President Eisenhower broke diplomatic relations with Cuba, and military plans for the operation began to take shape; the objective being to overthrow Fidel Castro much the same way as the CIA had succeeded, in July 1954, in engineering a coup d'état against Guatemala's president, Jacobo Árbenz.

The strategy for regime change in Cuba was as clear-cut as it was nefarious: an exile military brigade would secure a beachhead on the island, and members of the provisional government the CIA had assembled in Florida would go ashore, declare themselves the rightful leadership of Cuba, and provide a pretext for U.S. intervention in Cuba's "civil war." The operation's entire success, however, hinged on one indispensable assumption: that once a beachhead was established, large-scale defections from the Cuban militias would spontaneously materialize around the island and the Cuban people would immediately abandon Fidel Castro and join the invaders.

A time and place for the amphibious landing that was to oust Castro were selected: it was to occur on April 17 along a narrow bay—the Bay of Pigs—on the swampy coast of southern Cuba that gave out onto the Caribbean Sea.

Two days before the actual invasion, at dawn on Saturday, April 15, the CIA sent eight B-26 bombers, each heavily laden with bombs and missiles, from Nicaragua to Cuba to destroy Fidel Castro's air force on the ground. Staged to look like an internal revolt by Castro's own men, the bombers were made to resemble the B-26s in Cuba's air force, right down to the FAR (Fuerza Aérea Revolucionaria) markings on their fuselages and tails. They succeeded in destroying several of Castro's aircraft, but two of the B-26s had a different mission. They were to fly directly to Florida, where the pilots were to claim to be defectors and ask for asylum. Before they left Nicaragua, these two planes were shot up with machine guns to make it look as if they had been attacked when they escaped from Cuba. The ruse was quickly exposed in Miami by reporters who knew the difference between these B-26s and Castro's bombers.

The Cuban delegation at the United Nations accused the United States of an act of imperialist piracy, blaming it directly for the attacks against Cuba. The planes had come from Guatemala, Foreign Minister Raúl Roa charged, and the air raids were a prelude to a large-scale offensive financed by the United States. U.S. Ambassador to the United Nations, Adlai Stevenson, vigorously denied that the United States had any role in the bombings and stated that they had been the work of Cuban defectors. He reaffirmed his government's commitment to ensure that no U.S. citizen would participate in any actions against the Cuban nation.

Despite Stevenson's insistence that the United States would not intervene, two days later, during the early morning hours of Monday, April 17, 1961, a fleet of six cargo ships (borrowed from the United Fruit Company) and some 1,500 Cuban counterrevolutionaries—trained by CIA officers and supplied with U.S. equipment, executing a plan that had been approved by the Joint Chiefs of Staff and the president of the United States—landed on Playa Girón, just east to the entrance of the Bay of Pigs. They were to confront Cuba's professional army of nearly 30,000, with another 200,000 militia supporting it.

The ill-fated brigade never had a chance, having virtually no indigenous support within the island. Despite their extensive training and their elaborate equipment, the exiles were routed by Castro's forces within seventy-two hours. On the second day after the brigade's landing, it was apparent in Washington and Havana that the operation was on the verge of collapse. The invaders were trapped on the beaches, and they could neither advance nor retreat without U.S. assistance, which Kennedy refused to give, fearing that it would be revealed as U.S. interference in a sovereign nation. By the evening of the third day, Castro's forces had completely encircled the invading army of counterrevolutionaries. Of the nearly 1,500 Cubans who took part in the invasion, over 100 of them were killed and some 1,200 taken prisoner. The remainder were sent fleeing to the sea or else scrambled into the swamps, where the survivors were soon captured by Castro's army. It was at that moment that the exiles in Miami understood that they would be in the United States a long time.

The invasion had been an unmitigated military and political disaster—a "fiasco," to use the term that is often applied in reference to it—for the Kennedy administration. The United States had spent roughly $46 million, allowed itself to be humiliated by a small island-nation of 7 million inhabitants (compared to the U.S.'s 180 million at the time), and exposed itself as a bully in the eyes of the world. When it was over, the journalists Karl E. Meyer and Tad Szulc, neither of whom could be described as Castro supporters, wrote that the aborted invasion was more than a military defeat for the exile brigade. It "was a failure of mind, of imagination, of common sense—a failure that seems all the more grotesque now as the bright insiders in the Kennedy Administration discuss it with a certain mordant relish. It solved nothing. It won nothing."[18] But Meyer and Szulc did not blame the military, political, and intelligence miscalculations on particular individuals or agencies. Rather, evoking the characteristics that Max Weber detected in the modern bureaucracy, they attributed those blunders that led to the Bay of Pigs fiasco "to the insulated rationalism that infects a sheltered bureaucracy." Quoting directly from H. H. Gerth and C. Wright Mills, translators of *From Max Weber: Essays in Sociology*, Meyer and Szulc note that: "Every bureaucracy seeks to increase the superiority of the professionally informed by keeping their knowledge and intentions secret. Bureaucratic administration always tends to be an administration of 'secret sessions': in so far as it can, it hides its knowledge and actions from criticism. The concept of the 'official secret' is the specific invention by the bureaucracy, and nothing is so fanatically defended by the bureaucracy as this attitude."[19]

Thus, for Meyer and Szulc, the experts in the Eisenhower and Kennedy administrations who hatched and supported the invasion plan—CIA director

Allen W. Dulles; CIA deputy director Richard M. Bissell Jr.; presidential advisor Arthur M. Schlesinger Jr.; chief of Latin American affairs Adolf A. Berle Jr.—were, in a sense, unwitting victims, infected, as they were, by a bureaucratic obscurity and swept by an organizational momentum that became irreversible.

In contrast, and despite his thorough knowledge of what Weber had said about bureaucracy's tendency toward rationality without reason, Mills placed the onus directly on these experts, in particular on Kennedy, Schlesinger, and Berle, for which he had great animus. Thus, in the context of these previous and forthcoming events, Mills in *Listen, Yankee*, was no longer interested in explaining the behaviors of individuals as being caused by structural or social-psychological factors—by a "main drift," or a "managerial demiurge," or even a "military metaphysic"—as he had in his previous books, *White Collar* and *The Power Elite*. Now he was looking squarely, and almost exclusively, at the absurdity and irresponsibility of experts' actions due to their own volition: they voluntarily chose to become deaf to the truth and intentionally refused to listen to the facts.

CHAPTER THREE

Mills on Individuals, Intellectuals, and Interviewing

In one of his best-known passages in *The Sociological Imagination*, C. Wright Mills states, "What social science is properly about is the human variety, which consists of all the social worlds in which men have lived, are living, and might live."[1] These social worlds are all the social structures that have appeared in the course of human history. But to understand their essential characteristics, it is necessary that the sociologist undertake a comparative analysis: to observe social structures under a variety of circumstances and to examine them in contrast to other social structures, particularly those in other world areas and regions.

Just as importantly, the human variety also includes the array of men and women, as biographical entities, that have been known to exist and that currently do exist. For Mills, the sociologist must endeavor to understand these individuals by discerning the meaning that historical reality has for them—but always within the context of the political state. In sum, it was by studying the biographical experiences of the newly radicalized Cubans, Cuban national history, and the problems of their intersection within the political process of the Revolution, that Mills sought to understand what was really going on in Cuba in mid-1960. As Robert Taber put it, "the Revolution has been made not by parties or movements but by individual human beings, in all their living, breathing variety."[2]

Individuals

On his two-week trek through the Caribbean nation Mills spoke with and observed a wide variety of Cubans, from all walks of life, engaged in a number of endeavors, most of which were devoted to the construction of a new society. Whether or not it was the case when he was making his way through the island, by the time of the Bay of Pigs, he had clearly developed a sentimental affinity with the Cuban people. Indeed, just a few days after the military invasion, he wrote a letter to his parents expressing that feeling. Knowing that his mother, who had grown up in a ranch in South Texas, had "as her image of the human being—the men and women of Mexico," Mills explained to her that, "The Cubans are my Mexicans."[3]

It is noteworthy that, despite being a "North American aboriginal," as he referred to himself, Mills was remarkably free from national affections and ideological convictions, opposing, for example, U.S. participation in World War II and refusing to join any political party or association.[4] Nevertheless, after all his wanderings, and late in his life, Mills finally found his "emotional home," only 145 kilometers off the coast of Florida, in the Cuban Revolution.[5] And the Cuban *people*, who were making the Revolution, provided him with his idealized image of the human being, of the social being. But what exactly was Mills's view of individuals—both North Americans and Cubans?

Mills's sociology begins with the premise that individuals, whether peasants or bureaucrats, are first and foremost *social and historical actors*. But for us to properly understand their motives and behaviors they must be considered with sensitive reference to the social structure that is their context.[6]

He saw individuals as possessing a nature that is volitional and active, one that gives them the potential to be free. For Mills, humans have the ability, if not always the desire, to awaken from their political apathy, shake loose their feelings of fatalistic resignation, and engage in social action that makes a historical difference. His conception of human nature is that few limits can be placed on the capacities of individuals. However, in the postwar United States, most people's freedom, by which he means their "chance to formulate the available choices, to argue over them—and then the opportunity to choose," is constrained by power relations.[7] Simply put, those with the power to make the larger decisions for their society are freer than those without the power.

Mills draws two conclusions about individuals in their relation to the power structure of U.S. society. First, while all North Americans are free, some, by virtue of where they are placed within the social structure, are more powerful and free than others to shape human affairs. Second, and subsequently, history is made behind the backs of the majority of the U.S. populace.

Mills vehemently maintains that individuals in a mass society like the United States must refuse to remain "cheerful robots," apathetic automatons who blindly and complacently accept their life chances as being determined by fate. A true democratic freedom, declares Mills, can be realized only when individuals, in order to secure their freedom, must have not only the *power* but also the *desire* to make decisions concerning their own lives and their place in history. The passive spectators, the cheerful robots of U.S. mass society, must be transformed into a "community of publics"—scattered little circles of face-to-face citizens discussing their public business in the spirit of direct participatory democracy.[8] This explains why, in questioning the Cubans, Mills was particularly intrigued with how decisions were made and with the distinctly revolutionary notion of "direct democracy."

Mills's most penetrating characterization of North Americans, as individuals in the social-structural context of mid-twentieth-century mass society, is found in *White Collar*—his social-psychological study of the emerging new middle classes and their white-collar world. Here he reveals how the U.S. economy's rationalization and bureaucratization affect the psychological character, the social biographies, and the social roles of North American white-collar workers. In the major U.S. cities in the 1950s, these structural factors made for the subsequent rise of a world of big organizations inhabited by the "new middle class," or those propertyless white-collar workers involved primarily in sales and management and whose work situation was increasingly bureaucratized by the command hierarchies of business and government. The white-collar workers of the new middle class, mostly clerks, bookkeepers, and public relations specialists involved in sales and management, felt alienated because they lacked a sense of craftsmanship, of creating their own product. For the white-collar workers the enterprise had but one motive: to manipulate everyone and everything in order to make a profit. They had become bureaucrats, professionalized occupants of specified offices and specialized tasks, and were forced to accept the meaninglessness of their working life. In Marx's terms, they were alienated from power, work, and self.

Mills contends that by examining middle-class, white-collar life, something can be learned about what was becoming more typically "American." In this way, he states, we can "understand better the shape and meaning of modern society as a whole, as well as the simple hopes and complex anxieties that grip all the people who are sweating it out in the middle of the twentieth century."[9] This situation in U.S. society gave rise to what Mills calls the *new little man*, the product of these impersonal white-collar worlds, who "seems to have no firm roots, no sure loyalties to sustain his life and give it a center. . . . Perhaps because he does not know where he is going, he is in a frantic hurry; perhaps because he does not know what frightens him, he is paralyzed with fear."[10] It is instructive to compare the new little man of U.S. society with the Cuban revolutionary ideal: Ché Guevara's "new man."[11]

In stark contrast to North America's white-collar new little man, who works alone in some impersonal office, never talking loud, never talking back, never taking a stand, Guevara's famous conceptualization of Cuba's new man is of a man actively and consciously engaged in building socialism for the greater benefit of society; he is, in fact, making history. In this sense the new man is, at once, a unique individual as well as a member of the community. What is important in this context, writes the Argentine guerrilla, "is that people become more aware every day of the need to incorporate themselves into society and of their own importance as motors of that society."[12] This allows the new man to achieve total awareness of his social being, which is equivalent to his full realization as a *human* being. Guevara's new socialist man is not alienated; indeed, he "begins to see himself portrayed in his work and to understand its human magnitude through the created object, through the work carried out."[13] This new man, this new human being, is the "twenty-first-century man," yet to be formed, in the process of being formed. Mills provides glimpses of the formation of the new man in Cuba when, in *Listen, Yankee*, he has the Cuban revolutionary say: "We are *new men*. That is why we are so original and so spontaneous and so unafraid to do what must be done in Cuba."[14] And again, "The only real and true consolidation, of course, is the creation of the revolution by itself of *new kinds of men and women*."[15]

Guevara singles out the current crop of Cuban intellectuals, particularly, as *not* being new men; the reason—and it is a rather ambiguous one—is that they are not "authentically revolutionary," by which he presumably means that they had not been able to shake the old bourgeois idealism and adopt new communistic values. For Mills, by contrast, the North American intellectual had the potential, if not always the willingness, to be an authentic revolutionary, or at least an agent of social change. Mills, however, understood that it would not be easy to realize this expectation for the intellectuals.

Intellectuals

Much like Karl Mannheim before him, Mills fashioned a public—and a political—role for intellectuals. Before his Cuban sojourn and even before Fidel teamed up with Ché, Mills had concluded that intellectuals were the most viable agents for changing the conditions of sociopolitical existence. In his first major work, released in 1948, *The New Men of Power*, he contends that labor leaders, together with the labor intellectuals (i.e., the union's lawyers, editors of the union's newspaper, economists, statisticians, research directors), should form an alliance to stop the United States from becoming a corporate militarized state.[16] By the end of the book, however, Mills reveals his disenchantment with both the labor leaders and intellectuals because they had failed to raise the workers' level of political awareness to arrest the trend toward a permanent war economy. Given that labor intellectuals were woefully ineffectual in influencing the conditions of their work setting, Mills saw them as having virtually no chance to contribute to progressive politics.

In Mills's view, intellectuals must be motivated by a commitment to politics. Indeed, he frequently charges them to practice the "politics of responsibility" and act in a morally responsible manner. He sees it as the intellectuals' obligation, their moral imperative, to critique contemporary *overdeveloped society* and set forth general and detailed programs on how to attain the *properly developing society*.[17] An overdeveloped society like the United States, Mills explains, is an affluent industrial society where conspicuous production and consumption dominate and control the lifestyles of many individuals, but in particular those of the middle classes. Here the middle classes ignore their fundamental human needs as a result of being dazzled and distracted by technological gadgetry. Moreover, they are frequently preoccupied with competing for what is most important to them: status. As a consequence, the main features characterizing an overdeveloped society are emulatory consumption patterns, overproduction, and the deadening of human sensibility. In contrast, the properly developing society is a democratic order where troubles, issues, and problems are open to inquiry. It is a society that provides forums and other outlets through which all momentous decisions are made into public issues and openly debated by intellectuals before a community of free and knowledgeable publics.[18]

In *White Collar* Mills maintains that, like the labor intellectuals, middle-class intellectuals had also been rendered powerless due to three general trends of modern social and ideological organization. First, they had been transformed into bureaucrats, working in large organizations of state, business, and higher education. This meant that, as hired employees in the publishing and entertainment industries, they were no longer free to speak their minds in dissent. And in the large universities, the restraints on professors' academic freedom stemmed from a self-censorship that they unconsciously imposed on their own teaching and research. Further, the new bureaucracies had an ideological demand for intellectuals to compose symbols, representing various interests and passions, which serve the vested interests of the bureaucracy. Lastly, rather than actively resisting the cooptation of their intellect, intellectuals had become mere technicians, selling their ideas to the large corporations, the state apparatus, and the military establishment.

In addition to intellectuals needing to be independent of established institutions, Mills also expects them to be critics of their own country's political structures. He brought home this point in a March 1960 interview he had with the Mexican leftist intellectuals Carlos Fuentes, Víctor Flores Olea, Enrique González Pedrero, and Jamie García Terrés.[19] He exhorts them not to consider as the major source of Latin America's abject poverty the imperialistic and monopolistic machinations of the United States (though Mills insists that he was not an apologist for U.S. foreign policies), but rather the power elite in their own countries. He admonishes them for excusing their own political inactivity by reference to what the United States would and would not do. He chides them to conduct an honest sociological study that would, first, provide a penetrating account of the ruling groups in every Latin American country and, second, measure the extent to which these countries' underdevelopment can realistically be imputed to the imperialist policies of the United States. When the results are obtained, Mills tells his interviewers, they will have no more excuses for their political inactivity and will stop attributing all of Latin America's misfortunes to relations with the United States.

In *The Causes of World War Three*, Mills acquires a renewed faith that intellectuals could again be the agents of democratic renovation. And since a modern democracy necessitates an end to civic apathy and political indifference, it therefore requires a media of genuine communication open to the intellectual community. Mills believes that with the aid of this type of mass media, intellectuals could translate the private troubles of individuals into public issues, and public issues into their meanings for the private life. But until such time as genuine media becomes a reality, he instructs the intellectual community to "make the mass media the means of liberal—which is to say, liberating—education."[20] He acknowledges, however, that, in regard to Cuba's Revolution, this was particularly difficult to do, given that American television programming, newspapers, and magazines—but in particular "that weekly journal of fiction," *Time* magazine, for which Mills had particular contempt—were intentionally misrepresenting the truth about Cuba. Speaking through the Cuban revolutionary, Mills tells North Americans: "Everyone in the world who isn't limited to *Time* Magazine and the Hearst papers, and listening to your networks and all the rest of it, is getting to know something of the *truth* about Cuba today. They're getting to know that your press on Cuba is about as real as your quiz programs have been. They are both full of outrageous lies which may fool Yankees but don't fool anyone else. They are frauds, and other people are beginning to realize it, even if you do not."[21]

Mills holds an objective notion of truth, one that is politically informed. This was a *politics of truth*, by which he means that intellectuals have a moral and political obligation to tell the truth—to disclose the facts—about social reality; particularly since this reality was being distorted by the stultifying culture of mass society and the manipulation of the mass media. Thus, in *Listen, Yankee* Mills endeavors to explicitly present to the U.S. public—a public that largely had access only to information from the North American press—"the truth" about the Cuban Revolution. Indeed, one of the overriding political ideals is the value of truth, of fact. In a world of widely communicated nonsense, any statement of fact is of political and moral significance. But Mills is well aware that revolutionary truth is always volatile, mutable, and dangerous: "Like most Cubans, I too believe that this revolution is a moment of truth, and like some Cuban revolutionaries, I too believe that such truth, like all revolutionary truth, is perilous." What is more, he understands that the Revolution is tenuous and fragile and that events can easily take a turn for the worse: "Any moment of such military and economic truth [as exists in Cuba today] *might* become an epoch of political and cultural lies."[22]

And when it comes to truth, all intellectuals must be involved in the struggle between enlightenment and obscurantism. Mills's task in *Listen, Yankee* is to enlighten his fellow citizens about the achievements, aspirations, and aims of the Cuban Revolution. By contrast, those intellectuals most responsible for leading the U.S. public into obscurantism about what was really going on in Cuba were the "liberal obfuscators" in the Kennedy administration—namely, Adolf A. Berle Jr., the president's advisor on Latin America; Arthur M. Schlesinger Jr., the president's special assistant; and Adlai Stevenson, U.S. ambassador to the United Nations—who had actively sought to hide the facts about military intervention on the island.

But if Mills saw left-leaning thinkers as change agents, what role did they play in revolution? First and foremost, they were *catalysts* for revolution, particularly in the developing nations of the world. In fact, two conditions necessary for revolution in those countries were a continued, hopeless misery of the masses and "a disaffected intelligentsia with no place to go."[23] Indeed, in the case of Cuba, the ones who initiated the insurrection, Mills points out, were a handful of disaffected young intellectuals and students from the University of Havana.

There are a couple of characteristics of these young Cuban intellectuals that Mills particularly admires. First, they are pragmatic and thus original, fluid, and unafraid of what has to be done in Cuba. Mills describes their organization as a "do-it-yourself outfit," not oriented to any particular ideological blueprint, except perhaps by a vague kind of socialism. Second, and related, they are bereft of any rigid political dogmatism, and being of the younger political generation, they have no experience with old-left Stalinism. They are a *new* left and, as such, lack any sense of cynicism and futility about what they are doing. This nonideological and spontaneous praxis, this rather naïve political approach, was made evident to Jean-Paul Sartre: "In Paris I questioned a certain number of Cubans, but was never able to understand why they refused to tell me if the objective of the Cuban Revolution was or was not to establish socialism. Now I understand why they could not tell me. That is, that the originality of this Revolution consists precisely in doing what needs to be done without attempting to define it by means of a previous ideology."[24] Indeed, in March 1960, Castro, referencing Sartre, declared that, "we [Cubans] are not a people of high theory . . . we are a people of deeds and Jean-Paul Sartre has said as much. *This is not a revolution of the book.*"[25]

Such improvisation was partly rooted in the fact that the leaders of the Cuban government were, on the eve of the Revolution, all in their thirties or younger: Enrique Oltuski, minister of communications, was twenty-nine; Armando Hart, minister of education, twenty-seven; Raúl Castro, twenty-eight; and Ché Guevara and Fidel Castro were barely past thirty. In a chapter titled "The Kids Take Over," Sartre, in 1960, observed that youth was everywhere in Cuba, that the enfants terribles then in power were exactly the ones to rebel against a dictatorial regime: "Since a revolution was needed, circumstances willed that youth should accomplish it. Only the young had enough anger and anguish to accomplish it, enough integrity to succeed."[26]

Though youth may have been an asset in bringing about the Revolution, it became a liability, or at least an impediment, in creating a government, given that the Fidelistas lacked the political competence and administrative skills, to say nothing of the business acumen, needed to solve the country's many long-standing social problems, of poverty and destitution, illiteracy and disease. However, to provide a counterweight to that point, Huberman and Sweezy argue that one of the greatest *advantages* of the young revolutionaries is that they had *no* parliamentary experience, since it "takes no profound economic sophistication, no initiation into the secrets of government or administration, to understand what has to be done. What it does require is a sympathy for human beings, a passion for justice, and a vision unclouded by the fetishes and obfuscations of bourgeois ideology"—qualities that the young Cuban revolutionaries had in abundance.[27]

It was from these young Cuban intellectuals and revolutionaries that Mills took inspiration in writing his famous "Letter to the New Left," which he had drafted a few weeks prior to his visit to Cuba and then revised—no doubt as a result of his Cuba experiences—shortly after returning from the island.[28] It is to the rising generation of radicalized students, activists, and intellectuals that Mills addresses his letter, giving them hope for making a more democratic society. This was to be an international young intelligentsia—of students from Cuba, South Korea, Japan, Turkey, and even from the U.S. South—who would be the radical agents of social transformation. Mills's letter, in turn, became the inspiration to young activists like Tom Hayden, Al Haber, Bob Ross, Dick Flacks, and other leaders of Students for a Democratic Society (SDS) and its manifesto—*The Port Huron Statement*.[29] In encouraging this global leftist movement, made up of students and young people, Mills tells them reassuringly: "In Cuba, a genuinely left-wing revolution begins full-scale economic reorganization—without the domination of U.S. corporations. Average age of its leaders: about 30—and certainly a revolution without any Labor as Agency."[30]

But in focusing on the current crop of youthful Cuban leaders, Mills neglects the influence of the older political cohort of intellectuals—particularly the "generation of the Thirties" that had opposed the dictatorship of Gerardo Machado and to which the 26th of July Movement directly traced its roots.[31] Absent from *Listen, Yankee* is any mention of the intellectuals and students who took part in the revolution of 1933, such as Raúl Roa, Jorge Mañach, and Rafael Trejo.[32] What is more, Mills did not augment his research on Cuba's Revolution with any close examination of the island's past intellectual tradition; there are, for example, no references in *Listen, Yankee* to the works of Ramiro Guerra or Fernando Ortiz, or, for that matter, any detailed analysis of the ideas of José Martí.[33]

In the end, as Stanley Aronowitz states, "one may read *Listen, Yankee* as vindication of Mills's theory of intellectuals as social catalysts."[34] But before he could write about the revolutionary role of these intellectuals—and journalists, and soldiers, and workers—Mills had to first interview them.[35]

Interviewing

During the 1940s, Mills made extensive use of the interview technique in two major studies. In *White Collar*, he explained how certain structural and occupational changes taking place in mid-twentieth-century United States were affecting the psychological character, the social biographies, and the social roles of white-collar workers. For this project, Mills and his research team interviewed 128 white-collar workers on a number of occupational-related topics. What is more, Mills encouraged his interviewers to attempt to understand the respondents' deepest thoughts and feelings. This required that they ask intensive, probing questions, which meant that the interviews often lasted several hours and were frequently conducted in two sittings.[36] The other study, *The Puerto Rican Journey*, was one of the first social-scientific investigations on the adaptation and adjustment of Puerto Rican migrants in New York City. Mills designed the study and was in charge of its execution, which involved interviewing over 1,000 Puerto Ricans. The interviewers inquired about the respondents' experiences in Puerto Rico and New York and asked such incisive question as, "Would you tell me in your own words why you left P.R. and came to NY?"; "What do you personally want most out of your own life?"; and "What occupation would you like your children to follow?"

In both *White Collar* and *The Puerto Rican Journey*, Mills employed the interview to effectively understand the external conduct and inner life of different populations. But by the late 1950s and early 1960s, during his period of "pamphleteering"—when he published *The Causes of World War Three* and *Listen, Yankee*—he had allegedly come to reject empirical studies, preferring instead to take a broad critical analysis on a subject. For Mills, "much 'empirical research' is bound to be thin and uninteresting. Much of it, in fact, is a formal exercise for beginning students, and sometimes a useful pursuit for those who are not able to handle the more difficult substantive problems of social science."[37] If Mills had in mind interviewing as part of empirical research, then he was being disingenuous in his comments, given that he carried out a series of interviews, not only during his two weeks in Cuba, but also during his brief research trips to Yugoslavia (1956) and Poland (1957), and later, Brazil (1959) and Mexico (1960).

Mills was a confident and skilled interviewer and, for his proposed book *Contacting the Enemy*, for which he had queried approximately 70 Soviet intellectuals, he assuredly informed his research assistant, Saul Landau, "I'll show you how to conduct an interview, and how to put together the results."[38] To be sure, Mills was not opposed to interviewing as a social research tool, but rather to the philosophy—the abstracted empiricism—and the excessive focus on the interview protocol—"the fetishism of method and technique"—that prevented sociologists from seeing, much less studying, the major developments of the time.[39] Indeed, shortly before undertaking his tour of the Cuban island, Mills laid down specific rules on carrying out a series of interviews "with a small and highly selected number of inhabitants," specifically when on a short visit to a country:

1. Don't try to cover a great range of topics and of people.... Focus on one or two problems about which you've read a good deal....
2. Don't just converse at random, at least not all the time. Try to raise the same or very similar questions with each person interviewed. If you don't do this, you can't very well make comparisons between their views.
3. Don't try to find out the frequency ... with which some opinion or some type of person prevails. You can't do it. That requires a technique of sampling beyond the [visiting interviewer's] means. Try instead to find out the full range of opinion on each of your chosen topics of concern. Try to get an interview with at least one or two people who represent each type or each outlook that you come upon. But how do you do this?
4. First select someone who is known ... to represent one extreme of the range of opinion or of types being studied. Interview him, then ask him to refer you to someone else who might be able to give you an interesting or worthwhile view of the matter under discussion.... Now follow up the chains of these referrals from both extremes of the range....
5. Sometimes it happens that the answers from everyone you interview are quite uniform. That can mean one of three things: a) Opinion on the point is official and everyone, regardless of their true belief, is putting out the same line. The only safeguards against this are skill in interviewing and playing off facts previously known by you against what the person is saying in the interview. b) You have not gotten hold of people who hold "extreme" views; you've not covered the range. In this case, all you can do is to try again to find the other end of the range of opinion. c) There really *is* uniformity on the point in question; the range is quite narrow. In that case, if you're sure, then you've made a finding, but be very careful about this point.[40]

As Mills states in *Listen, Yankee*, his major aim in the book "is to present the voice of the Cuban revolutionary, as clearly and as emphatically as I can." This was a collective voice that he derived from the composite style of presentation, and so, in regard to the fifth rule above, it is certainly possible that he was merely parroting the Cuban government's dogma. Indeed, one of the Revolution's chief detractors, Theodore Draper, who had been on the island just a few months before Mills, contends that the revolutionary leaders "talked in much the way Mills recorded them. Sometimes the words in [*Listen, Yankee*] were so close to those that I had heard that I felt I knew the name of the source." Draper may perhaps be correct in saying that Castro and his associates were promoting the party line and that, as a consequence, "Mills made himself the vehicle of the purest and most direct propaganda."[41] But this is not evident among the Cubans whose interviews are transcribed in Chapters 4 and 5 of this book. Though they all showed strong support for the revolutionary process, and the direction it was taking at that point, it is difficult to discern a pervasive official viewpoint among them. So the other possibility in reference to the fifth rule is that Mills truly *did* find uniformity among several points with his respondents; a uniformity that arose not from propaganda, but from the interviewees' shared opinions and lived experiences. Still, that Mills did not find opinions at variance with the official party line not only engenders incredulity, it also raises the question of whether he was simply seeking confirmation of his a priori beliefs.

However all this may be, one thing is certain: Mills's experience with the Cuba interviews wasn't only a matter of adhering to research guidelines while briefly visiting a foreign country, whether Poland, Brazil, or another. In this case, Cuba was unlike any country Mills had ever been to: it was very much a society in *revolutionary transition*.

In any event, Mills sought "to ask a few of the fruitful questions, and then to seek out and to listen well to as full a variety of answers as I could find."[42] He explains that he formulated his queries by reading everything he could on the current situation in Cuba and then summarizing it in the form of questions to which he could find no answers in published sources. Some of these fruitful questions that Mills posed to the recorded respondents may be articulated as follows:

1. What is the character of the anti-Yankee sentiment present in Cuba today?
2. What is the character of the counterrevolutionary sentiment and activities such as exist in Cuba today?

3. What is the role and influence of the communists in Cuba and how organized is the Cuban Communist Party?
4. Who are the Cuban intellectuals? What was their role before the Revolution and what is it now?
5. Is there a lack of competent administrative personnel in the Revolutionary government? If so, how is this vacuum being filled?
6. Is the 26th of July Movement, in effect, a political party?
7. What are the greatest dangers the Revolution faces? What are the most important challenges confronting the Revolutionary government?
8. What is the probability of a military invasion of Cuba by the U.S. government?

And as a sort of experiential question he would frequently ask the interviewees:

9. When did you first become aware of or come in contact with the Fidelistas?

Robert Taber states that Mills posed one key question to all the revolutionary officials whom he interviewed (but did not tape), and that was: "If you were to have your fondest dreams realized—and here we do not speak of probabilities or possibilities, but only of dreams—what would you like to have the United States do?" According to Taber, the consensus response was: "If the United States cannot come to negotiate its differences with us, honestly and on the basis of mutual respect and equality, then our wish must be: stop harassing us, stop haranguing us, stop trying to interfere with our affairs. In plain words: go away and let us alone."[43] But Mills had to have known, should have known, contrary to whatever hopes he may have harbored, that the Cubans' appeal for a modus vivendi with the United States could never be realized; not given that North Americans had for too long regarded the island as a kind of extra state, an economic and political colony; more, as their personal *playground*.

Another theme about which Mills repeatedly questioned his interviewees concerned the influence that the Cuban Communist Party (officially, the Partido Socialista Popular or PSP), with almost 18,000 members, was having on the revolutionary process and government. Though in mid-1960 the Castro regime was not yet in the Soviet camp, Mills feared that it might be moving in that direction. Thus, his abiding interest—his *concern*—in the potential Communist influence in Cuba stemmed from two factors. First,

Mills wanted, above all, to tell the truth about Cuba; not, "The Whole Truth about Cuba"—for he did not believe that anyone, Cuban or North American, could yet know the whole truth about its evolving Revolution—but the plain truth. This meant that he had to, as accurately as possible, describe for a North American public what was happening in Cuba. And he knew that U.S. readers would plainly want to know if the Soviets were establishing a political and military base a mere 145 kilometers from the U.S. shoreline. Second, Mills—who was at the time drafting the manuscript for what would become his posthumously published book, *The Marxists*—was much concerned with the uses of the distinct varieties of Marxism by Cuban intellectuals, such as Ché Guevara.[44] Would the Cuban revolutionaries, as Mills no doubt hoped, become *plain Marxists* and emphasize the human being's freedom in the making of history, and confront in Marx's work the unresolved tensions of humanism and determinism, of human freedom and historical necessity? Would they instead become *sophisticated Marxists*, displaying greater flexibility and being mainly concerned with Marxism as a model of society and with the theories developed with the aid of this model? Or would the revolutionary leaders, as Mills feared they might, turn to *vulgar Marxism*, becoming apologists for the Soviet Union, exhibiting a strong party allegiance, and operating within the strict confines of Marxism as a dogmatic ideological system? To be sure, the communist question was of the upmost concern to Mills, and he broached it in detail with no fewer than four of his interlocutors.

In addition to the aforementioned questions of wide scope, Mills would at times ask his interviewees for biographical information—name, education, occupation, age—usually prefacing these with the request, "May I ask you a few personal questions?" He inquired about the marital status of all of his female interviewees (a not uncommon practice for the time). He continuously queried his respondents about the specific time—the year, the month—when events occurred. He always endeavored to get an accurate chronology of events and frequently asked, "And then what happened next?"

Equipped with a wire recorder and two Nikon cameras, he had discussions and intensive interviews with many Cubans, both government officials and private citizens. He also took careful notes when speaking with everyone. Apparently at every conversation, Mills would automatically and unobtrusively slip his notepad out of his jacket pocket and write down everything people were saying. About these jottings, "no one seemed to notice," remarked Saul Landau, who saw Mills take notes in a restaurant setting. "It didn't isolate him from the group or conversation."[45]

According to Mills, he was given complete access to information and experience by "Cubans close to events," who gave him their trust "because of their acquaintance with previous books of mine," but in particular *The Power Elite*.[46] Indeed, one of the recorded respondents, Franz Stettmeier, makes oblique reference to *The Power Elite* (see chapter 5, interview 6).

It is significant that Mills did not speak Spanish, nor did he have any adequate understanding of the language. For all communications—from spontaneous conversations to formal interviews—involving Spanish (which were the majority of them), he relied on the interpretation skills of Juan Arcocha, primarily, but also at times those of René C. Vallejo, head of INRA in Oriente. Mills's Texas drawl, mixed with a mid-Atlantic accent, produced a marked Yankee enunciation of his Spanish, in those few occasions when he did attempt speaking it. He employed the long "I," and thus said "Fīdel" and "Fīdelistas," as well as the long "e," and, for example, pronounced the province in Cuba as "Orientē." As the conversations progressed, he began to change his pronunciation of these words to more closely conform to the actual Spanish. He also seems to have grown bolder in attempting a few Spanish words—*señora, ranchera, casa*—that he likely picked up while growing up in Texas.[47] Though quite good at remembering proper names, the pronunciation of the Spanish digraph "*ll*" was lost on him. Thus, when he verbally referred to Vallejo, with whom he was apparently well acquainted, he either mangled the name or simply called him "V."

While Mills was generally patient and courteous with his interlocutors, he did not hesitate to interrupt if he sought clarification, wanted to pursue in more detail a thread in the conservation, or if he felt that the issue had been exhausted and wanted to shift the conversation's direction. In those interviews that required translation, he would frequently speak to his interpreter directly and refer to the interviewee in the third person.

At times Mills would probe, tactfully but firmly, as he did, for example, during an interview when he felt that he was again hearing the same "line" about the insignificance of the Cuban Community Party: "You must realize that I need, the kind of information you give me now, the truth about the communist thing because I write for a Yankee audience." Only in one instance was Mills somewhat impertinent with an interviewee, Stettmeier, when he facetiously inquired about his competence as a clinical psychologist for social analysis:

MILLS: Do you consider your position as a clinical psychologist a very good one for the study of counterrevolutionary activities? [Chuckling]

STETTMEIER: I think, yes. You know why?

MILLS: No sir, I don't. Why? [Chuckling] I was joking, but you take me seriously!

Generally, however, Mills was tactful and respectful, and at times even courtly, with his interviewees, particularly the female ones. On wanting to end one interview, he instructs his interpreter to relay the following to the interviewee:

Tell the Captain that one thing I have found is that all Cubans will talk about the Revolution almost forever but that I must save some of my tape for Fidel Castro because I understand he speaks ten or fifteen minutes at a time. That is why I have a four-hour machine here ready and so I must save it for him!

At another interview, as he was ending the conversation, Mills realizes that he had not properly introduced himself to his female interviewee, Isabel Rielo, who had recently married: "I have been very rude. I have not asked the Captain's name. Could she please give it to me? And spell it please." He ends with, "Although we do not have the honor of knowing your husband may we congratulate him nonetheless." In addition, he often used humor prudently to create rapport.

Mills spoke deliberately, with a strong sonorous voice, presumably to make himself understandable to his interviewees and interpreter, but also, no doubt, to produce a clear audio record of his conversations. He would often intersperse his replies to his interlocutor's statements with, "Yes. I understand" or "Aha." Many of the interviews were seemingly conducted near busy roadways and other public places with loud noises in the background (barking dogs, revving engines, honking horns, horse hoofs on pavement, planes flying overhead); the louder of these noises would sometimes interrupt the discussion or make it difficult to be heard.

Mills had obviously prepared questions in advance, which he read to the interviewees, but many, perhaps most, of his questions arose from the flow of the conversation. His queries were, at times, perhaps too long, too wordy. He tended to be formal with Spanish-speaking interviewees and more relaxed and easy with the English-speaking ones. Concerning the latter, of particular note is his repartee with Arcocha and Stettmeier, punctuated with laughter and joking. The English-speaking interviews tended to be twice as long (an average of thirty-three minutes) as the Spanish-speaking ones (an average of fourteen minutes).

It is not known how Mills arrived at the "small and highly selected number of inhabitants" he interviewed. It may have been Robert Taber who, while acting as his guide through Cuba, put him in contact with them. It is known, however, that Mills had discussions with most of the leaders of the Revolutionary government, including Prime Minister Fidel Castro and Co-mandante René Vallejo. He also met with Osvaldo Dorticós Torrado, the president of Cuba; Enrique Oltuski, director of organization of the industrialization of INRA; Ché Guevara, president of the Cuban National Bank; Raul Cepero Bonilla, minister of commerce; Armando Hart, minister of education; and Carlos Franqui, editor-in-chief of the daily *Revolución*. In addition, there are the seven interviewees Mills electronically recorded and that he mentions by name in the book's foreword: Juan Arcocha, Franz Stettmeier, Isabel Rielo, Juan Escalona, Elvira Escobar, Elba Luisa Batista Benitez, and Lauro Fiallo Barrero. Other interview participants also taped, but not identified, are two "captains." Through it all, Mills was extraordinarily busy, having to jam all of these discussions and interviews with these and countless others into about two weeks' time. In the estimation of Arcocha, who accompanied Mills throughout his journey in Cuba, "Mills had a right to speak in the name of the Cuban people because he had made a superhuman effort to understand them, and he had earned it."[48] This same sentiment was expressed to North American Beat poet Lawrence Ferlinghetti, when he visited the offices of *Revolución* a few months later. Several of the newspaper's writers—doubtless Arcocha being among them—told Ferlinghetti that even though Mills had seemed "pretty naïve" about the events of the Revolution to that point, they nonetheless respected him for his diligence, having "gone everywhere and talked to everyone."[49]

Yet, for all his efforts—his firsthand observations and intensive interviews—there are several major criticisms that can legitimately be leveled against Mills. To begin with, he did not, as he put it in his rules on interviewing, "cover the range of opinion." He spoke only with Cuban revolutionaries, not with Cuban *counterrevolutionaries*, whether in Havana or Miami. Also, and related, while he quite accurately captures the revolutionaries' character structure, he appears to have a partisan view of revolutionary Cuba's *social structure*. For example, he does not consider how the new regime's suppression of freedom of expression—in effect at the time through the rigid control of information services, and even intellectual life—was impacting the arts and media, to say nothing of religious life, in Cuban society. On these two points Theodore Draper is quite correct to state, in reference to the Cuba interviews Mills conducted to write *Listen, Yankee*: "A reader has a right to expect that the author should do some work of his own beyond listening only to one side, and that a sociologist would be able at least to give a reasonably accurate report of the social structure of the country."[50] Finally, Mills seems not to have spoken with any *campesinos*, thus failing to get the story from the other half, the uneducated half of the population, that made the Revolution.

In the two chapters that follow, we hear from these Cubans who spoke with Mills and who were close to events; first from the public officials and then from the private citizens.

CHAPTER FOUR
Recorded Interviews with Cuban Officials

The five interviews presented in this chapter were all conducted with people in some way attached to the Revolutionary Government, four of them associated with the military. Though some respondents did at times express their own sentiments (and in fact, Mills asked specific personal questions of two of them), they were generally speaking ex officio to a citizen of a country they perceived as a menace to their efforts to create Cuba as a sovereign state. Juan Arcocha worked for the newspaper *Revolución*, the official organ of the 26th of July Movement that aimed to organize, guide, and disseminate revolutionary ideology to the Cuban people. The two army captains—whom I'm calling Captain 1 and Captain 2—had long been involved in military and administrative capacities. Isabel Rielo, also a captain, had been a rebel soldier in the women's platoon. At the time of the interview, she was working at the Camilo Cienfuegos School City in the mountains of Oriente. Comandante Dermidio Escalona had been appointed by Fidel Castro as commander of the rebel forces in Pinar del Río, on the western end of the island. He was, at the time, acting military commander of the province. In all, Mills's taped recordings include three "captains" and one "comandante" (i.e., Escalona), military ranks held by about 200 and 40, respectively, at the time.[1] None of these interlocutors, however, was a member of Castro's inner circle.

Interview 1

Time: Approximately thirty minutes
Interviewee: Juan Arcocha
Appropriately enough, Mills began his series of interviews by talking with the man who would serve as his interpreter and companion during his entire time in Cuba, Juan Arcocha. In the Note to the Reader, I, Mills thanks Arcocha and describes him as the man "who interpreted for me in many long interviews and during much hard travel, and more than that, helped me to understand many things in Cuba." Arcocha is the only one of his recorded interviewees who would eventually break with Castro and go into self-imposed exile.[2]

Thirty-three years old, tall, prematurely balding and wearing black horn-rimmed glasses, Arcocha possessed a bookish, sober look. But as is evident from this interview, he had an easy laugh and good humor, occasionally taking time off from his official duties as interpreter to play guitar for his traveling companions, Vallejo, Taber, and Mills. Being fluent in both English and French, Arcocha had served as interpreter to Jean-Paul Sartre and Simon de Beauvoir on their first, and well-publicized, visit to post-Revolution Cuba during February–March of 1960, and just a few months before interpreting for Mills.

Early in the interview, Arcocha, who had known Fidel Castro since they were university students (and who initially rejected him as an ambitious and irresponsible opportunist, then accepted him at the time of the interview as the sincere leader of Cuba, and ultimately would come to reject him again as a dictator on par with Stalin)[3] describes his astonishment concerning Castro's personality transformation from student days to the present.

Many years after speaking with Mills, Arcocha would record the details on first meeting Castro:

> It was during the early days of October 1945. It was the start of the academic year at the University of Havana. A group of us, friends and recent graduates of the Colegio de la Salle [a Catholic preparatory school], had agreed to meet at a café near the School of Law. We were afraid to go to the University alone as it had the well-earned reputation of being a den of gangsters who used it as a springboard to enter into politics according to their own understanding—that is to say, their enjoyment of dubious privileges, and they usually obtained at gunpoint the grades that their intimidated professors dared not deny them.... We were approached by a tall, strapping fellow with a penetrating look, greasy complexion, with the beginnings of a double chin, who had a profile reminiscent of a Greek statue. Though his nose was not straight, it extended down from his forehead, wide and intelligent.... He came straight to the point: "Guys, all of us graduates from Catholic schools ought to unite to clean up the University. I hope that you will vote for me for class delegate." He triggered in me an immediate and almost allergic dislike of him; of course, I did not vote for him.[4]

In the interview, Arcocha states that Castro's remarkable transformation—Castro's character, he says, is marked by sincerity—is most clearly exhibited in the latter's numerous televised appearances, particularly through his didactic and garrulous speeches. Mills is skeptical that Castro's sincerity can be ascertained electronically, since many charismatic personalities are adroit in "the television technique." Later in the interview, Arcocha uses Sartre's notion of "direct democracy" to describe Castro's particular form of governance; given Castro's skillful use of the television technique, his concept of democracy has also been referred to as "government by television."[5]

Mills begins by asking for some biographical information. Arcocha gives his occupation as secretary for Carlos Franqui, the editor-in-chief of *Revolución*. He states that he graduated from Havana High School, a private Catholic school, and then attended the University of Havana, where he studied law and journalism. Arcocha completed his law degree in 1950 and began working as a journalist. In 1955 he studied French literature at the Sorbonne in Paris, where he first became interested in politics.

After some discussion about Arcocha's father, who had been a lawyer working for the Batista government, Mills then asks Arcocha, "When did you first meet Fidel Castro?"

ARCOCHA: At the University [of Havana].

MILLS: What was your impression of him?

ARCOCHA: Very bad. I thought he was a cheap politician who wanted to use me. He always wanted me to vote for him. He wanted to be the class delegate. Because the University was sort of a springboard. And it was like this: first of all you were elected delegate of the class, then you were a delegate of a year, then you were a delegate of a faculty, then you were a delegate of all the faculties that was a [inaudible] of the FEU, which means Federation of the Students of the University.[6]

[...]

ARCOCHA: ... I had been strongly trying to fight against [Castro] in Paris.

MILLS: Figuring out how to get rid of him if he did win?

ARCOCHA: Exactly. I was convinced the only thing he wanted to do was to put Batista down and put himself in his place and go on exactly like before.

MILLS: The replacement of one with the other.

ARCOCHA: Exactly. A change of men.

MILLS: Yes. And what caused you to change your mind on that? I take it you have changed your mind.

ARCOCHA: Yes, I have. [Laughter]

MILLS: Given your position on *Revolución* we may assume that. [Laughter] Unless, you are a secret counterrevolutionary. [Laughter] That's not likely.

ARCOCHA: [Laughter]

MILLS: OK, now, what was it that made you change your opinion?

ARCOCHA: Well, the first time he appeared on television it was agreeably shocking.[7]

MILLS: I see. Why?

ARCOCHA: Because I realized that he was sincere.[8] That all those things he had been telling for so many years, he had meant them all of the time.

MILLS: But surely you can't tell from one or two television appearances that suddenly the man is sincere. There are many people who are expert at the television technique.

ARCOCHA: Yes, but first of all, the things he spoke about. He had already won, so he didn't have to keep his promises.

MILLS: Oh, I see. He had power after all. With such military force as existed in the country he could then have done anything he wished, if he wanted to.

ARCOCHA: Before, all the politicians had made many promises until the day they were elected, and then they didn't even speak about it anymore. It was completely forgotten.

MILLS: So first he spoke of the agrarian reform.

ARCOCHA: He spoke of the agrarian reform, but those were not only words. Everybody was watching television that night. Absolutely everybody. We wanted to see how he was. He was such a legend. It was a normal curiosity to see how he was, what he was going to say. So he insisted very, very much on the poor conditions of the peasants, of the workers. But it was not a scientist discussing things in a cold way. He was discussing that from a very human point of view.[9]

MILLS: And so not only what he discussed but also the manner of his discussion.

ARCOCHA: Exactly, the way in which he participated. And I think that you can feel on television.[10]

MILLS: What other aspects of Fidel at this time impressed themselves upon you?

ARCOCHA: Well, he had his [inaudible] at the university period.

MILLS: So perhaps history will absolve him but we will never know...

ARCOCHA: No. I asked him. I called him and I told him, "Well, I'm very disappointed that the conversation hasn't gone further." Because I wanted to know something which I hadn't found. And he said, "Well, what do you want to know?" And I told him, "Well, I want to know in which moment the Fidel I knew at the University became today's Fidel?"

MILLS: Did he tell you the moment?

ARCOCHA: Well, he looked me in the eyes and said, "Well, you know, the Fidel you met at the University was a very primitive one. I was a product of all the frustrations that there were in Cuba. After that there was a long evolution." Actually, he never explained, so I don't know why the change took place.

MILLS: Well, perhaps those are things that a man doesn't become aware of until a little later.

ARCOCHA: Perhaps. But he made such a spectacular change. It's incredible.

The conversation then turns to those features that Arcocha found particularly attractive about Castro in the early months of the Revolution. Arcocha mentions his humanity, sincerity, intelligence, and courage. He describes Castro as speaking, not demagogically, but in a low conversational tone. This type of simple and human conversation was "a new invention in Cuba." Arcocha mentions that he particularly liked Castro speaking on television because it was as though he were chatting with the people. Castro assumed a different intonation when he gave a public speech, Arcocha explains, but even then it was unique from that of any other public speaker.

MILLS: To what extent was [Castro's] kind of nationalism at that time, in the spring of 1959, based upon his anti-Yankee remarks?

ARCOCHA: Well, even at that very moment, it was a very human and a very particular nationalism because all he said was, "We have been exploited for so many years by the United States. We are human beings. We have rights. So all we want is that the United States recognize these rights and treat us like human beings."

[...]

MILLS: Now may I ask you a few general questions about your attitudes and opinions?

ARCOCHA: Yes.

MILLS: What is your real attitude now towards the possibility of the Cuban Communist Party increasing in power? I don't mean internationally now, but strictly within the Cuban political scene.

ARCOCHA: Well, that's a very interesting point. First of all, I don't think they are increasing in power.[11]

MILLS: You do not think they will?

ARCOCHA: No.

MILLS: Why not?

ARCOCHA: Because, first of all, nobody likes them here.

MILLS: Well, you have undoubtedly heard the argument that there is a lack of competent administrative personnel. And they seem to have some administrative competence. Hence, do you think there is a possibility that they will, sort of by default, move into the vacuum?

ARCOCHA: Of course there are Communists which are occupying positions because of that vacuum you mention. And you hear a lot of talk about infiltration—Communist infiltration. But the point would be to see who's infiltrating whom.

MILLS: Well, that is indeed the question I am asking.

ARCOCHA: Exactly. Well, I might say that the Communist Party[12] is very strongly infiltrated by July 26 and it's in a very dangerous position. I wonder if they have realized that.

MILLS: What sort of evidence do you have for that? Because American readers of the Yankee press certainly are not aware of the infiltration of the communists. Indeed, it's a world historical development and I'm perfectly prepared, don't misunderstand me, to believe that that might happen in Cuba. [Laughter]

ARCOCHA: [Laughter] There's a very popular joke here. It's, by the way, a counterrevolutionary joke. The counterrevolutionaries here, and the middle class and the bourgeois, they, of course, are convinced that we're all communists. My poor father is convinced that I am. And the joke goes like this: When Mikoyan came to Cuba he went back to Moscow and he spoke with Khrushchev.[13] And Khrushchev asked him, "Well, what do you think about Cuba?" And he says, "Well, I'm a little worried because there's so much infiltration from the July 26 in the Communist Party." [Laughter] Actually, it isn't a joke anymore, I think. I mean I have no proof for that.

MILLS: Are the Communists quite a competent organization, in your impression of them?

ARCOCHA: No. The trouble is they are frozen.

MILLS: Rather dogmatic and inflexible, do you mean?

ARCOCHA: Yes, exactly. Very dogmatic. They simply don't understand what's happening here.

MILLS: Well, have they not learned from Fidel's leadership and the actual course of the Revolution, anything?

ARCOCHA: The trouble is they have old leaders and there's no hope that they will change. They are old Stalinists.

MILLS: And the younger men who are bright do not go into the party?

ARCOCHA: They have no young people.

MILLS: Really?

ARCOCHA: For instance, from the intellectual point of view. I am in the intellectual circles thanks to *Revolución*. And they have just one young intellectual who's not very bright. The only one they have. The Communist intellectuals in Cuba are people over fifty years [old]. They have no one single young voice.

MILLS: If they do not recruit younger people ...

ARCOCHA: They're trying desperately to recruit them.

MILLS: Yes, but if they do not succeed, and it's your impression that they will not, presumably, because of the many opportunities for leadership and everything else political within the 26 Movement and other revolutionary organs, then it is a question of waiting a little while and they will fade away.

ARCOCHA: Exactly. For instance, there is no such thing as a political apparatus in Cuba. And they have one, so it has been necessary to take some of the low- and middle-level members just to fill that vacuum.

MILLS: How do you mean there is no other political apparatus in Cuba? Isn't the militia a political apparatus?

ARCOCHA: No, I mean a political organization like a political party, for instance.

MILLS: There's no party whatsoever, in your opinion?

ARCOCHA: The Communist Party only.

MILLS: Well, don't you think that the July 26 is, in effect, a party?

ARCOCHA: No. It's something very strange.

MILLS: Yes, I know. That's what I came to find out.

ARCOCHA: It is not a party.

MILLS: Why?

ARCOCHA: Because it has no ...

MILLS: Because there have been no elections?

ARCOCHA: No, that doesn't mean anything. [...] For instance, take China or Russia, how it's organized. There's a political party and you have functionaries and functionaries [...] and it's a very complicated organization. That doesn't exist [here].

MILLS: I see. So what you have here ...

ARCOCHA: It's a direct contact between Fidel and the people.

MILLS: And ministers, of course, and governmental agencies.

ARCOCHA: It stops at the level of the Council of Ministers, and then it goes to the people.

MILLS: In terms of decision.

ARCOCHA: Exactly, exactly. In the middle there are people who work and want positions in government but it isn't organized. It is not a political organization.

MILLS: In what sense do you think of that as dictatorial? A dictatorship?

ARCOCHA: Well, perhaps a [inaudible] dictatorship but I mean we have never had such real democracy here.

MILLS: In other words, in terms of the realization of interests, which the people have at heart, and which are the people ...

ARCOCHA: Exactly, exactly. That's what Sartre calls "direct democracy."

MILLS: Aha. Sometimes called "guided democracy."[14]

ARCOCHA: They're troubling words. When an American says "democracy," well, you mean elections and so on and so forth. Personally, I think it's a fraud. If you say that in the United States you're automatically considered a communist.

MILLS: Not necessarily. I've said it very frequently. [Laughter]

ARCOCHA: Well, then, perhaps you're considered a communist. [Laughter]

MILLS: On the contrary. It's well known that I am not. This is the most worrisome thing about me, I think. [Laughter] What's your attitude toward the real possibility of a military invasion of Cuba by the U.S. government?

ARCOCHA: Well, I think it's very possible.[15]

MILLS: Even now?

ARCOCHA: Even now. It's not so probable as it was some weeks ago. Until Khrushchev said he would send the rockets. Then it was rather a sure thing to come.[16]

MILLS: Oh, you do believe that it is the Khrushchev threat of retaliation that is keeping the U.S. Marines in Florida?
ARCOCHA: Yes.
MILLS: You really do?
ARCOCHA: Uh-huh. I wonder for just how long he will keep them there.
MILLS: You mean that they will still come to Cuba despite the Khrushchev warning?
ARCOCHA: They might. It depends on who's running things in the United States.
MILLS: Do you think the [presidential] election will make a difference in the United States, coming up?[17]
ARCOCHA: I don't think so. That won't change anything. Well, I have read something in a French newspaper about the possibilities of a kind of mild revolution in the United States.... For some months I just don't expect anything else from the United States so it doesn't matter if it's a Republican or a Democrat. They're all the same. But then I read in that French newspaper it seems that Mr. Kennedy has some advanced ideas, which are considered very advanced in the States about, for instance, state planning and better organizing the whole economic structure of the country.
MILLS: I believe that this is [inaudible] dreaming, personally.
[...]
MILLS: And what is your considered opinion, Juan, of *Time* magazine?
ARCOCHA: Oh, it's horrible. It's the most dangerous thing for the United States.
MILLS: How so?
ARCOCHA: Because it so cleverly distorts truth.
MILLS: The truth about Cuba, for example?
ARCOCHA: About anything...

Arcocha goes on to explain that he initially experienced at firsthand *Time*'s distortion of the news when he visited Greece in 1958. According to *Time* magazine, there was supposedly a great communist danger in Greece, with the Greek people and government being implicated in adopting a communist ideology. He discovered that *Time*'s reporting about the Greek situation was completely false. Arcocha's second experience of *Time*'s distortion of the truth happened when it started writing about Cuba and Castro.

In this case, Arcocha was in the country and knew what was happening there. Since then he had resolved to stop reading the magazine.

Interview 2

Time: Approximately fifteen minutes. Juan Arcocha interpreted.
Interviewee: Unknown
The following interview is with an unidentified captain of the Rebel Army that probably took place in Oriente province. The captain's identity cannot be deduced from any information provided in the interview or in *Listen, Yankee*. I will refer to him as "Captain 1."

> MILLS: Capitan, when did you first get into the Rebel Army?
> CAPTAIN 1: Well, the Rebel Army was a modification of the struggle and it was formed during the tyranny.
> MILLS: During 1958?
> CAPTAIN 1: Well, I have been a soldier of the Revolution since 1952.
> MILLS: Fifty-two? How old are you, Captain?
> CAPTAIN 1: Twenty-nine.
> MILLS: You started very early then, didn't you?
> CAPTAIN 1: There are others who started before me. There are *comandantes* who were seventeen and eighteen years old at the time.[18]
> MILLS: I see. And what jobs did you have before you became a soldier?
> CAPTAIN 1: Well, office clerk. Then I was a factory worker. I have had many other jobs.
> MILLS: You were telling me a little while ago that there were militia attached to various enterprises here in this district and you are the captain of the army. What is the relation between these militia and your command of the army?
> CAPTAIN 1: The relations between the militia and the Rebel Army are the relations that exist between different units of the same army.
> MILLS: So they are sort of like a reserve, the militia is.
> CAPTAIN 1: Well, we could call it a reserve army because we are currently working now. While there is no war, we work.
> MILLS: Do your rebel soldiers, under your command, work in different enterprises?
> CAPTAIN 1: There is a part that devote themselves strictly to indispensable military issues. There are other parts that belong to different state institutions.

MILLS: Such as?

CAPTAIN 1: Well, INRA, other public activities, and some of them are ministers. The official leader of the Revolution is the commander of the Rebel Army and prime minister.

MILLS: You, of course, train the militia—that is part of your duty.

CAPTAIN 1: Yes, of course. . . .

MILLS: I've heard some of the governmental officials and other people in Cuba say that there may come a time when the militia would be more important than the army as such. What is your opinion concerning that?

The captain states that he doesn't understand the question and sets out to explain how the Rebel Army is different from any other army in the world. He contends that Cuba considers any citizen who is a good revolutionary to be a good soldier for the country. Mills replies that he doesn't quite understand that because armies in many parts of the world issue from the people, that is, they are voluntary armies. The Cuban Army is voluntary, and so Mills doesn't see how it is unique in the world. The Cuban Army is different, explains the captain, because the other armies fill their soldier's heads only with unconscious discipline. For example, the U.S. Army goes to war without being aware of the motives, consequences, and the general significance of those wars. Mills then asks if the difference is that the Cuban soldier knows what he is fighting for. Of course, says the captain, the soldiers are taught about the causes and motives that produced the Revolution. Mills again interjects that many armies, including the Chinese Army, for example, do that. The captain acknowledges that other armies provide that sort of education, but at the moment he's wanting to consider the Cuban Army in particular. The Cuban Army, the captain insists, possesses a disciplined consciousness [*conciencia*][19] because the rebel soldier understands that his cause is just. He therefore has a higher consciousness compared with the soldier who is just fighting for a salary or for his country's false beliefs.[20] Echoing the captain's sentiments, Mills, in *Listen, Yankee*, writes in the voice of the Cuban revolutionary: "So ours, we think, is not like any other army in the world."[21]

MILLS: Do you think that there are any other differences that are unique to the Cuban Army?

CAPTAIN 1: This is an army that is born from the most humble level of society and that guarantees the rights and the aspirations of the dispossessed classes. So, that is a right of the majority as democracy demands.

MILLS: Do you have classes in which the history and the causes of the Revolution are explained? You have many very young boys that are now only eighteen coming into the army and the militia. So, do you have classes to train them in the meaning of the Revolution?

CAPTAIN 1: Yes. But not only to the boys in the Rebel Army. Our leader, Fidel Castro, speaks to all the people every week.

MILLS: Are there no special classes for the army?

CAPTAIN 1: Cuban history, geography, economic geography, the thoughts and works of José Martí, political economy, and all of the other studies that complement the minimum cultural base that we should all have.

MILLS: And does the captain teach such a class himself?

CAPTAIN 1: Yes, and there are many *compañeros* who teach these classes.

MILLS: That's part of the training of the soldiers?

CAPTAIN 1: Yes.

MILLS: What sort of books do you use in teaching the political economy of Cuba?

CAPTAIN 1: There are many books in political economy—French, North American, German. It depends on how much progress the class has made.

Interview 3

Time: Approximately fifteen minutes
Interviewee: Unknown. Juan Arcocha interpreted.
Like the previous interview, this short one was also with an unidentified captain of the army. The captain's identity cannot be deduced from any information provided in the interview or in *Listen, Yankee*. I will refer to him as "Captain 2." The captain had only been at his present command post for a few days when Mills spoke with him. Prior to that he had been a coordinator in the 26th of July Movement in the province. In this capacity he provided revolutionary orientation and organization to the civilian population.

As in the interview with Juan Arcocha, the likelihood of an invasion of Cuba with the backing of the U.S. government is again raised. Another issue discussed is that of industrialization, particularly the role of the Cuban military in building the industrial sector of Cuban society. If Captain 2 is vague about his actual involvement, and that of the soldiers under him, in the construction of a factory nearby, it is perhaps because, given the nonexistent preconditions for industrializing in Cuba, "what had been done along this line to date has been almost wholly in the realm of study, planning, preliminary preparations."[22] The first step toward financing industry had been articulated by Fidel Castro in a television interview earlier that year: that all workers should contribute 4 percent of their wages, and in this way raise $40 million for industrial development.

The interview begins with a brief discussion of a raised cultural awareness among the workers and also of their involvement in self-government—a concept that had been foreign to Cubans up to that point.

> MILLS TO ARCOCHA: You were saying that the captain was just at a little town near here and he found a farmer...
> ARCOCHA: A peasant in this place, and although he was illiterate he was saying many interesting things at a worker's assembly.
> CAPTAIN 2 TO ARCOCHA: Do you want me to explain about the *campesino*? Well, I was profoundly impressed by the way in which a man without any education or culture could achieve such a clear conception of the historical moments through which the country is living and of the position a worker is supposed to have. And he was explaining that he had not received that conception at any school, given that he could neither read nor write.
> MILLS: What was his conception?
> CAPTAIN 2: It concerns the position that the Cuban revolutionary worker should have regarding the events and development of our Revolution. He explained that he loved the Revolution and defended it. The education he received had been of coming home, late in the evening after a hard day's work, and finding his children asking him for food, which he was unable to provide for them. Because the large sugar monopolies provided work only three months, and sometimes only two months out of the year. And there was no other place to work after that. And so during the dead season [*tiempo muerto*] they borrowed against their future salaries and went further into debt. The same company would take advantage of the situation by extending them credit that they could only use in company-owned businesses.

MILLS: Yes, I'm familiar with that situation.[23] How is this worker living today?

CAPTAIN 2: With the hope and satisfaction of knowing that the imperialistic monopoly belongs to him now.

Mills asks how it is that the peasant feels that the sugar mill now belongs to him, and if the peasant is actually making decisions about how it is to be run. The captain states that at the aforementioned worker's assembly, the newly appointed administrator told the workers that they were the ones to decide when they would begin readying the sugar mills in the district. Mills then asks who appointed the administrator. The captain explains that he had been an ice cream vendor who studied and made sacrifices, and the Revolutionary government and the worker's assembly from the district appointed him.

MILLS: How long does that worker that you were telling me about, that was so happy in that hope that he entertained because he now had a share in that sugar mill, how long does he think it will be before his material standard of living goes up quite materially?

CAPTAIN 2: That depends on Yankee imperialism. If they attack us, if they continue to choke us economically, we will have to devote forces to the country's defense.

MILLS: Does the captain really believe that there is any probability that the United States will actually invade Cuba?

CAPTAIN 2: It's difficult for them to do it directly, but we have conclusive evidence that they provoke aggression with Cuba. In addition, they disrespect the American people by taking before the U.S. Senate the war criminals [Cuban exiles] who murdered 20,000 people in Cuba.[24]

MILLS: Do you believe that if there is any kind of actual military action against the Revolutionary government it will be indirectly, in the sense that these exiles and war criminals will be the ones to actually do it?

CAPTAIN 2: And anyone else who sells himself to the imperialist's money and wants to participate in these armies.

MILLS: You mean mercenary armies.

CAPTAIN 2: Mercenary. Although we now have U.S. citizens who have died in the aggression against Cuba—those who came by plane. That's an alarming matter because it shows the complicity of the U.S. government because they could have stopped these attacks.[25]

ARCOCHA TO MILLS: The captain wants to highlight the opinion of the Cuban working classes concerning the general state of the Revolution.

CAPTAIN 2: They are aware that it is not an issue of sectors but of the entire Cuban people. They know that the Revolution has to progress evenly for all. And that is why it has not been possible to achieve rapid progress in one particular sector. In other systems, in the capitalist system, certain sectors may grow rapidly in wages and a better standard of living. But there is a consequence to that, and that is the impoverishment of other sectors. In Cuba we are vigilant that that doesn't happen. And we are industrializing the country to create other sources of work for those other sectors.

MILLS: Yes. Now, what is the role of the army in this industrialization program?

CAPTAIN 2: To work and cooperate with the people. The worker is giving 4 percent of his salary for the industrialization of the country. In all the municipalities, in all parts of the country, they are working for industrialization.

MILLS: That is to say, actually soldiers under the captain's command will help build an industry?

CAPTAIN 2: Well, we will cooperate in everything we can. I'm thinking about getting some tools and going to where they are constructing a factory where the industry will develop. I'm thinking that one Sunday or Saturday I will go there to do some work. I will not order my soldiers to work. I will go, and those who want to help can come.

[. . .]

Interview 4

Time: Approximately ten minutes
Interviewee: Isabel Rielo. Juan Arcocha interpreted.
Mills's next interview was held in the Sierra Maestra with Isabel Rielo, the only one of his interviewees that Mills mentions by name in *Listen, Yankee*. Rielo was a thirty-two-year-old rebel soldier with angular features, high cheekbones, deep-set eyes, her dark-brown hair pulled back. When Mills spoke with her she was wearing her soldier's uniform, holstered gun swinging at her hip. Captain Rielo had a quick smile and spoke animatedly in rapid-fire sentences to Mills, Taber, and Arcocha.

Originally from Oriente, Rielo came from a large peasant family of eight brothers and sisters. She was the only one of her siblings to enter university, in 1952, where she studied pharmacy. After the *Granma* landing, she became part of a clandestine cell in the 26th of July Movement involved in underground work. Later, she and her younger sister, Lilia, joined the rebel soldiers in the Sierra Maestra to work as nurses, treating the wounded and assisting in surgery.

During the interview, Rielo tells Mills that she had been in charge of the Mariana Grajales, the Rebel Army's first all-women's platoon and the only women organized into combat during the insurrection. The details of how the platoon was formed and how Rielo became its leader are as follows.[26] In May 1958 Batista launched a large military offensive against the Rebel Army, and by July of that year the dictator's forces had been badly beaten by the greatly outnumbered guerillas. By that point in the insurgency women like Teté Puebla, Eloísa Ballester, Celia Sánchez, Haydée Santamaría, Isabel Rielo, and Lilia Rielo had proven themselves to be as capable as any of the male rebel soldiers. Though they had not yet been organized as combatants, they had helped with cooking, sewing, tending to the wounded, and even taught some of the *compañeros* (comrades) to read and write. After Batista's offensive had been defeated, some of the women asked Fidel Castro to let them fight with a rifle, face-to-face with the enemy. Castro agreed that the women had earned the right to fight, and on September 4 he formed the eleven-woman Mariana Grajales Platoon, armed them with lightweight M-1 machineguns, and taught them to shoot.[27] In target practice, with a Garand rifle, the women (now called the "Marianas") were to try to hit a U.S. quarter from twenty to thirty meters away. Isabel Rielo hit the coin and split it. She was named commanding officer as a result. The Marianas saw combat three times; first, at the battle of Cerro Pelado on September 26; then at La Presa, Holguín province, on October 21; and finally at the battle of Los Güiros on November 2. Rielo finished the war with the rank of first lieutenant and in 1960 was promoted to captain.[28]

In 1971 Rielo recounted the conviction that compelled the women to participate in combat:

> Those of us who had formed the women's battalion never felt we should have any different treatment from the men; we wanted them to look on us as just one more soldier. So we made them understand that we had suffered the same privations as they had, we'd confronted the same hardships, we'd endured the machine gun fire from the planes,

we'd dragged the wounded back to safe positions and got them to the campaign hospitals so they wouldn't be killed by the bombs....

Combat was just another front you couldn't deny our women, since it grew mainly out of our own desire to fight. We used to see a man go out and later they'd come and tell us, "They killed him," and our anger made us want to go and share that danger.[29]

At the time that Mills interviewed her, Isabel Rielo was implementing the material and ideological foundations of what would become the Camilo Cienfuegos School City. Mills spoke with her on the campus, while she was serving as a teacher in makeshift buildings. The school cities were intended to provide education to the underserved children of peasants "in those rural, mountainous areas [where] the people are so scattered that it's not really possible to build regular schools in such a way that they are convenient."[30] Part of the education these schools provided the children was an *encuentro*, an experiential nexus between city and country.

An educational complex composed of several units, with buildings of bioclimatic architectural design, the Camilo Cienfuegos School City was situated in the foothills of the Sierra Maestra, about forty kilometers inland from Manzanillo. Its inauguration had taken place on July 26, just a few weeks prior to Mills's visit, with 5,000 peasant children already enrolled. That day hundreds of people showed up, including Fidel Castro, to celebrate the first phase of construction. Loud speakers on towers were set up in the midst of the crowds, a mobile unit with television crew was stationed among the throngs. Pennants on tall poles fluttered in the wind, bunting with triangle patterns draped over the sides of buildings—all this with the towering Sierra Maestra mountain range as the backdrop. The initial plan was for the School City to include 40 schools, 2 to prepare teachers and nurses, and a 200-bed hospital, with the ultimate goal of matriculating 20,000 students, offering them a complete education from first grade to high school.

Rielo is the only informant whom Mills mentions by name and quotes directly in *Listen, Yankee* (see chapter 7, "Culture in Cuba"). In this interview Mills asks a question of Rielo that he would repeat with subsequent interviewees: "When did you first become aware of the Fidelista movement?" Before beginning his conversation with Rielo, however, Mills spoke the following into the recorder:

MILLS: I am at the military establishment of the women Rebel Army in the Sierra. I've just had an interview with two of these young women. Their situation seems to be as follows: There are about fifty of them who went into the Sierra in 1956 and 1957 and formed a Rebel Army unit and fought with Castro. What is now happening is that they are being trained. There are high school teachers here who are giving them grammar school or other kinds of education. And this Rebel Army unit will now become a military reserve unit, but its major function will be to do social work and teaching in the new centers [the school cities] in the Sierra Maestra. It can also be seen as a sort of cadre and is an excellent illustration of the way in which army and militia units are being transformed into organizations for more positive social functions, nonmilitary functions.

The interview with Isabel Rielo begins at this point and is conducted at the Camilo Cienfuegos School City.

MILLS: How long have you been building the [school] city?
RIELO: We brought the first children here in the middle of December.
MILLS: In last December [1959]. And had the construction started at that time?
RIELO: We're just starting it now. The problem here is that the children help us to found the city. I personally brought the first children here from the Sierra. When we first brought the children only the first classrooms were built.
MILLS: And how did you select the children?
RIELO: The children were selected by Fidel personally who was here with us for a few days and he would go to the Sierra and knew the children of the humblest origin. I also knew the Sierra and I went to the places that he indicated to me: La Plata, La Plama Mocha, the lower slope of Turquino, Santo Domingo, El Jigüe, where a big battle took place . . .
MILLS: What was the attitude of the parents of the children when their children were selected to come to school here?
RIELO: Imagine. The selection must be intense. I stayed in the countryside for a year and the peasants would recognize me. When I arrived I would explain the reasons why I was there and the future for the children if they came to the [school] city, and so they consented very agreeably.
MILLS: Very agreeably. What arrangements are you going to make to have the parents and the children visit one another?

RIELO: There are no perfect arrangements. But we allow the parents to visit their children and we will build a hotel for each unit so that the parents will have facilities when they come visit the children. In addition, the children will get vacations so that they can go and visit their parents.

MILLS: Three months in the summer?

RIELO: I think less. Because we are going to use part of the vacations to take the children to travel to different places and then go home. So far we have decided that they will stay one month with their parents.

MILLS: And what grades of school do you have now operating?

RIELO: Imagine. All the children who are here are illiterate. Some of them who were brought in the month of December can manage the printing press. They know how to read and write. They know how to add and subtract. A project in the future will be basic high school. In addition, there will be a teacher-training school, a nursing school...

MILLS: But it's now a primary school only, so far. When do you expect to complete the buildings themselves?

RIELO: This unit [right here] is complete from the point of view of children. We have 576 children. It was inaugurated on the 26th of July. If you are referring to the construction of the building, yes, there are things missing like sports camps, swimming pools, the hotel we were talking about, green areas. This area on the street on the right will all be a green area.

MILLS: How many such units as this will there be in the Sierra?

RIELO: Forty units will form the school city, with a capacity for 20,000 children. Twelve thousand males, 8,000 females.

MILLS: Does the captain think that this sort of boarding school—and I take it she will not object to our calling it that, a boarding school—is going to be the prototype for the whole of Cuba, eventually?

RIELO: Well, I think so. Because I understand they are going to create ten more school cities like this one. This is a system of life very suitable for children. We can't call this a vigorous boarding school, because here they live as if they are at home.

MILLS: Will they have older women to take care of them, sort of housemothers, we might call them?

RIELO: No, no, no, of course not. The only women here are two *compañeras* and myself. We function as a cooperative. We cooperativize the units of the school city. Each unit will function as a cooperative. When there is a situation of administration in the cooperative there is [inaudible] an administrator, school police, even an economical board and the children themselves work with the teachers.

MILLS: May I ask the captain two or three personal questions?
RIELO: Delighted, if I can answer. [Giggles].
MILLS: When did you first become aware of the Fidelista movement?
RIELO: I became aware at the university. I was at the University of Havana.
MILLS: In what year was that?
RIELO: The same year that Fidel landed [1956].
MILLS: How old are you now?
RIELO: I am now thirty-two years old.
MILLS: Do you intend to dedicate yourself in the future to building new school units or will you stay and operate this one?
RIELO: I love the cause so much. I believe I'm being useful enough in that sense. If they are going to build ten more school cities I'd like to have the privilege of being in all of them—helping the children of the *campesinos*.[31]

At this point, Rielo details all the many services the teachers provide the children. She informs Mills that she is in charge of ordering shoes, clothes, toothpaste, medicines, and so forth for them. Rielo says that there are eleven former guerilla fighters working with her, in addition to two young women soldiers. Including her, there are three women in all.

MILLS: How long have you been a rebel soldier?
RIELO: Since I joined the insurrection. I went to countryside [the Sierra] in February. In 1958.... After we were in the Sierra they organized the feminine battalion.
MILLS: Oh, she was in the feminine battalion?
RIELO: I have historical photographs from the Sierra when we went to the plains. I was the one who founded the Mariana Grajales. I left the battalion last December [1959] because I wanted to come here and work with the children.
MILLS: I have been very rude, I have not asked the captain's name. Could she please give it to me? And spell it, please.
RIELO: Isabel Rielo....
MILLS: Has the captain ever been married?
RIELO: I am married. [Giggle]. I have been married ten months.[32]

MILLS: Although we do not have the honor of knowing your husband may we congratulate him nonetheless. [Laughter]

Interview 5

Time: Approximately eight minutes
Interviewee: Dermidio Escalona. Juan Arcocha interpreted.
Escalona was the highest-ranking government official whose interview Mills recorded electronically. Inspired by the Moncada attack, Escalona took part in what was perhaps one of the earliest armed military actions in the province of Holguín: the failed assault on a munitions depot in order to obtain explosives. Involved in the founding of the guerilla force in Pinar del Río, he participated in several combat missions, including the battle of Seboruco on July 17, 1958, where he was wounded. Just a few months before the interview, Escalona had served on the tribunal that tried Comandante Huber Matos for treason.[33] The interview with Mills likely took place in Pinar del Río, where Escalona was serving as military commander of that province.

Mills had been talking with Escalona before turning on the recorder. He then activated the device and summarized what had been discussed.

MILLS TALKING INTO THE RECORDER: I've been talking with a captain of the security, Escalona, E-S-C-A-L-O-N-A. He confirms the general point that because the insurrectionary period was rather short, therefore there was not a great deal of time as was true in the, for example, Chinese Revolution, to build administrative and other kinds of personnel.[34] However, from the very beginning there were schools set up in the Sierra and on the Second Front also for peasantry.[35] And in November 1958 there were schools set up for the soldiers themselves. Not only schools to train them how to fight better, but also schools having to do with peacetime, after the insurrection was over. That is, to prepare cadres of an administrative ... [At this point Mills asks Arcocha, "Was it also technical nature?" Arcocha replies, "[inaudible] ... from the middle, eh. To prepare them from the civic point of view and revolutionary orientation."]

Mills resumes questioning Escalona.[36]

MILLS: Just a moment ago, the captain mentioned that there was some ideological difference between the underground leaders in the city, during the insurrection, and the rebel soldiers. And that this became apparent in the variety of opinions when the victory had been won. Would he please tell me a little something about what those differences were?

ESCALONA: Fundamentally, the army leaders had a more radical sense of the Revolution. The people from the city were from the [inaudible] and by nature they were more conservative. For instance, when the agrarian reform was applied, there were initial differences, and then when the Revolution became more radical, before the aggressions—because the aggressions have been the determining factors that made the Revolution more radical—the desertions started.[37] Those leaders belonging to the bourgeoisie and to the wealthy classes got scared.

MILLS: Is it his impression that most of the defectors from the Revolutionary movement were people who had been in the cities, in the underground at most, rather than among rebel soldiers?

ESCALONA: The defections have an origin of class, of fear. There is no one single peasant or worker in exile yet. But the fundamental nucleus of the underground resistance against Batista in the cities came from the working classes, the bourgeois classes.

MILLS: The labor movement did not do very much in that period.

ESCALONA: The labor movement had suffered decomposition since the period of [Carlos] Prío, almost from [Ramón] Grau. Because of the intervention in the syndicates, the imposition of leaders, they stopped syndicalist democracy since then.

MILLS: In other words, the unions were not democratic.

ESCALONA: Goodness, no. And then later on when Batista came, they were even less democratic. They had imposed leaders on the unions under the direction of Mujal.

MILLS: Who was he?

ESCALONA: He was secretary general of the CTC [Confederación de Trabajadores de Cuba] from the beginning of Prío's government to the end of Batista's government.[38]

MILLS: I understand also that the Communist Party during the Batista regime had been rather corrupted in the same sense as you mentioned.

ESCALONA: I don't know the details of the process. I know that those imposed directors presented as something fundamental the problem of anti-Communism. There was no Communist leader leading the unions. What existed during Batista's first government, when he appeared as a democrat, was a packing by the Communist Party in Cuba to participate in Batista's government. But at that time Batista pretended that his government was democratic.

MILLS: This was in what time? You mean before he took over in 1952, back in 1933?

ARCOCHA: Yes. During the first government of Batista from 1940 to 1944.

ESCALONA: From March 10 [1952, when Batista took power], there was no support or any kind of relationship between Batista and the Communists because Batista solidified his elite position as a great democrat in his anticommunism. And that justified the military missions from the United States—the bombing, the murdering of peasants in Cuba, the loans when Batista needed money, all the support he received from the American government until the end of his government.

MILLS: They were very useful to him then. They were a legal party, however, under the Batista dictatorship, were they not?

ESCALONA: Yes, to the first government of Batista [1940–44], yes.

MILLS: But not during the second government? [1952–59].

ESCALONA: No, no. It was President Prío who made the Communist Party illegal.

MILLS: And they existed then. Did Batista persecute the Communist Party?

ESCALONA: Yes. Batista also murdered Communist leaders. There was an event in the province of Oriente called the "Bloody Christmas," where Colonel [Fermin] Cowley murdered twenty-nine union leaders, most of them were Communists.

MILLS: What year was that?

ESCALONA: That happened in 1957, sometime after Fidel landed. 1956 or 1957.[39]

CHAPTER FIVE

Recorded Interviews with Cuban Citizens

Though Mills tape-recorded more interviews with civil servants than he did with private citizens, the three presented here provide unique insights into life in Cuba before and during the Revolution. The interviews took place in or near Santiago, the second city of Cuba after Havana, with a population of about 160,000. Santiago had been the site of several pivotal events during the insurrection: the 1953 armed attack on the Moncada army garrison, the 1956 uprising intended to help usher in Fidel Castro's *Granma* landing, and the 1959 victory proclamation that Castro delivered from the balcony of its city hall. What is more, all of the interviewees witnessed most if not all of these events firsthand. As Mills puts it, in the voice of the Cuban revolutionary in *Listen, Yankee*, "I was in the revolution almost from the beginning, and I will tell you about it from the inside."[1] These interviewees were also familiar with many of the main actors directly involved in making the Revolution. The clinical psychologist Franz Stettmeier, who taught at the local university, knew Celia Sánchez, rebel soldier, close friend, and trusted assistant to Fidel Castro. Stettmeier's wife, Elvira Escobar, who also taught at the university, had helped some of the Moncadistas escape after the attack and was well acquainted with Frank País, who had led the Santiago uprising. Stettmeier and Escobar were both actively involved in the civic resistance. Another interviewee, head housekeeper Elba Batista, originally from Manzanillo, knew René Vallejo, who operated a successful medical clinic and private practice in that port city; she attended to Castro, Vallejo, Celia Sánchez, and other dignitaries when they visited the ranch household near the town of San Francisco where she worked. Thus, the civilians Mills interviewed were indeed those "Cubans who were close to events."

Interview 6

Time: Approximately thirty-seven minutes
Interviewee: Dr. Franz Stettmeier
A psychiatrist and clinical psychologist, Franz Stettmeier was a leftist who had fled Nazi Germany for Cuba. With help from Raúl Roa and others, Stettmeier was hired at the University of Oriente and was, at the time of

the interview with Mills, supervising a course teaching sixty peasants about techniques in agriculture. Prior to marrying his current wife, Elvira Escobar, Stettmeier had been married to the psychiatrist Rosa Lenz. He and Rosa were good friends of Ernest Hemingway and his wife. The Hemingways would stay at Franz and Rosa's house at Santa María del Rosario while they were away. During the Revolution, Stettmeier served as consultant to the Ministry of Education and the Makarenko Educational Program.

The interview with Stettmeier is one of the longest and most informative conducted by Mills. Of particular interest is that Stettmeier provides psychological insight into the disappointment—the "anticipation of loss"[2]— experienced by the bourgeois sectors of the Cuban population after the Revolution.[3]

In speaking with Stettmeier, Mills again raises several issues that he first broached with Juan Arcocha (see chapter 4, interview 1) and that he would revisit several times with other informants: the role of the Cuban intellectual in the Revolution, the influence of the Cuban Communist Party in the political process, and whether the 26th of July Movement operated as a political party.

Another issue about which Mills queries Stettmeier concerns the likelihood that Castro would forge a "neutralist" or "third" system of industrialization for Cuba, one independent of the United States and the USSR. Indeed, five months previous, when Mills had been interviewed by several intellectuals in Mexico City, he made it clear to them that he didn't particularly care for either of the two overbureaucratized state structures and thus, "that is why I look very much to various countries in the underdeveloped or pre-industrial world—as they try to get some 'third pattern.'" For Mills, at the time, such a noncommunist, noncapitalist pattern of development largely depended on one country: India. But, he quickly told the Mexicans in the spring of 1960 that "maybe Cuba will turn out that way; I haven't been there yet."[4] Mills was therefore keen to know if Stettmeier thought that Castro would pursue the nonaligned option.

Shortly after returning to the United States from Cuba, Mills again invoked Stettmeier's name in a letter that he wrote to Fidel Castro, telling him that "When I was in Cuba last month, Dr. Franz Stettmeier of the University of Oriente asked me to try to get some young professors for him, to teach there and possibly to work with INRA."[5]

The interview with Stettmeier took place on August 12, 1960, in or near Santiago de Cuba. Stettmeier was fluent in German and Spanish, and though he speaks passable, if heavily accented, English in this interview, he frequently delivers his sentences haltingly, and a couple of times Arcocha intervenes to clarify certain words and phrases.

> MILLS: Dr. Stettmeier, what would be your opinion of inside Cuba today the major elements that are involved in the counterrevolution?
>
> STETTMEIER: I think that is easy to say. What we call in Spanish *lastimados*,[6] people who lost materials, power ...
>
> MILLS: Do they have any ideological basis, or is it simply a material and power loss in that sense?
>
> STETTMEIER: I would say they cannot be separated this way. They lost just the style of life. It was an easy life in a material way, but it was a whole manner.
>
> MILLS: Do you consider that the statement which they always make when they do defect, let us say, something like that, it's always in terms of anticommunist statements?
>
> STETTMEIER: I think it is just a label. It is not real anticommunism. This is just a panic to lose an old, and I would say, many years ago, a fine style of life—a feudal style of life and some high culture some sixty years ago. And all this way of living is now destroyed and being destroyed against all expectations. It was a surprise that they suffered. Many of these people were active in the Revolution, helping the Revolution.
>
> MILLS: In the beginnings of it, yes.
>
> STETTMEIER: In the beginnings [inaudible] ... materially, ideologically, and personally. And for a time it looked like even that the middle class and higher middle class would participate in the Revolution....
>
> MILLS: What period are you speaking of now?
>
> STETTMEIER: I would say more or less the time from the beginning of the invasion, the coming of Fidel to the Sierra to the whole civil war, the whole fight in the Sierra. The turning point was when Fidel on the 31 of December of 1958, he, in the city hall, said, "¡*Golpe de estado, no! ¡Revolución, sí!*"[7] It was a turning point, and from this moment people were frightened.
>
> MILLS: Was it that even at that early period, in early 1959, that counterrevolutionary sentiment began to appear among middle- and upper-class elements?

STETTMEIER: At the beginning, very few. Later, more counter-revolutionaries tried to [appeal to the middle and upper classes] by theoretical "permanent revolution," as Trotsky would call it.[8] It is the process of radicalization that went very fast and much deeper than, for example, myself, and people around myself, expected.

MILLS: It went much faster, didn't it, than the Cuban Communist Party would have expected?

STETTMEIER: Much ahead of the Communist Party. It's the real reason why Fidel has no problem with the Communist Party because they are running behind and crying: *Nosotros también!* "We too, we too!" They have no power, no influence.

MILLS: You know, there's one problem that I've run into in talking to various people about that, and that is, there is, of course, a lack of adequate personnel in the 26 [of July Movement]. Do you agree with that?

STETTMEIER: In the administration?

MILLS: Yes. In all areas, you know.

STETTMEIER: It is incredible how fast many of them learned. For example, in one year a young man learned from writing in the sixth grade.

MILLS: So you do not give any belief to the idea that because of the lack of administrative personnel, an inheritance from the old order, that the Communists, being an apparatus with some training, would move into a sort of vacuum?

STETTMEIER: I think, in part, you are right. I don't know the number, but the Communist people, trained by the Communist Party, have a high training in administration and discipline and just understanding orders. But I think there is no danger that these people will be a great deal of administration apparatus and will have some influence. They have no influence as Communists.

MILLS: Yes. But as individuals.

STETTMEIER: As individuals and, of course, in facilitating the process of radicalization.

MILLS: Do they tend to be older people, the Communists?

STETTMEIER: Older people.

MILLS: Are they able to recruit young men today?

STETTMEIER: I think not.

MILLS: Your impression is that they do not.

[…]

MILLS: What are the major countermeasures which the government has and probably will have to take to these counterrevolutionary forces we were speaking of?

STETTMEIER: I would say, the general idea is very keen not to use physical oppression. Not in prison and not in concentration camps. It is one of the real ambitions and I think it is a success 'til now. Not to take it too serious. To have relevant control in a small country. The whole country is a militia. There is an absolute control without police. A spontaneous control, unofficial control. For example, not so much in Havana maybe but in Santiago, you know anything about everybody. And so it is a real control to get these people in the beginning and have no need to repress them in a physical [inaudible] communist way.

MILLS: To your knowledge has anyone, Cuban, a counterrevolutionary, been arrested because of counterrevolutionary opinion?

STETTMEIER: No. Of activity.

MILLS: Activity. What sort of activity?

STETTMEIER: Nearly all to make mimeograph papers.

MILLS: They have arrested people for that?

STETTMEIER: Yes, I think. I have no absolute proof. But I have a dear friend, for example, a patient and friend, a young man not very intelligent, not very adapted to reality who just began to make mimeographed papers and he was caught.

MILLS: Do you consider your position as a clinical psychologist a very good one for the study of counterrevolutionary activities? [Chuckling].

STETTMEIER: I think, yes. You know why?

MILLS: No sir, I don't. Why? [Chuckling]. I was joking, but you take me seriously!

STETTMEIER: I take you very serious because I am discussing this much with my friends and pupils. The real force behind the counterrevolution is a psychological force. Not what they have lost really, but in what they have lost in expectations.

MILLS: Disappointment with what the Revolution is not giving them?

STETTMEIER: Disappointment about what they cannot dream about now.

MILLS: Aha. Meaning a bourgeois life.

STETTMEIER: A very bourgeois, very easy life. They dreamed about it but they never would have got it. It's just like a weekly lottery. You have always a chance to dream that now you will get there, with a thousand dollars on a Saturday afternoon. The destruction of this dream on which the middle class lives.

MILLS: You speak of the lower-middle class mainly now?

STETTMEIER: I would say all people, because several school teachers to get a license without work. This, what you call, a corrupt style of life, you know, is now destroyed, absolutely.[9]

MILLS: That's a very interesting point.

STETTMEIER: It's the only point, I think, would be a little original.[10]

[. . .]

MILLS: Dr. Stettmeier, may I ask you a question that I know requires a lengthy answer. But give me just an idea about it. What have been the roles of Cuban intellectuals and semi-intellectuals, first, in the fifties and then in the Revolution, and in the regime now, and finally the ideal for the role of the intelligentsia in Cuba if everything went as the 26 [of July Movement] and Castro and prorevolutionaries wished it to go?

STETTMEIER: I don't know if I'm competent to answer.

MILLS: I just want an impression.

STETTMEIER: You have to speak with my wife [Elvira Escobar]. She knows much more because she's stayed in these circles in the 1930s in the University [of Havana] when so many people came out like Raúl Roa, like [Carlos] Prio, like [Jorge] Mañach, what you would call, probably, intelligentsia.

Stettmeier goes on to note that the best example of an intellectual is Raúl Roa, who had been appointed foreign minister of Cuba by Castro shortly after the victory of the Revolution in 1959. Roa, whom Stettmeier had known personally for twenty years, had been imprisoned in the early 1930s under the dictatorship of Gerardo Machado and was now being discovered more or less by Castro. Aside from Roa, Stettmeier tells Mills that he cannot, at the moment, think of anyone who would be important as a member of the Cuban intelligentsia. Mills then asks, "In other words you don't agree that this Revolution was made by intelligentsia when they came into contact with peasantry. How do you characterize the young men who led the revolt, Castro himself?" Stettmeier remarks that it is fortunate that Castro is not a member of the intelligentsia.[11] Seeking clarification, Mills then asks, "What

Recorded Interviews with Cuban Citizens 81

do you mean by intelligentsia then? I would consider him an intellectual." Stettmeier explains that Castro is not of the communist, Stalinist lineage. He states that Castro really doesn't know about that old type of communism and that he was never a true believer of it. Stettmeier explains that the Cuban Revolution was instead born of a heritage that makes Cubans practical and spontaneous—a sentiment that Mills would echo in *Listen, Yankee*, declaring, "We're practical men, not theorists."[12]

This pragmatic heritage, devoid of ideology, is what makes it "a social and economic and military do-it-yourself."[13] Stettmeier asserts that it is not a revolution prepared by intellectuals; it was done by people who had "the good luck not to know too much." While people like Castro are very knowledgeable, because they are well educated, they do not have personal experience with communism, or revere it as a religion. This gives them a freedom, says Stettmeier, to, for example, engage in affairs with Russia without any doctrinaire encumbrances. Stettmeier then refers to Nietzsche's notion of the use and abuse of history, that Nietzsche's wish for the (German) people to be able to start again with no memory of their past is what was essentially happening in developing the new Cuba. Mills tells Stettmeier: "I would like to say that although I have only had half a dozen interviews, this squares with my impressions up to this point. This idea."

> MILLS: Dr. Stettmeier may I ask you this question? Apart from securing sovereignty for Cuba, that is, the international fight, and apart from great economic problems which the country must now confront and solve, what do you think are the major problems that the government faces as far as the building of a free Cuban society is concerned?

Stettmeier identifies two problems: first, the need, as a developing country, for technical education; and second, the need to train young people from the lower classes and the militia for administrative work and on how to deal specifically with the Cuban people.

> MILLS: What do you see as the major problem in terms of political construction? What I have in mind now is that there is one theory, at least, of the governmental structure of Cuba as it exists at the present moment, which is Fidel Castro, and then not too much of a strong organizational link, and then the people. And he, of course, educates, guides, leads, reasons with, and so on. But that clearly can't go on forever. That is what I might call, "camping out." You

can do that only for so long.[14] Now, what is the political problem of constructing a durable, free society?

STETTMEIER: Well, let me say, I think it is no problem, this Cuban way of Fidel. Since I was educated in the German state apparatus, I was very frightened at the beginning. I thought, "It must be destroyed tomorrow. It can't work, it doesn't work." This spontaneous work, in a small nation of 6 million people, can be done, and must be done for a long time, exactly in this way without breaking down this spontaneous, flexible way. You know, the 26th of July is not a party.

MILLS: In what sense is it not a party?

STETTMEIER: It's just that people go in and go out and some have a function and some not. And you have no special obligations. I am convinced that it is difficult for everybody who comes from a big country, an organized country, an old country, to understand how well it works. This way of spontaneous government working so flexible, it works. And do not forget it is the second luck of Fidel (he had two or three special kinds of luck to get into this position); this second luck is exactly that it is a small country. You can't do it in a big country.

MILLS: Well, the inevitable question is, What happens if Fidel should die for some reason? Natural reason, or accident, or what not. This could happen. Then what would be the outlook? I mean, how much really depends on Fidel as an individual as against, let us say, the upper ten or twelve people? It is a reasonable question, is it not?

STETTMEIER: I think it's a very reasonable question. I would say it is the work of Fidel. Of one man.

MILLS: In other words, it could all go to hell.

STETTMEIER: Yes. I don't think that the time exists now, and with each day it exists less.

MILLS: Why does it exist less every day?

STETTMEIER: Because people come up uneducated and ... many kinds of leaders from the poor people.

MILLS: Well, then you must see in the future—ten years, five years, fifteen years—you must see a transition from this form of politics to one that is somewhat different.

STETTMEIER: I wouldn't look so far ahead.

MILLS: You're living on the two-year plan. [Chuckles].

STETTMEIER: Just now it works well. We have no obligation to change it. On the contrary, let us cultivate it. Because the danger now may be technical administration and a lot of rationalization and a lot of calculating, how much things cost. I think the danger is mainly to lose its spontaneity.

MILLS: But the idea, realistically, politically, is to keep plunging ahead.

STETTMEIER: Yes. But I wouldn't dare to look so many years ahead. In two months all you think and tell about the Cuban Revolution can be terribly antiquated. Some days ago, with my wife, we read some articles of Sartre, whom I saw some hours here, when he passed through Santiago [earlier that year], and he grasped the situation in a genial way, very fast and, I think, very correctly. But now if you read it two months after, it is antiquated.[15]

MILLS: In what senses is it particularly...

STETTMEIER: Economic danger. Sartre, he told in my presence about the economic pressures [that] will make the standard of living very low. Administrative people will live very easy. It will be a new class. I think it is theoretically constructed, you know. We don't dare much to make theoretical constructions.

MILLS: Well, yes, and Dr. Stettmeier, Sartre, after all, is a literary man.

STETTMEIER: And he is a genius.

MILLS: A brilliant literary man.

STETTMEIER: He's not very, I think, trained.

MILLS: I'm talking against our friend Juan here, when I say that. [Laughter between Mills and Arcocha. Obviously an inside joke.]

STETTMEIER: I'm laughing because it is so simpatico to hear him and to see his brain work. He learned about Cuba, I think, in three days, what I needed ten years [to learn].[16]

MILLS: Oh, come, that must be an exaggeration.

STETTMEIER: It is not so much an exaggeration. Let me tell this, and I'm not thinking I am such a slow working brain, in general, no. This is more or less all I can say to you.

MILLS: May I ask one more question of a general sort? What is the extent, if any, of what the Indians would call "neutralist" sentiment inside Cuba? In other words, "*Cuba sí, Yankees no, Russia no.*"

STETTMEIER: I think there never was people in general in favor of this.

MILLS: It's too abstract and...

STETTMEIER: It is too abstract and it is too avoiding the fact. You know, Fidel, probably you have studied him. You can be sure that he cannot be a neutralist, [he is] just attacked, always attacked. You saw here [in Santiago de Cuba] probably the Moncada [barracks] and ... how he is attacked. He's a valiant, brave man and it would be no ideological ... him just to keep out or to take money from the two sides.

MILLS: It would be too passive a role for him.

STETTMEIER: All these various enemies. I think it was never a chance for this third power, third party, or how do you call it, neutralist, ideology. Because he was attacked in such a way that he had no chance to form it. Just as anti-Yankeeism was not made and not planned by Fidel. It was just philosophical.

MILLS: Of economic realities.

STETTMEIER: Economic and before economics, ideological, I think.

MILLS: Is there anything else that you think of, just in this kind of a preliminary talk like we're having, that I should know, in your opinion, about the entire Cuban scene today? What's it like in Cuba today?

STETTMEIER: In a general way I would like to explain to you the reasons that affect about our optimism. It is not an easy optimism. It is not an optimism to cut off problems in the sense of clinical psychology. I think the Cuban Revolution must be considered very strong and for the enemies, very dangerous. And the people decided to die tomorrow ...

MILLS: They mean this?

STETTMEIER: They mean it as the Russian soldier might on the front. "Here I am, you have to kill me."

MILLS: That certainly is my impression.

STETTMEIER: That makes the Cuban Revolution very dangerous for all enemies. But really dangerous for all counterrevolutionary movements and ideology. The moral, the physical, the economical. I think this should be explained better by people who know more, you know.

MILLS: In your opinion, in the realities of the case, what are the three or four greatest dangers that the Revolution faces as it tries to succeed and consolidate itself?

STETTMEIER: The first I would say, the death of Fidel Castro. The death or some transformation by chronic illness or something, of Fidel Castro. I think that he is mentally a very healthy man—as studied by a psychologist in the sense of the book. Much healthier than any other leader I saw in fifty years in Europe and America. So this is the first danger. He wouldn't admit it. I say it to you because it is my opinion. The second, I would say, these kind of administrators and functionaries who do not understand the Cuban style, the style of Fidel: to respect the people, to work with the people, to believe in people, to use the people, to educate the people, and to respect the people. I think the great difference, for example, like a comparison, that Stalin never believed in his people. And even Hitler, probably, didn't believe so much. But Fidel really had a reason to believe, and this belief makes people better. I think the second danger would be this: that all administration, like all Spanish, Latin American way, who comes from above. I don't think it is a real danger at this moment. But let me tell you something, it is most irritating but it is not a matter of the highest danger. Well, in the third place, I really couldn't say.

MILLS: You don't see any insuperable economic obstacles, do you, that cannot be taken care of in due course?

STETTMEIER: Not at all. Speaking one word about the economy, there are two or three factors of the good luck of Fidel. The consumption is very flexible here. You can live on 30 dollars and can easily spend 3,000 dollars without living very well. You must know it. This flexibility and the flexibility of production too. It is a good country. Things have gone rather easy, not a lot of illness of plants and animals. And the people do not need much consumption. I think this flexibility, parallel to the flexibility of the mind in the case of the economic sphere, is a guarantee.

MILLS: And do you believe that the revolutionary euphoria,[17] enthusiasm, that we were speaking of, that that would carry the movement and the people generally over any kind of setback, economically, that might occur?

STETTMEIER: Absolutely. In addition, it would be weeks and months before it would be explained by Fidel. Explaining and preparing in this patient way, a highly pedagogical way, educational way. People believe in him, he says the truth. And prepares people. For example, we are not prepared for a socialistic revolution or how you call it, you can give it any name to this Revolution.

MILLS: You said a moment ago, as a clinical psychologist, you have not known any political leader that is as sane, or as mentally healthy, as Fidel Castro. Would you elaborate on that just a little bit?

STETTMEIER: I would say what we call mental health is to stay well into reality, not to form aggression without reason, a brain that works in the reality and not in imaginations, that doesn't expect too much, that doesn't expect too many. Of course a diagnosis is made against other leaders. I saw Hitler, Mussolini, Stalin himself.

MILLS: Eisenhower?

STETTMEIER: Well, I wouldn't dare to speak about him.

MILLS: You wouldn't analyze at such a distance?

STETTMEIER: No. I have no material about it. I know only his book about the *Crusade in Europe*.[18]

MILLS: May I say, then, that he is a crackpot. [Laughter]

STETTMEIER: You really think? I don't know.

MILLS: I've examined him rather closely and I think so.[19] [Laughter]

STETTMEIER: I don't speak about it. I don't know much. The book [*Crusade in Europe*] that come out about the administrator of war. It's a book that he wrote.

MILLS: He didn't write the book.

STETTMEIER: I don't know much more about it. But, Fidel. Anyhow, I know very well Celia Sánchez [Castro's secretary], who's a friend of my wife for twenty years, a friend of mine of fifteen years, more or less. I stayed in her house, and I know how she thinks. Intellectually she knows some clinical anecdotes about [Castro's] healthy mental and maybe even his physical state. I don't know exactly so much about him. Much of this is clinical impression and not based in scholarly work. Let me say the last thing, our ideology, I say my wife and mine, is based about the high school. We lived six months, or less, three months, between the [the Batista army and the rebel soldiers].[20]

MILLS: In 1958?

STETTMEIER: In 1958. In a place nearly like this but on the other side. Between the hills there's a town and all people are running away. And we're just not running away and I don't know why. But we saw, at that time, Batista men, and I tend to repel them. I think this gives you a fine and real impression of how people are and they have not changed. They have not changed by power. They are not corrupted by power. This I cannot explain. The only secret I can explain to myself is how these people have so much power and [are] not corrupted. After the famous verse that all power corrupts. I think you said it in your book [*The Power Elite*].

MILLS: Well, power not only corrupts sometimes, but it also ennobles. [Laughter]

Interview 7

Time: Approximately forty-seven minutes
Interviewee: Elvira Escobar. Juan Arcocha interpreted. Robert Taber was present at the interview.
Mills took up Stettmeier's recommendation that he talk with his wife, Elvira Escobar, age forty-eight, whom Mills interviewed near Santiago de Cuba. At the time of the interview Escobar was professor of domestic economy at the University of Oriente. She had recently completed a sociological study in which she interviewed 115 *campesinos* as well as some Communists in Oriente province.

In terms of recording time, this was the longest interview Mills conducted (though the interpretation process does add time), and perhaps the one that yielded the most information for him. Escobar is the only respondent of whom Mills relays in broad outline the personal story she told him: "Now there was a woman living in a house outside Santiago de Cuba, in the Oriente. She was an educated woman in her forties.... She was with us, she was a revolutionary. She came from Manzanillo, where many revolutionaries have come from."[21]

Stettmeier and Escobar had been involved in supporting the insurrection, not as recognized combatants, but as private citizens in the civic resistance. Being a physician, Stettmeier, along with Escobar, owned a medical clinic in the center of Santiago, which they used to clandestinely supply the rebels. In her interview with Mills, Escobar mentions the clinic a couple of times in passing but does not provide specific details as to its use, though she probably provided the rebels with medical supplies. Robert Taber tells of another Santiago physician, the one who headed the underground network in that city and who also had a clinic, which he employed for purposes of aiding the rebels: "In Santiago, the private laboratory and pleasant home of Dr. Angel Santos Buch, a prominent physician, served a similar purpose, being used as a way station for rebel couriers and important fugitives, on their way to or from the Sierra. Similar underground stations were established in each city, throughout the island, and slowly, almost reluctantly, the business and prosperous professional classes began to turn their considerable means and influence into revolutionary channels."[22]

What is more, thousands of Cuban women, particularly of the middle classes like Escobar, were active in the urban underground, collecting military provisions for the guerrilla fighters. For example, Jules Dubois tells of how Señora Enrique Menocal and Señora Felipe Pazos (both of whose husbands were prominent in Cuban politics) would frequently drive from Havana along the Central Highway as far eastward as Holguín to deliver a shipment of bullets for relay to Castro. "This was a cause in which Castro inspired faith and confidence in the women," states Dubois. He could easily have been describing the clandestine activities of someone like Elvira Escobar, whom Mills describes as providing the rebels with "bullets scattered among the beans," when Dubois writes: "In Santiago de Cuba, society women would call at homes of friends, ostensibly to pay a social call, and leave a gift of a large can of crackers. The can would be filled with .45 caliber bullets and, if luck were at hand, also with a .45 caliber pistol. The same day or the next the cargo of crackers would make its way to the Sierra Maestra, but this time they would become firecrackers."[23]

MILLS: May I ask you first, a few personal questions?
ESCOBAR: As you wish. It's a pleasure.
MILLS: At what year did you marry Dr. Stettmeier?
ESCOBAR: In the year 1952.
MILLS: And what was your education then?
ESCOBAR: High school, doctorate in Pedagogy. I didn't finish the Philosophy. I teach domestic economy. And I've always been a dilettante sociologist.
MILLS: Aha. Yes, everyone is an amateur sociologist. [Laughter] At what time did you first come into contact with the Fidelistas?
ESCOBAR: Directly, when Fidel attacked Moncada, in 1953. With some of the boys [Moncadistas] who remained after the attack.
MILLS: And they came into your home? Or you helped them?
ESCOBAR: I helped to take some of them out of the city with a group of women friends.
MILLS: To get them out.
ESCOBAR: I am going to confess something. At that time I didn't know Fidel and I didn't understand him. It was because I had a sentiment [compassion] for those lost young men.
MILLS: You were just helping them in that way. Because of a sentiment for some lost young men. And then what happened to you?

ESCOBAR: I can't say I was born a rebel, because being a teacher of psychology I know nobody can be born a rebel. But I was formed as a rebel.

MILLS: We are colleagues, madam.

ESCOBAR: I am from the most rebellious city in Cuba, one involved in every movement.

MILLS: With a tradition of rebellion. What was that city?

ARCOCHA: Manzanillo.

ESCOBAR: From there arose every revolution, every social movement.

MILLS: Well then, for a long time, after 1953, not very much happened, is it not true?

ESCOBAR: After the killing of those boys from Moncada we had already protested against that and then everything began. There was a moment of expectation: Fidel's trial, his speech of his defense.[24] Personally, I was at a distance from the revolutionary groups until just before November 30, some days before Fidel landed [in the *Granma*] in 1956. There was an uprising in Santiago, and the boys took the city.

MILLS: And what did you do then?

ESCOBAR: I did nothing. I couldn't even make my house available to make the [red and black 26th of July Movement] flags.

MILLS: What work were you doing then?

ESCOBAR: I worked as a teacher.

MILLS: In the university?

ESCOBAR: Now, yes. Not then. At a high school. And after that I did what everyone from Santiago and Manzanillo did, which was to take and bring weapons, messages, food, medicines.

MILLS: Up into the hills, you mean?

ESCOBAR: No. Taking those things from here in the center of the city to my house, which I called "Parallel 38."[25] And from there I had a messenger. I personally did not go.

MILLS: And where did [you] get them?

ESCOBAR: The medicines were bought. Because I had a clinic I was able to purchase them in large quantities.

MILLS: And took them to her house which she called Parallel 38.

ARCOCHA TO MILLS: And then there was a messenger there who took them to the rebels. She wouldn't do it herself because she would have been noticed and then she wouldn't be useful anymore.

MILLS: I wonder if she would sort of back away from her personal participation for a moment and tell me what she considers the pivotal events of the Revolution as a whole. What are the three or four, you know, turning points?

ESCOBAR: First Moncada. Because, for us, it obligated Batista to remove his mask. Not me, since I was a revolutionary, but for the people. The thirtieth of November...

MILLS: What did Moncada show the people?

ESCOBAR: That Batista was truly a murderer. Younger people or those with poor memories had forgotten the period that led to the Revolution. I was in Havana the day of Batista's coup [March 10, 1952], and I was insulted that the people accepted it. We older ones had not forgotten the things Batista had done [in the 1940s].

MILLS: And this now showed them that. And that was the first pivot of the Revolution. What was the second?

ARCOCHA: And then she mentioned November 30, the uprising several days before Fidel landed [in Cuba].[26]

ESCOBAR: That proved that a group of young men could take a city, even for a few hours.

MILLS: Yes. And then the third event that she thinks...

ESCOBAR: Fidel's arrival [December 2, 1956].

MILLS: Aha. But that was not known to everyone, was it? Did everyone know about his arrival?

ESCOBAR: Yes. And it was also revealed that he was not dead [as had been publicly announced by Batista].

MILLS: And then the next dramatic event?

ESCOBAR: I can't remember. Those were years of seeing loved ones die, a young man who helped me. Each day we asked, "How many today?"

MILLS: And that went on up until what point?

ESCOBAR: Each day it was more and more serious until the day of the thirtieth [of November 1956]. We were living in a war zone [in Santiago].

MILLS: And how was the fact that the Revolution was triumphant brought home to her personally? What was she doing when it occurred? Was it a gradual realization or was there some real turning point that gave her that realization, "We're going to win." How did she know, "We are going to win," and when?

ESCOBAR: I always knew we were going to win. I didn't expect it so soon.

MILLS: And under what circumstances did the news come to her that it was going to be soon?

ESCOBAR: I expected a quick fall of Santiago de Cuba, because I lived in a place surrounded by rebels that I would see because I would sometimes go to their camp. Each night they would come to my house. The [Rural] Guard would come to my house by day and the rebels by night, and they would shoot at the Guard from my house. And we expected the fall of Santiago, but we also believed we could take Oriente. But no one, not even Fidel, expected the fall. The day Fidel entered Santiago [January 1, 1959], he said that the war had been over a year before it should have been, a year before the time it would have been convenient for the Revolution to take flight.

MILLS: Meaning by that, that the number of men who were formed by the revolutionary process would be larger.

ESCOBAR: Yes. Because there was an unfortunate incident in Santiago—the death of Frank País.[27] I personally felt lost when he died. Until I again became connected with the people, the revolutionaries. I did not belong to the formal organization [the 26th of July Movement]. I served from the outside without belonging in order to maintain my anonymity.

MILLS: Yes. Now you are, of course, a member of the intelligentsia by your training and by your work. How do you see the role of the intelligentsia as a whole in the different phases of the Revolution?

ESCOBAR: I am disappointed. The intellectual class is less brave than I expected.

MILLS: Who does she include in the intelligentsia in terms of their work?

ESCOBAR: I consider them to be the persons of intellect, journalists who write about public opinion, the best persons that we had as representatives of Cuba abroad. They were afraid because of social laws[28] and of being labeled [Communists].

MILLS: So she includes in intelligentsia many of the officials. And how is she using the word, in short?

ESCOBAR: Those who represented us abroad, yes. Miró Cardona.[29]

MILLS: In other words, the educated class.

ESCOBAR: The educated classes. The educated classes have been the most frightened of the social laws and of being called Communists.

MILLS: Do you understand that Fidel Castro and the five or six men who have been closest to him during the Revolution, in your opinion, are they intelligentsia?
ESCOBAR: Celia [Sánchez] yes. She belongs to the upper-middle class.
MILLS: But Fidel himself and his secretary...
ARCOCHA: Raúl Roa.[30]
MILLS: Raúl Roa. Was he with the Revolution from the beginning?
ESCOBAR: Yes. And his son [Raúl Roa Kouri] was in the Sierra also.
MILLS: Yes, I know his son.[31] Now, in what other respect have you been disappointed in the role of the intelligentsia apart from their lack of valor and apart from their fearing to be labeled and apart from the losses—these are characteristics you had named. What other characteristics would you give to the Cuban intelligentsia in all of this process?
ESCOBAR: I think that they never had a chance to get to know the people, especially the peasants. They can't value how much there is.
MILLS: Would you think that it is a proper way to define the situation would be like the following: That one small branch of intellectuals went into the hills, including Fidel, and that most of the intelligentsia did not do so. That is, the Revolution was made by young intelligentsia in contact with the poor people.
ESCOBAR: Yes, exactly.
MILLS: Would you tell me what sort of work you are doing now?
ESCOBAR: Forming teachers by teaching psychology and sociological techniques at the University [of Oriente]. That, officially. Unofficially, I am where the Revolution needs me, no matter where.
MILLS: Of course, but besides teaching and forming teachers, what is she doing with peasants, for example?
ESCOBAR: Listen, I don't think we need to form *campesinos*, I think the *campesinos* form us, including me.
MILLS: What does she mean by that, exactly? Because as an overdeveloped society member, I do not understand this, although I wish to.
ESCOBAR: I have found a type of *campesino* with such a high human quality. I have just finished conducting 115 interviews, of the sociological type, of *campesinos* in the entire province [of Oriente]. And from different places, trainings, and educations. In all of them there exists a real sense of the Cuban problem, the socioeconomic problem, that is much clearer than the sense held by the educated

classes. And a sense of responsibility to the country. And the disposition to absolute sacrifice for Cuba, without partisanism. Because in addition I interviewed leaders of the socialist party.[32] Cuba first, party second.

MILLS: Are the leaders of the Communist Party, they tend to be older people do they not, or are they younger also?

ESCOBAR: Well, the leaders that I knew, because they were from my town, they are old, but there are some young ones. I interviewed from seventeen years old. They're not afraid of me, and they show me their [membership] cards. They know that in Cuba there is nothing to fear. They make no impression. It doesn't matter. Just one more who wants to help regardless of the label, whether red, white, or blue.

MILLS: Is it her impression that the Communists are rather well organized, or are they not so well organized?

ESCOBAR: I think that at this moment it is not a very organized party. They've always been an organized party. But [now] it has no importance in the country as a party.

MILLS: It's merely individuals from it who assume positions?

ESCOBAR: No. They belong to that party as others belong to the 26 [Movement], and others to traditional parties. Today the Communist Party in Cuba has an air that looks like an old traditional party.

MILLS: Some communist parties are under quite close discipline by a party and some are not, and as I understand what you are saying, the Communist Party in Cuba as a whole is not a very disciplined kind of organization. For example is it easy to get into the party if I wish to join and I'm a Cuban?

ESCOBAR: Yes, very easy. You just have to fill out a form.

MILLS: So it's not a very disciplined organization.

ESCOBAR: Yes. First, for example, they make an investigation. But nobody cares. Apart from the Catholics and the counter-revolutionaries who use it as a political weapon, in the eyes of the people the 26 [of July Movement] is much more new [inaudible].

MILLS: So the better young men, the more qualified young men, they go into the 26th of July?

ESCOBAR: Yes. And also the most radical, the newest. The other is old fashioned.

MILLS: That would seem to be very important, yes.

ESCOBAR: This [the 26th of July Movement] is more radical and newer. The other [the Communist Party] doesn't matter anymore.

MILLS: You must realize that I need, the kind of information you give me now, the truth about the Communist thing because I write for a Yankee audience.

ESCOBAR: The truth, the truth! It's someone [the person she interviewed] who knows well the Communist Party. He was a close friend and in my family was a Communist mayor of the town.[33] In my town, in 1933, there was the first soviet in [Latin] America.[34] The Communist leader is a personal friend of mine. He has always been, even when they were prohibited.

MILLS: Is it your opinion that in the next year or two, perhaps, the Communist Party inside Cuba would assume decreasing importance, because of the growth of the 26 [Movement]?

ESCOBAR: I think that importance was given to them in the United States. Not here.

MILLS: Is there anything else she can think of that she believes I should know, as an outsider, in order to understand the character and role of the Cuban Communist Party?

ESCOBAR: It's a party that I consider to be organized that has valuable members, valuable persons, but I don't consider it to have decision-making influence in Cuban politics as a party. I also don't think it is going to decide. Except if being a Communist becomes so important that every day we are called Communists, then maybe one day we may desire to be Communists.

MILLS: I agree that the U.S. policies, publicity, would be an important factor in increasing the power of the Communist Party.

ESCOBAR: Furthermore, the Communist Party would increase if it were persecuted. If it were condemned. But one very young Communist leader who became a Communist in the early days of the Revolution when Fidel went [to the United States], then that immature adolescent man joined the party.[35] And the other day, he told me that it [being a Communist] has now lost its charm. He believed it was a great thing. There is a concentration and up to that point everything goes well. Everybody's welcome.

MILLS: At that time it was a symbolic act to join?

ESCOBAR: No, he joined because Fidel went to the United States [and] as a protest against his parents—it was a personal adolescent problem. When I was young, then it was a matter of rebellion. That's why I say that this anticommunist struggle is thirty years old.

MILLS: And have no relevance, really, to what is going on?

ESCOBAR: Absolutely not. But they cannot be underestimated either. They are regular people.

[...]

MILLS: What do you think are the most important tasks, jobs, in the next year or two that are going to confront the revolutionary government of Cuba?

ESCOBAR: First of all, to fight against the external oppression.

MILLS: Yes. Let us assume that they win that.

ESCOBAR: To produce. That's the only word in Cuba, to produce.

MILLS: To produce. You mean industrially and agriculturally?

ESCOBAR: Industrially and agriculturally. In all aspects.

MILLS: What are the greatest problems in the building of a free, political society or maintaining it in Cuba?

ESCOBAR: A great political society? What do you mean by that?

MILLS: How do you build and maintain, after you have built, a free, political society? You can have high production, you can have military safety, and yet you might still have a tyranny.

ESCOBAR: No, not here. Not here.

MILLS: Why not here?

ESCOBAR: The Cuban is always free. No one has ever imposed himself on the Cubans.

MILLS: Even under Batista? This was a tyranny.

ESCOBAR: If someone imposes himself on us we will fight. Even if I'm in a wheelchair. [Laughs]

MILLS: Yes. [Laughs] You do not see any particular problem of political organization as being a task, the construction of a political organization of some kind, to guarantee freedom?

ESCOBAR: Do you mean the democratic type [of political organization] for example, with free elections?

MILLS: Free elections are one mechanism whereby you maintain freedom. They're not the only one. But I was speaking of that sort of thing, yes. What are the mechanics of freedom?

ESCOBAR: I don't know what opinion to give. I feel so free for the first time in my entire life. And I see a lot of people who talk and say things and they forgive each other. I have never in my entire life seen so much freedom. True freedom. Not like the period of [President Ramón] Grau and [President Carlos] Prío; that wasn't freedom, it was debauchery.

[...]

MILLS: And this existed in Cuba at one time? What time?

ARCOCHA: Yes. In the time of Prío, Grau [1944–1952].

ESCOBAR: Every person lived without directed activity, without purpose. Today each life has a purpose. The majority is for the Revolution, the minority is against. Each life has meaning.

MILLS: And what are the major countermeasures which she thinks the government is taking and should take against counterrevolutionary sentiment?

ESCOBAR: We don't take them [counterrevolutionaries] very seriously. They are taken seriously in the United States. As long as they don't attack a life, a property, it's not important. What they say is believed abroad, not here. Here we see what is happening. And everyone knows they can speak.

MILLS: What does she think is the most serious threat, if any, inside Cuba to the success of the Revolution?

ESCOBAR: None, unless it comes from abroad.

[There is a gap in the recording at this point.]

ESCOBAR: ... the worst moment? The day that Frank País had some moments of indecision. But the worst moment for me is that I did nothing for the Revolution. I did what every Cuban woman.... I wish you would understand this. I was one in a thousand, one in a thousand. I did less than many thousands of others. Understand? Here, to risk one's life was very natural. And each one played the role that life demanded.

MILLS: And that role was revolutionary?

ESCOBAR: No, no, within the Revolution. Each one played the role according to his position. For example, my husband and I were not braver than the others by staying at the house [inaudible]. But there we had a unique position. We owned a clinic. I could pass through. The people knew me. The [Batista] soldiers respected me. They knew I had lost money because of the Revolution. They didn't imagine I had feelings for the Revolution. I had a file with SIM in Havana since 1956.[36] It was noted that my father's cattle had been taken by the revolutionaries. That saved my life. That was something else to thank Fidel for. [General laughter]

MILLS: May I ask a question about Catholicism in Cuba? To what extent, if any at all, do you see Catholicism as a basis among the people for counterrevolutionary sentiment?

ESCOBAR: The people are not apostolic Roman Catholics. The Cuban people have a strange mixture of religions, consisting of saints, [African] images, and cults. Yes, it's a mixture of Catholicism and [African] spiritualism.

MILLS: And the Roman Catholic clergy is not very important?

ESCOBAR: The clergy influences a social class, nothing more.

MILLS: You mean the upper classes?

ESCOBAR: Yes. And perhaps a little bit the middle classes. Here we don't call the clergy *sacerdotes* but rather *curas*.[37] In my generation we were leftist and anticlerical. I was Catholic until I was a teenager and was educated in a very exclusive Catholic school. I was distressed during a religious crisis in my adolescence. But my own son is [religiously] neither one thing nor the other.

MILLS: He did not have to go through such as a crisis because it never took as a religion.[38]

ESCOBAR: I was brought up in a very strict Catholicism. I took Communion every day for six years.

MILLS TO ARCOCHA: Would you please tell her that so did I. I was an altar boy. [Laughter]

ESCOBAR: But my son today is not one thing nor another.

MILLS: How old is he?

ESCOBAR: He is twenty-six years old. He is a doctor. He has requested to go to the Sierra [Maestra to care for the peasants]. So when someone says something to him, he'll say, "Don't you understand. I love Cuba."

[There is a gap in the recording at this point.]

MILLS: How old is the madam at the present time, may I ask?

ESCOBAR: Forty-eight years old.

MILLS: Do you think that what you have been telling me about Cuba, that it is more characteristic of Santiago and the Oriente, or do you think it is generally true of Cuba?

ESCOBAR: I would say that in order to understand the Revolution very well you need to understand the [civil] war very well. I think that all of Cuba identifies with the Revolution. But those of us from Oriente had more opportunities to witness firsthand more [war] crimes. In addition, they say that we are more unruly.

MILLS: Does she think that most of such counterrevolutionary middle-class sentiment as exists is probably in Havana rather than elsewhere?
ESCOBAR: To be honest, I haven't been in Havana long enough to know. I have spent very little time there after the Revolution.
MILLS: You went to school here in Oriente, or in Havana?
ESCOBAR: At the University of Havana.
MILLS: What years did you go there?
ESCOBAR: I entered in 1929. I knew Trejo, we were friends.[39] I am of the generation of the thirties.[40]
MILLS: And what was your father's social position?
ESCOBAR: Manager at a sugar mill.
MILLS: He was a rich man?
ESCOBAR: Not very. My uncle was rich. And my godfather. Today I'm very happy that my father was financially comfortable and nothing more. Had he been a *latifundista* he would have been of the same disposition as my uncle and perhaps today I would feel *siquitrillada*.[41] [Laughter]
MILLS: I do not believe that! [Laughter]
[...]

Interview 8

Time: Approximately twenty-four minutes
Interviewees: Elba Luisa Batista Benitez and Lauro Fiallo Barrero. Juan Arcocha interpreted.
As Mills notes in the foreword to *Listen, Yankee*, his discussions and interviews while in Cuba were with rebel soldiers, intellectuals, officials, journalists, and professors. Indeed, Mills had always been interested largely, or perhaps even exclusively, in the more educated classes. For example, in his 1950 study on Puerto Rican migrants to New York City,[42] one of his coauthors revealed that Mills "did not interview migrants or try to share their views. He interviewed English-speaking officials and intellectuals."[43] Theodore Draper criticizes Mills for not having spoken to workers or *campesinos*: "Without exception, his informants were middle-class intellectuals and professionals of the type in power."[44] But there *was* one exception. The interview that follows is the only one recorded by Mills in which he has a conversation, not with a mandarin of Cuban society, but with an uncomplicated thirty-eight-year-old woman of peasant stock: Elba Luisa Batista

Benitez. It is important to note, however, that this woman's words, ideas, and sentiments are altogether absent in *Listen, Yankee*. Much as he derided the powerful, Mills preferred to speak to them, and to the intellectuals, instead of the masses.

While true that the rebel soldiers were, as Mills states, "formed of peasants and led by young intellectuals,"[45] it was, in fact, the *campesinos* who were the backbone of the Revolutionary Army. The rebel soldiers were *peasant* soldiers, and hard-working people from the countryside, like Elba Batista and her husband Lauro Fiallo, had played a vanguard role in winning and consolidating the Revolution. As Huberman and Sweezy observed just a few months prior to Mills's interview with Batista and Fiallo, "owing to the tremendous achievements of agrarian reform the bond between the regime and the peasantry has never been so strong as it is today."[46]

At the time that Mills was on the island, it is estimated that there were some 200,000 peasant families. Alongside this large peasant population, there were over 300,000 cane-cutters, employed only seasonally, usually during harvest time.[47] Elba Batista and Lauro Fiallo were more fortunate; they were part of the several thousand rural workers who held jobs on various estates and cattle ranches. As head housekeeper and farm mechanic, respectively, Batista and Fiallo were permanent workers, "servants," attached to a cattle ranch that had been recently appropriated by the new regime and was now functioning as a dairy center with 1,500 head of cattle, mostly milk cows.[48]

In his interview with Elba Batista, Mills's tone is of respect, with no hint of condescension. Indeed, it is one of the most straightforward and personal discussions he had with his Cuban informants. Though Mills is sitting during the discussion, Batista refuses to do so and remains standing the entire time. Lauro Fiallo Barrero is present but contributes only a few comments, and the audio recording ends abruptly when he is finally about to respond to a question from Mills. The interview is conducted in the house of Batista's and Fiallo's former employer, a Dr. Rousseau, at a ranch located on the outskirts of Manzanillo near the village of San Francisco.[49] The estate, which had been appropriated by the new regime the previous year, was likely a state farm. It consisted of 30,000 acres, and a mansion with rooms for 60 guests. The near-desolate condition of such large estates, which served as seasonal resorts for the wealthy owners, was quite common before the triumph of the Revolution. Sartre describes the situation: "What did those who visited a large estate up to 1958 find there? An empty palace, a manager, a team of agricultural workers. The palace remains empty today. The master won't return there any longer. The manager preferred to disappear or change his job."⁵⁰

MILLS: How old are you now?
BATISTA: Thirty-eight years old.
MILLS: And how long have you been married?
BATISTA: I was married for nine years.
MILLS: Nine years. And how old was she?
BATISTA: I was fourteen years old. We lived together for nine years and then we divorced.
MILLS: They divorced. And how old are you now?
BATISTA: Well, now, if we figure it, since the time when I was fourteen years old that I married and I have been divorced for fourteen years.
MILLS: So she does not know how old she is now?
BATISTA: No, I don't know. I have a notice, a, what do you call it? But I don't have it, my mother has it.
MILLS: All right. We can figure that out and that is not important.⁵¹ Where did you go to school?
BATISTA: In Manzanillo.
MILLS: And how far did you go in school?
BATISTA: Until sixth grade.
MILLS: And after you got out of school, what did you then do?
BATISTA: Nothing. I was in the house.
MILLS: In whose house?
BATISTA: My mother's.
MILLS: What did your father do to earn money?
BATISTA: My father is *campo* [of the fields].
MILLS: He worked in the fields. And did your mother work too?
BATISTA: Yes, she is *campo*.
MILLS: In the fields?
BATISTA: Yes, in the fields.
MILLS: And then you got married after you had worked in the house of your mother for a while?
BATISTA: Yes. After I left school.
MILLS: You got married then?
BATISTA: Fourteen years old.
MILLS: And what did your husband do to earn money?

BATISTA: Shoemaker.

MILLS: A shoemaker. In the city?

BATISTA: In Manzanillo.

MILLS: And how was your life then?

BATISTA: Well, normal.

MILLS: And then what happened? How did you get into this house?

BATISTA: Well, after the divorce he was going to marry someone else. That's how men are. Then I returned to my [mother's] house with my daughters.

MILLS: How many daughters?

ARCOCHA: Two daughters.

MILLS: How old were they when you divorced?

BATISTA: They were little. Six and seven years old.

MILLS: And you went back to the house of your mother?

BATISTA: Yes with her. But then when he sued for divorce I had to turn them [my daughters] over to him.

MILLS: Aha. He got both daughters?

BATISTA: So he could educate them well. I wanted to take them to the countryside with my parents but I couldn't educate them. There was no school over there or anything.

MILLS: Was it very difficult for him to get the divorce?

BATISTA: No. He was the one who asked for the divorce. It was very difficult. I didn't want the divorce. [At this point Arcocha offers that it seemed to him that she didn't care very much about the divorce.]

MILLS: But she could not do anything on the divorce?

BATISTA: Me, yes? If I didn't want to, I wouldn't have divorced.

MILLS: Aha. So she was willing to go along with it. *Señora*, please, sit down, eh? [Sound of chair scraping on floor] Eh? Why do you not sit down?

BATISTA: I don't have to sit down.[52]

MILLS: But why?

BATISTA: Because that's how I am. They tell me that's why I'm not fat, because I'm always standing.

MILLS: Ay! [Laughter] Well, and then what happened after the divorce and the man to whom you had been married took your two daughters? Then what did you do?

BATISTA: I went to my mother's house and then I went to my sister's house where I stayed a period of time. I realized that my parents did not have a way to make a living. I started working in Manzanillo.

MILLS: And what kind of work was that?
BATISTA: Like I'm doing here—serving in the house.
MILLS: And when did you first come to this house? What year?
BATISTA: This house? Well, in September it will be four years.
MILLS: Four years ago this coming September?
BATISTA: In 1956.
MILLS: In 1956. And at that time, who ran this house?
BATISTA: Well, Dr. Rousseau.
[At this point Arcocha spells the name Rousseau.]
MILLS: Like the philosopher.
ARCOCHA: Like the philosopher.
MILLS: And what sort of man was he?
BATISTA: A very nice person.
MILLS: A very nice person. Did he have a wife?
BATISTA: Yes. She was also very nice.
MILLS: Did he have children?
BATISTA: Two daughters.
MILLS: Two daughters. How old were they?
BATISTA: Fourteen, fifteen, something like that. They were young.
MILLS: And *Señor* Rousseau and his wife treated you very well?
BATISTA: Very well. Very well. I have no complaints.
MILLS: Yes. How long did they stay in this house during the year?
BATISTA: They rarely stayed here. He more than she. He would come at the end of the month to sign the bills. He would spend the weekend here and then leave.
MILLS: Yes. Were you in charge of the house while they were gone or was there somebody else in charge of the whole *ranchera*?[53]
BATISTA: There were others. I was here to serve them [the Rousseau's] when they came. There was a cook.
MILLS: What did you do when they were not here?
BATISTA: Well, nothing. Because . . .
MILLS: You just lived?
BATISTA: Yes.
MILLS: Yes, and that was a pleasure, right?
BATISTA: I took care of the house. I always had the keys.
MILLS: The keys to the house. You were the majordomo, the chief person in charge of the house?
BATISTA: Yes.
MILLS: And then how did you first learn about the Fidelistas?

BATISTA: Well, because, how do you say it, like we were here, so near, and they always . . .

MILLS: Yes, but how did you hear about them? Did you help them? Did you give them food?

BATISTA: Everybody was interested in them. Because Fidel was over there in the Sierra. At first they didn't come down [from the mountains], then they did.

MILLS: And when you first heard about them, what did you think about them?

BATISTA: Well, I heard that they said bad things about the [Batista] government. One hears things and you don't have enough experience so you go along with what you hear other people say.

MILLS: Yes. So you were against them at first?

BATISTA: No, I was not against them. They would visit us. At night they would visit us at the house.

MILLS: And what did they say to you?

BATISTA: The Fidelistas? They would visit us at night and then we were afraid.

MILLS: Why were [you] afraid?

BATISTA: Well, that the other [Batista] people would come and find . . .

MILLS: And then when they came down very often and they were out of the hills and they were beginning to go out into the plains, what did you then think and what happened to you?

BATISTA: Well, we now saw them as being very brave and every day they would advance, advance.[54] And they led the people from here up to the Sierra. Every day they would take more and more people from the army over there.

MILLS: Did some of the Batista soldiers go with them to the Sierra?

BATISTA: Yes, I think so. Many of them. Many of them.

MILLS: To follow Fidel?

BATISTA: Yes, to follow Fidel. They would join the Fidelista troops.

MILLS: And when did *Señor y Señora* Rousseau leave the *casa*?

BATISTA: Towards the end of the war he left and could not come back, did not dare come back.

MILLS: What did you think about that?

BATISTA: Well, I didn't think anything.

MILLS: What do you mean, you must have thought something?

BATISTA: They abandoned [the house]. It was like a shot in the [rebel] victory. When they [the rebels] started to descend [from the mountains] they were near Manzanillo. They had taken several villages, and they were starting to surround [Manzanillo]. And then those of Batista's people who were not going to join Fidel would surrender.

MILLS: And were you glad about this or were you just worried?

BATISTA: Sometimes when they [the rebels] came I would be happy but with that panic that there might be an encounter [with the Batista troops] and there could be a battle.

MILLS: Did you ever think that you might personally be hurt by either the rebels or by Batista's soldiers?

BATISTA: No, I never thought that. On the contrary, I thought about the idiots in Batista's army here. Remember, because of them I had such a terrific fall at the airport that I had a buttock like this!

MILLS: How did that happen?

BATISTA: Because I had to walk since there was no traffic [no cars available].[55]

MILLS: Why was she going from Manzanillo to here [the Rousseau ranch]?

BATISTA: I walked there to see my daughters and my family.

MILLS: She was walking back and what happened next?

BATISTA: And then to come back I had to walk because I didn't have a car to come from Manzanillo. And to the airport I brought a little package with an apple and some cigars for my husband. He was here at the house. And then there were [Batista] guards on both sides of the road at the airport who were intolerable. They were rude and disagreeable, even with the women.

MILLS: Did they whistle at you or what?

BATISTA: Yes, of course! I had to show them, in any case, what I had in my package. The police car wouldn't descend because there were rocks there. So I had to go down to where they were. They thought I was bringing something to the Fidelistas.

MILLS: Now what time did this happen? The year, the month.

BATISTA: I think it was the same year that the war ended.

[At this point Batista's husband, who had not previously said anything, interjects.]

FIALLO: About three months before.

MILLS: September 1958?

ARCOCHA: Yes.

BATISTA: I slipped with the apple and cigars and fell. They were scared because I hit myself and my buttock turned purple. I fell on a rock. And the others on the other side said to me, "Ay, see here, Señora, why were you so daft?," and they all laughed a lot.

MILLS: And it hurt you?

BATISTA: Of course! I've already told you, I fell on a big rock!

MILLS: What did the soldiers then do?

BATISTA: Nothing. They just stayed there. Laughing a lot.

MILLS: You showed them the apple that you had and then what?

BATISTA: I showed them that it was an apple and cigars that I had. Because they had to see what you had in your hands. They had to see it there at the airport. If not, they wouldn't let you pass.

MILLS: And then they let you pass through and you came back to this house?

BATISTA: Yes. I walked.

MILLS: And was Señor Rousseau still here then?

BATISTA: No, he wasn't. He didn't live here much.

MILLS: When did you first know about Dr. [René] Vallejo?

BATISTA: Of Vallejo? Well, since he left Manzanillo for the Sierra. I knew him from before.

MILLS: Was he your doctor?

BATISTA: No, no. I never consulted him but I knew him. Good doctor, good doctor.[56]

MILLS: When was this *ranchera* intervened?

BATISTA: It's going to be a year next month [September]. In 1959.

MILLS: And what have you been doing that year that it has been intervened?

BATISTA: Well, I've been attending to all these people [visitors]. Fidel. He started coming here in December. In December was the first time that he came.

MILLS: He comes here for weekends or what?

BATISTA: Fidel? No. He comes once a month. Then two months pass without being here. He comes often.

MILLS: To talk to the Comandante?[57]

BATISTA: In January he came twice. And then in March. I have counted the times.

MILLS: And in general, her life, the way she lives and what she does, it is not very different yet?

BATISTA: Yes, quite a lot.

MILLS: How does it differ?

BATISTA: In everything. Because they are very kind.

MILLS: Yeah, but Señor Rousseau was also.

BATISTA: Yes, he was a very nice person. He liked us very much. Not like others who hire you and treat you very bad. He didn't.

MILLS: But he did not?

BATISTA: No, he was a very nice person.

MILLS: And so how is your life? How is it different?

BATISTA: Well, because I'm better off with these people [the Fidelistas]. They're all very nice and they help me.

MILLS: What do you think you are going to be doing—you and your husband—oh, let us say, a year from now?

BATISTA: I think that we will prosper much more but we intend to remain in the house with these people. I don't intend to leave and neither does this clumsy person [her husband]. Never.[58] The first time Fidel came here he didn't tell me anything. But the second time, while he was eating there at the table, he said, "Come here." In front of all the *comandantes* and Celia [Sánchez]. "Tell me, how much are they paying you?" I told him the same that Rousseau gave me.

MILLS: And how much was that?

BATISTA: Rousseau? Twenty-five *pesos* [a month].

MILLS: And her food and board?

BATISTA: Yes.

MILLS: And her husband, how much did he make at this time?

BATISTA: When? Rousseau?

FIALLO: Eighty *pesos* a month.

MILLS: What sort of work were you doing, sir?

FIALLO: Mechanic.

MILLS: Tractors and other things, yeah?

FIALLO: Yes.

MILLS TO BATISTA: And what did Fidel say to you then? When he came over?

BATISTA: Fidel said, before Vallejo and the other *comandantes*, that because I hadn't complained...

[There is a gap in the recording at this point.]

MILLS: ... name five of the best things.

BATISTA: The agrarian reform.

MILLS: The agrarian reform. How has that affected you?

[Inaudible]

MILLS: Positively affected.

FIALLO: Benefits? Yes.

MILLS: Sure, and many other people also.

FIALLO: All of the people who live around here. More than 500.

MILLS: Yeah. People that you know, that you see.

FIALLO: Yes, of course.

MILLS: May I ask you one more question, and then I'm through. What do you most want to do with the rest of your life that remains? She first, then he.

BATISTA: I would like to prosper. Without abandoning, how do you say it, attending Fidel and serving him when he comes [to the house].

MILLS: Right. So she wants to live as she now lives.

BATISTA: Yes. I'm doing very well.

MILLS: She's in a well condition at the present time. And you, sir, what do you most want to do with the rest of your life?

FIALLO: Me?

[The recording ends at this point.]

Militiamen, employees of the Hotel Habana Riviera, drilling. Photograph by C. Wright Mills. Copyright © 2017 by Nikolas Mills. All rights reserved.

Cuba Sí! Yankis No! Havana, Cuba. Photograph by C. Wright Mills. Copyright © 2017 by Nikolas Mills. All rights reserved.

Traveling with René Vallejo in a small aircraft. Photograph by C. Wright Mills. Copyright © 2017 by Nikolas Mills. All rights reserved.

Reviewing troops with Ché Guevara and Fidel Castro. Photograph by C. Wright Mills. Copyright © 2017 by Nikolas Mills. All rights reserved.

Revolution is to build. Photograph by C. Wright Mills. Copyright © 2017 by Nikolas Mills. All rights reserved.

Here was born Cuba's freedom. Photograph by C. Wright Mills. Copyright © 2017 by Nikolas Mills. All rights reserved.

Juan Arcocha (playing guitar), René Vallejo, and Robert Taber. Photograph by C. Wright Mills. Copyright © 2017 by Nikolas Mills. All rights reserved.

Women rebel soldiers at military establishment, Sierra Maestra. Photograph by C. Wright Mills. Copyright © 2017 by Nikolas Mills. All rights reserved.

Captain Isabel Rielo. Photograph by C. Wright Mills. Copyright © 2017 by Nikolas Mills. All rights reserved.

Juan Arcocha, Robert Taber, Isabel Rielo. Photograph by C. Wright Mills. Copyright © 2017 by Nikolas Mills. All rights reserved.

Isabel Rielo and Juan Arcocha. Photograph by C. Wright Mills. Copyright © 2017 by Nikolas Mills. All rights reserved.

Student at Camilo Cienfuegos School City. Photograph by C. Wright Mills. Copyright © 2017 by Nikolas Mills. All rights reserved.

Buildings of bioclimatic architectural design, Camilo Cienfuegos School City. Photograph by C. Wright Mills. Copyright © 2017 by Nikolas Mills. All rights reserved.

At a cattle ranch, Isle of Pines. Photograph by C. Wright Mills. Copyright © 2017 by Nikolas Mills. All rights reserved.

The rainy season, Isle of Pines. Photograph by C. Wright Mills. Copyright © 2017 by Nikolas Mills. All rights reserved.

Shooting pigeons. Photograph by C. Wright Mills. Copyright © 2017 by Nikolas Mills. All rights reserved.

Discussing agricultural matters and military preparedness, Isle of Pines. Photograph by C. Wright Mills. Copyright © 2017 by Nikolas Mills. All rights reserved.

Transforming the Isle of Pines to the Eucalyptus Island! Photograph by C. Wright Mills. Copyright © 2017 by Nikolas Mills. All rights reserved.

The counterrevolution might occur on the Isle of Pines. Photograph by C. Wright Mills. Copyright © 2017 by Nikolas Mills. All rights reserved.

The advantages of a pistol machine gun. Photograph by C. Wright Mills. Copyright © 2017 by Nikolas Mills. All rights reserved.

A drive through the Cuban countryside. Photograph by C. Wright Mills. Copyright © 2017 by Nikolas Mills. All rights reserved.

Fidel Castro, the center of attention. Photograph by C. Wright Mills. Copyright © 2017 by Nikolas Mills. All rights reserved.

Looking in on the Comandante. Photograph by C. Wright Mills. Copyright © 2017 by Nikolas Mills. All rights reserved.

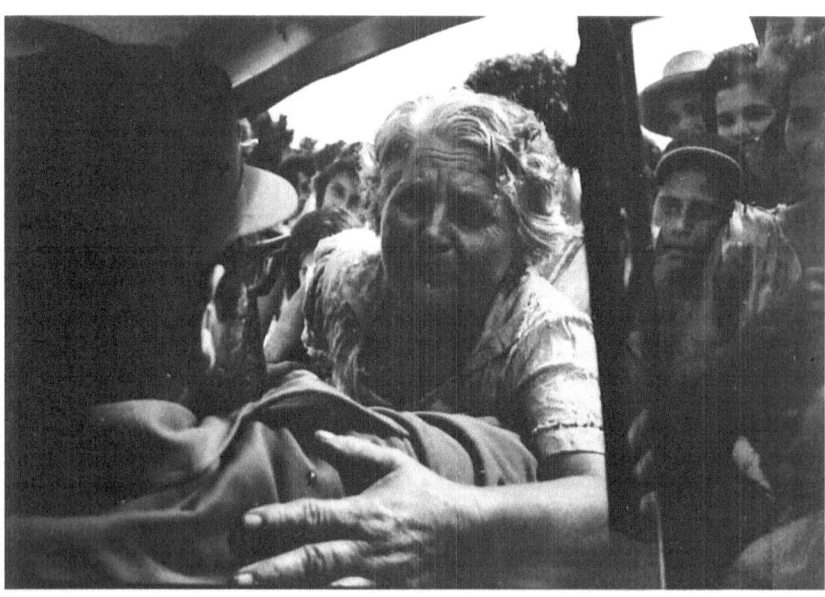

Fidel! Fidel! Photograph by C. Wright Mills. Copyright © 2017 by Nikolas Mills. All rights reserved.

Converging around the Maximum Leader. Photograph by C. Wright Mills. Copyright © 2017 by Nikolas Mills. All rights reserved.

Campesinos, soldiers, farmers, teachers. Photograph by C. Wright Mills. Copyright © 2017 by Nikolas Mills. All rights reserved.

Stopping at a cooperative. Photograph by C. Wright Mills. Copyright © 2017 by Nikolas Mills. All rights reserved.

Fidel Castro firing a Belgian rifle. Photograph by C. Wright Mills. Copyright © 2017 by Nikolas Mills. All rights reserved.

René Vallejo and a *campesino*. Photograph by C. Wright Mills. Copyright © 2017 by Nikolas Mills. All rights reserved.

A Cuban *bohío*. Photograph by C. Wright Mills. Copyright © 2017 by Nikolas Mills. All rights reserved.

A girl and two women in their *bohío*. Photograph by C. Wright Mills. Copyright © 2017 by Nikolas Mills. All rights reserved.

CHAPTER SIX

Fellow-Traveling with Fidel

In the foreword to *Listen, Yankee* Mills states that he spent three and a half days traveling with Fidel Castro and five or six days with René C. Vallejo. Though he had never met either of these two men prior to his visit to Cuba on August 8–24, 1960, nor any of the other top government officials with whom he spoke, most of them were already familiar with Mills's reputation, or at least with *The Power Elite*, the most controversial book he had written to date.

The Power Elite is a social-psychological study of stratification focusing on a tripartite ruling stratum in the United States. Its central theme is that, as the institutional means of decision, information, and power became more centralized, and as the public became more politically uninformed, there had arisen a national group made up of a governing triumvirate—a power elite— with tiers and ranges of wealth and power of which the North American people knew very little. According to Mills, the power elite was constituted of "those political, economic, and military circles which as an intricate set of overlapping cliques share decisions having at least national consequences. In so far as national events are decided, the power elite are those who decide them."[1]

In November of 1958, while still in the Sierra Maestra, Castro had read and discussed Mills's book with his band of guerilla fighters. According to Jules Dubois, *Chicago Tribune* reporter and major critic of Mills and Castro, while in the mountains Castro had read and carefully annotated his personal copy of *The Power Elite* and presumably showed it to a friend (whom Dubois does not identify) and remarked: "If the American consul should visit me here I hide this book under the bed, no?" Again, according to Dubois, writing in late 1960, many of the book's "opinions have been used, without attribution, by Castro time and again in his speeches and in his controlled press."[2]

However all this may be, the Cubans clearly had grave concerns about what the Washington administration, the U.S. corporations, and the Joint Chiefs of Staff had in store for their country. But could they have identified the specific actors, those particular members of the power elite, which they feared had and could have intervened, militarily and economically, in their national affairs? If we take Mills at his word, that he was accurately relaying the thoughts and sentiments of the informed revolutionary, then the answer is largely no. As concerns the political directorate, Mills's hypothetical Cuban protagonist does indeed single out President Eisenhower, presidential candidate Kennedy, vice president Richard Nixon, diplomat A. A. Berle, and U.S. ambassadors to Cuba Arthur Gardner (who was a vigorous admirer and close, personal friend of Batista) and Earl E. T. Smith (who was the dictator's guest at cocktail parties and receptions) as among those responsible for Cuba's woes. But regarding the other circles of power—the chieftains of the major corporations and the warlords of the Pentagon—*Listen, Yankee* does not provide names.[3]

On the Isle of Pines

As an accomplished author and a tenured Ivy League professor, Mills possessed the intellectual solidity to provide North American readers of *Listen, Yankee* with a credible and authentic voice, one that would perhaps not be immediately dismissed as mere communist propaganda. Indeed, Mills was associated with the independent Left—the "New Left" as he would come to popularize the term—with no ties whatsoever to the Stalinists of the "God That Failed" camp. Furthermore, as Tom Hayden has pointed out, "In those days Mills was the intellectual parallel to Bob Dylan. Their every page and every lyric were explored like tea leaves."[4]

However, Mills was indeed fortunate to have spent time with Castro and, even luckier still, to actually have had at least two extended conversations with him: one while both men were trekking through the Viñales Valley and staying at a hotel in Pinar del Río province, another while riding in Castro's car on the remote and desolate Isle of Pines.[5]

The two transcriptions in this chapter are from separate recordings made by Mills when touring with Castro in the Isle of Pines. Shaped like a swollen comma, the 2,000-square-kilometer island is located 80 kilometers off the southwest coast of mainland Cuba. During Mills's visit a number of U.S. citizens were living there, descendants of North American families who had settled on the island after the Spanish-American War in 1898, most of whom were citrus farmers. Much of the land was wilderness, and aside from the forests of conifers that covered the island and gave it its name, there were also grapefruit groves, cucumber fields, and cattle farms. The isle had several banks, department stores, and hotels, mostly in the capital city of Nueva Gerona. But perhaps most significant for Mills, because it was thought to be a likely invasion target, the isle was being transformed into a virtual armed fortress when he was there.

The Isle of Pines was most famous for its model penitentiary, the Presidio Modelo, where Fidel Castro, his brother, Raúl, and the other rebels who had survived the failed Moncada attack were imprisoned, from 1953 to 1955. Indeed, at the time that Mills was there, prisoners made up about one-half of the resident population on the isle. Erected by the dictator Gerardo Machado, the Presidio Modelo was built as a military prison in accordance with the Panopticon architectural design—consisting of circular blocks, with cells constructed in tiers around central observation posts—first proposed by Jeremy Bentham, and whose major effect was "to induce in the inmate a state of conscious and permanent visibility that assures the automatic functioning of power. So to arrange things that the surveillance is permanent in its effects, even if it is discontinuous in its action; that the perfection of power should tend to render its actual exercise unnecessary; that this architectural apparatus should be a machine for creating and sustaining a power relation independent of the person who exercises it."[6] Despite the constant prison surveillance, Castro managed to recreate from memory his *History Will Absolve Me* defense speech, write it in invisible lemon juice, and smuggle it out for publication. Twenty-thousand copies were clandestinely distributed.

In the first transcription, Mills is talking into the recorder and describing what is happening, in real time, at a cattle ranch that Castro is visiting. Mills is with a group consisting of Castro, Vallejo, and several military men, including an unknown "Captain" with whom Castro has an ongoing conversation about what to do with the pine trees in the forest. As it is the wet season, it begins to rain heavily. Castro, who is wearing an ankle-length rain cape and looking vaguely like a Roman centurion, leads the men through the muddy countryside. Later, the men take shelter from the downpour under a porch with a corrugated tin roof—most stand while Castro and a few of the officers sit in rocking chairs. The conversation turns from agricultural matters to military preparedness, with each man making a report. At one point, Castro shoots pigeons, positioning his rifle on the slats of a corral.

While these activities are transpiring, Mills frequently asks Juan Arcocha to tell him what Castro and his men are discussing, with Mills alternately speaking into the recorder and taking photographs.

MILLS [TALKING INTO THE RECORDER]: I am standing with Juan [Arcocha] behind a group of military men—1, 2, 3, 4, 5, 7, or 8—with

Fidel Castro in a new cattle ranch which INRA has taken over. These fierce-looking *barbudos* are discussing the number of eucalyptus trees that have been planted and will be planted in the near future.[7]

MILLS: Juan, what is the content of their animation? Why are they so excited?

ARCOCHA: Well, because Fidel is feeling very optimistic about the results of all these agricultural plans they are starting. So he is encouraging. It's nothing very curious because he speaks with enthusiasm that all the men who are speaking with him get like an injection of that enthusiasm. And so everything is going to be alright and they are going to plant many hundreds of thousands of trees, and so on and so on.

MILLS: Do they also speak about the cattle that are going to be run here?

ARCOCHA: Well, not yet.

MILLS: They'll get to that a little later, perhaps.

[Recorder is turned off and then turned on some time later.]

MILLS: Juan, would you get me a little bit of the running conversation between them, if you can do it?

ARCOCHA: Yes, it's rather comic because during that conversation about trees Fidel has been asking several times about a number of pines. It seems that at the center of this territory there is a wood of pines and Fidel wants them out. He's asking "What are we going to do with them?"

MILLS: Why does he want them out?

ARCOCHA: I don't know. He wants to plant something else, more productive. And so the officer in charge of this territory says, "No. We will need those pines for later in order to build houses for our soldiers." But then [Castro] doesn't say anything and later he comes again, "Oh, those pines, I still feel like cutting them."

MILLS: And he wants to plant eucalyptus trees and such things?

ARCOCHA: Probably. Well, eucalyptus grows very fast. In fact, here they are already productive.

MILLS: In ten years you can cut them, I've just noted.

ARCOCHA: Yes, yes.

[Recorder is turned off and then turned on some time later.]

MILLS [TALKING INTO THE RECORDER]: It is raining very hard, a kind of tropical rain which pours down.

MILLS: How often in the year does it rain like this?
ARCOCHA: Well, in the rainy season, about once a week, at least.
MILLS: That's very good for growing, isn't it?
ARCOCHA: Yes, very good.
MILLS: What is the Captain saying, Juan?
ARCOCHA: He's still speaking about pines.
MILLS: Don't you know they're transforming the Isle of Pines to the Eucalyptus Island?[8]
ARCOCHA: I think so.
MILLS: What has Fidel just said?
ARCOCHA: Well, he was telling about once there was a fire in the pine woods and then he went up to the men to put the fire out. Now he's describing the conditions for the neighbors, these people who live in a very uncomfortable way without any means of communication.
MILLS: What is the Captain now saying, Juan?
ARCOCHA: Well, he's still arguing in favor of the pines. He thinks that there are many good carpenters here that can do many good furniture and houses and everything from the pines. I think he's saying already his pines are in danger.
MILLS: So the real ideological conflict under discussion is pine trees versus eucalyptus, and carpenters as a labor force come into it.[9]
[Recorder is turned off and then turned on some time later.]
MILLS [TALKING INTO THE RECORDER]: Several more soldiers came up onto the porch where we're standing to give some reports on some martyr installations. There have been rumors that the counterrevolution might occur on the Island of Pines. A soldier tells Castro that should he hear that the Isle of Pines has been taken, and if it is confirmed, he will then know that there is not one living soldier on this island.[10]
MILLS: What is he asking now, Juan, to the soldiers?
ARCOCHA: Well, they are reporting to him that they are instructors with different weapons, mortars and so on. And so he's asking them just how many weapons they have, how are the ammunitions and everything. And just how is the work going on.
MILLS: He's getting a detailed report, in other words.
ARCOCHA: Yes, very detailed.
MILLS: So first we had eucalyptus trees and now we have martyrs.
ARCOCHA: Exactly.
MILLS: What is the paper that Castro is now reading?

ARCOCHA: It's a receipt for the weapons they have received.

MILLS [TALKING INTO THE RECORDER]: They are discussing the advantage of a pistol machine gun which Castro is examining with some care. And, may I say, abandonment.

MILLS: Do they like this particular gun, here?

ARCOCHA: Yes, it seems like they may like it very much and so all of them want to have it.

MILLS: Is he saying that they will get it?

ARCOCHA: No. He hasn't said it.

[Recorder is turned off and then turned on some time later.]

MILLS [TALKING INTO THE RECORDER]: There are now about twenty men on the porch making a report. They are going over [replacement?] parts which they require. Fidel answers that this man acts as if he would like to go to Havana to get them. The soldier replies that he has just come back from Havana.

MILLS: What did Castro then say?

ARCOCHA: He laughed.

MILLS: I have been photographing. What have they been talking about, Juan?

ARCOCHA: Now they have been talking about men. Each man was making a report. They told him just how many men they have and those that they thought should be sent here. And then they have been discussing generally about the quantity of troops that should be or shouldn't be here, all the time entering into particular details about that particular man . . . who has been acting very well, so on and so forth.

MILLS: Were they speaking of army personnel for military dispositions or for the agricultural work that the army is doing here?

ARCOCHA: Both of them.

MILLS [TALKING INTO THE RECORDER]: He [Castro] told them a moment ago that they did not need so many men for a given task. That this was the American way. The way of waste.

MILLS: What is he talking about now, Juan?

ARCOCHA: Well, in general, now he is giving them advice so that they learn how you can obtain the best from men.

MILLS: Morale problems, you mean?

ARCOCHA: No, no. How they can work best and how they can produce the most they can.

MILLS [TALKING INTO THE RECORDER]: I have been photographing again.

MILLS: What has he been talking about, Juan?

ARCOCHA: They have been long discussing military tactics and at the same time the process of the occasion to make advice to the men. They must have discipline and so on.

MILLS: Any other new themes in the conversation?

ARCOCHA: No, just the same. Weapons and military tactics.

MILLS: And eucalyptus trees?

ARCOCHA: No, not anymore.

MILLS: Not anymore.

A Drive in the Countryside with Fidel

Mills made another recording (transcribed below), likely on the evening of the same day. On returning to his hotel, Mills, who had taken detailed notes on a conversation he earlier had with Castro, dictated those notes into the recorder. The conversation with Castro took place in a car while driving in the countryside. In addition to talking with his hospitable host, Mills also took several photographs of him.

A conversation with Castro, the American journalist Lee Lockwood explains, is an extraordinary experience, and, he adds, "until you get used to it, a most unnerving one." Mills does not provide an account of his experiences conversing with the Cuban leader, but his rules for conducting interviews (discussed in Chapter 3) were likely of little use, given Castro's gift for overpowering oratory. According to Lockwood,

[U]nless you are very firm, it is not properly a conversation at all, but something more like an extended lecture, with occasional questions from the audience. This is not to say that Castro is rude, for he is not; in fact, socially he can be as courtly as a Castilian nobleman. Nor does it imply that he is not interested in what you have to say. It is simply that he is one of the most enthusiastic talkers of all time. A ten-word question can program him for an answer lasting fifteen or twenty minutes....

For Castro, trained as a lawyer, and an orator and a politician since his university days, the primary use of speech is demagogic: that is, its purpose is not so much to exchange ideas with someone as to convince another of his own. This is true whether he is addressing half a million people in public or conversing privately with one man. It is not enough that you understand; you must, if at all possible, be convinced. To this end he bends his considerable energy and intellect with enormous concentration. As the carefully formed sentences flow out in cadence, every word has the ring of absolute conviction, the product of a mind never in doubt.

But what is even more compelling than Castro's mind is his manner, the way he uses his voice and his body, especially his eyes, to reduce a listener to surrender. If he is effective in a public speech, where the listener is at a relatively safe "aesthetic distance," in a private conversation, focusing the full force of his personality upon you at close quarters for hours at a time, he is formidable.[11]

And what was Mills's general experience of traveling with Castro? Though he does not give an account, a good sense of it can be gotten from photographs taken by Mills of his excursion with Castro as well as from a record provided by Jean-Paul Sartre when he and Simone de Beauvoir accompanied Castro on a similar *vuelta*, a drive through the Cuban countryside, five months before Mills.[12]

To begin with, a drive with invited guests served at least three purposes. First, it routinely doubled as a tour of inspection for Castro. He would talk with *campesinos*, soldiers, farmers, teachers, anyone and everyone, about work in progress. This meant there were constant interruptions to conversations he had with guests accompanying him. Second, Castro would encourage and boost morale among those people with whom he came in contact. Third, it was an opportunity for him to propagandize and show his guests the most pleasing aspects of the Revolution.

On these *vueltas*, the cigar-puffing Castro would usually sit in the front seat of the car, which he would drive as often as not, and his guest would sit in the back, usually with an interpreter and, sometimes, his secretary, Celia Sánchez.[13] This front seat–back seat arrangement makes sense, given that Castro and Mills were large men—both over six feet tall. In this case, Castro went in front with his chauffeur, with Mills and Arcocha in the back.

At every village, every cooperative, people would gather to greet Castro and converge around his car, wanting to touch him, talk with him, complain, make suggestions. The "Maximum Leader" would hold long conversations from the car window or else emerge to be surrounded by men, women, and children, always the center of attention. Huberman and Sweezy describe these encounters, which they experienced a few weeks after Mills, as follows:

> Accompanying as he goes among his people, one not only sees [his charisma]; all of one's sense are overwhelmed by it. To watch the faces light up as their owners suddenly recognized the driver of our car; to hear the delighted cries of "Fidel, Fidel"; to experience the rush of people, young and old alike, whenever the car stopped, even if only for a red light, people drawn like iron filings to a magnet, wanting to shake his hand, touch his sleeve, wish him well; to smell the sweaty bodies of hundreds of construction workers who swarmed around the car when it was halted by an obstruction in the road, ... —these were indeed unforgettable experiences.[14]

At one point, Castro, his entourage, and Mills stopped at a private airfield that had been previously intervened. Here, Castro, in the company of about a dozen soldiers, fires a Belgium rifle from the roof of a small concrete building with a pole on which is attached a flaccid wind sock. It is a windless, sunless afternoon—perfect for target practice.

As K. S. Karol observed several years later after spending many hours in Castro's company: "There is nothing like a dinner or a vuelta with Fidel to help explain the optimistic mood of his entourage, and the devotion he inspires wherever he appears."[15]

Building and Defending the New Society

What follows below is a verbatim transcription of Mills's dictation of the conversation he had with the garrulous Cuban leader while riding in his car earlier that day.[16] I have set in quotation marks those passages that I surmise Mills wanted to attribute to Castro. I have also placed within parentheses those asides Mills makes to himself; indeed, several times he says "parenthesis" and "close paren" to indicate those places. As though he is writing while speaking, Mills also indicates which punctuation to use—comma, exclamation—and where to place it. He also tells where he wants to begin a new paragraph, which instructions I have followed in the transcription below. In short, Mills was dictating—indeed, *composing—Listen, Yankee* while still in Cuba.

One of the general themes that recurs in the colloquy is that of increasing and diversifying production and of engaging in productive work. This was obviously foremost on Castro's mind—the building of the Revolution by constructing a new society. Indeed, Mills saw for himself that everywhere, in the cities and in the countryside, Cubans were working hard in making a new life for themselves.

Another pervasive theme is that of defending the nation against U.S. hostilities, expressed in the Caribbean island's motto, *¡Patria or Muerte, Venceremos!* Interesting in this respect is that Cuba had a well-armed population and at one point Mills tells of Castro firing a new kind of Belgium rifle that obviously existed in great numbers in the area. Arcocha describes the event as Mills "watching with inexhaustible interest for a long time Fidel Castro having shooting practice with a group of soldiers from the Rebel Army."[17] In the third edition of the Spanish translation of *Listen, Yankee*, Mills wanted North Americans to know that the Cuban people were well armed and possessed first-rate weapons. "And I implore you," he tells his readers, "let's not insult each other with sad lies about Cuban rifles not working properly, that they are not loaded, that they are snatched from their owners under cover of night, etc. I have seen with my own eyes how automatic weapons work in Cuba."[18]

> I am now back at the hotel. It's 9:30. One question asked to Fidel was the largest economic problem that he saw in the immediate future. His answer was, "There is none. If the United States does not buy sugar, we will have, here in our hands, we will hold the world price of sugar. We are very efficient sugar producers now.[19] We will also have on the sugar cooperatives a diversified agriculture. The sugar coops will be diversified, not simply sugar. They already now have enough cows in a few places. And soon we will take one man from each of these cooperatives, from each of them, to a central place where he will be taught artificial insemination so that there will be pure milk available at all sugar coops. Who can compete with Cuba in sugar?," he asked. "We have in our hands the world price. And guilt for the fact that the world price will go up will be clearly laid at the door of the United States."[20]
>
> (Paragraph.) I asked him the rate of investment. He clearly does not know. I suggested to him that perhaps in order to calculate the rate of investment he would need journalists with daily reports rather than a statistical central board. He then told me, concerning the rate of investment, that, "In the first year of the Revolution, when we had just broken the chains, the economic situation was not too clear. Everybody wanted jobs if they didn't have them and those who did have them

wanted increased money, wages. Prices tended to be high and rent in particular was high. Where the wage workers were free, they now started a wage fight. The rights of the wage worker were established in Cuba by this Revolution, independent of economic matters. That was a matter of political science. So the increase in the consumption began. Everyone saw a magic formula to solve all questions, and that was to get more money. I got all the sugar people in the industry together and explained the economics of it to them. We raised the living standard, I said, only by increasing production. More money will not accomplish anything. Also there must be some limits to the wage workers' standard for the time being. So I put the social and political consciousness as well as economic consciousness into the wage worker stratum. And they then, very soon, voluntarily, gave 4 percent of their wages for industrialization." We were interrupted, while riding in the car, to talk with a worker standing alongside the road who had been a policeman in the jail [the Presidio Modelo] when Fidel Castro had been there [as a prisoner] on the island. He asked him how he was and how his condition was. This policeman apparently had been a fairly decent kind of man. We passed a coconut field. Coconuts seem to bear in some three years a fantastic tropic richness. (Compare notes on eucalyptus trees bearing in ten years). The discussion of the wage worker and his relation to the peasantry, and especially the problem of the rate of investment, continued as a thread with these interruptions. The point seems to be that immediately after the matter was explained properly, the wage workers began to give to the agricultural development, in particular a great number of tractors are involved in this. We then had a discussion concerning state ownership of certain enterprises versus the cooperative farm. Castro's general criterion would seem to be that in situations in which there is a big investment in proportion to the number of wage workers involved, those wage workers had better remain wage workers, in short, to keep it a state-owned property. In cases where things are growing—vegetables, corn, sugar—and where there are many wage workers involved and the rate of investment is not great, the amount of investment is not great, then a cooperative farm makes more sense, as he sees it.

(Paragraph.) He continues that, "The big problem, of course, was to give everyone employment, and it is still a major problem. So there's a need to invest in agriculture and in industry. So some public works had to be immediately put into operation. The big reason for the rate of investment being up is because here in Cuba we increase production immediately. Now about 100,000 people were put to work in reproductive capital. Private riches that existed in Cuba were also put to (Can't make the damn thing out) . . . were put to consumers goods that were used in short to raise the standard to living as well as to invest. Tax was placed upon alcoholic beverages and the money gotten from this tax was used to invest in the expansion of the tourist industry. I also opened up all factories that had been closed as well as beginning to build some new ones. I also put soldiers into productive work. Five thousand teachers (No, kill that). In the budget there was money for 5,000 new teachers. But the matter was explained fully to them. Ten thousand teachers who were unemployed were put to work on the same budget that had been intended for 5,000. They were willing to do this for a while. And an arrangement has been made with them, an understanding has been come to with them, that in future years they will be compensated for the lack of full salary at this time. It used to be in Cuba that 35 million dollars a year was spent on the importation of automobiles and 5 million a year on agricultural machinery." (Parenthesis, Check these figures with Oltuski, close paren).[21] Castro remarks that, "We have reversed this proportion. In other words, mere distributing, or redistributing, what we already had in Cuba made for a rather large investment reserve. We don't need to sacrifice the present generation for future generations. We are not in that big a hurry anyway. If certain things take fifteen years instead of ten years, and by taking fifteen years we can give two more houses that are needed in a given spot, well, we will take fifteen years. We do not know the rate of investment yet, but we are working on it in the statistical Central Planning Board of INRA. In all other revolutions the agricultural reform in them failed because they divided the land. But in the case of Cuba it was not politically necessary to do this as it was in those other places because the Cuban peasantry was already greatly scattered in rather huge concentrations. In short, he did not own land to begin with as was the case in other revolutionary situations." Castro is quite well aware that this was a political chance in Cuba that does not exist in all places. "If we had had to divide the land for political reasons," he said, "what would happen was that the people would, for example, eat the cattle, slaughter them and eat them. In the Sierra Maestra we had during the war a small experiment in such distribution schemes and that is what happened.[22] We didn't have to do this for political reasons in Cuba and so we have a big head start on all other revolutions." We now arrived at a, it seemed to me, a prototype of fruit, an experimental farm for fruit production, citrus and other such fruits, and there were many discussions about the number of acres that should be planted in this and that kind of fruit. The idea is to make this particular region, as Castro put it to the workmen in charge, "a paradise of fruits." When you listen to him talk, even if you do not know Spanish, three phrases tend to recur: How many? When? and Why? In appearing as he does in the middle of productive work as well as among soldiers at various posts where one stops, he is doing two things, at least, at once. He is sustaining and building morale and enthusiasm, and he is, secondly, actually getting reports on what is going on in order that he may be informed, and thirdly he is actually giving advice, suggestions, or at least getting ideas that may later be implemented. (Parenthesis: Expand list of functions of Castro personally in all areas of Cuban life, close paren.)

(Paragraph.) Whenever it becomes known that Castro is in some zone of Cuba, all varieties of responsible people converge, and the automobile train, of which the car he is riding in usually leads, becomes slightly longer as you proceed during the day or the evening. We went driving over a new airfield which had presumably been intervened recently—some small private outfit—and is now going to be greatly expanded. It reminds one of the fact that in the mountains a small group of men did it themselves and learned how the hard way. Now they do not fear any sort of task with which they may be confronted in any area: economic, military, or political. And they are, of course, teaching many others and fast. How we are learning (exclamation). So many things (comma), every day (comma), how we are learning (exclamation). And how easy it is, really, if someone only shows you how to begin, how to follow through.

(Paragraph. Set up a new page bit.) He does a quite thorough inspection examining a house on the edge of the airfield where presumably men who will guard or work in, or both, at the airport, are to live. At the airport, standing on top of the small concrete building, he tries out a new Belgium rifle, remarking that he has seen it abound and for two hours now he has wanted to shoot it. (Compare photographs of him with gun.) The first photographs with gun were pigeon shooting at the corral of the cattle ranch. The second, he wanted to try the range of the gun, presumably for its defensive value of the airport.

They are laying out a great expansion of this intervened airfield and also the defense system for it in this area as well as the airport itself. We then went to an army post which he inspected and which was quite poor and in which the men are only going to be for a short time, presumably. Again, he shot the rifle and the people at the army post, the soldiers, told him that they almost shot at his plane this morning. At Castro's plane. Because it circled the area two or three times and it was strange to them. He said to them that he was circling it in order to study the terrain around the army post and that the next time, if they see a strange plane, to shoot up at it as a warning.

(Paragraph.) Vallejo, that's V-A-L-L-E-J-O, tells me that the Isle of Pines was a free zone and that people smuggled from this island to Cuba. Another source of their income, before the Revolution, was tourism, which was centered, like most tourism in Cuba at that time, around gambling. The land was not used much at all. Another source of income was the big prison because relatives of the prisoners came. That too is tourism of a sort. [Castro] asked at the army post for the teachers, and two men came up who were presumably high school students, and they need more seats and various little things like this were discussed. Apparently seven men in this troop or group are illiterate and the rest are first- and second-grade people. He asked a question then of a man who came up. Why did the prison on the island, which used to be quite large, according to Commander V., some 5,000 prisoners in the Batista period. He said, "Why did they sell 25 pigs to Havana? They should have a slaughter plant here and make ham . . . ." [garbled].

[End of recording]

Mills and Gerth aptly captured the sociological essence of the revolution-making enterprise—as experienced that day with Castro on the Isle of Pines—when they had written, seven years previously: "In interpreting contemporary social change, we have found ourselves more and more interested in those roles and technologies that involve violence and which involve economic production. Like many other observers we believe that revolutions in these [social] orders are now central to the course of world history. Tools and arms, industrial machines and military weapons, factories and armies, skill levels and practices of violence—how these interplay with each other seem to us most immediately relevant to the course of twentieth-century societies."[23]

The Charismatic Leader

Mills cultivated close relationships with Castro and Vallejo. It seems that Mills and Castro first cemented their friendship shortly after Mills's arrival in the Cuban republic. As the story goes, Mills, along with Juan Arcocha, Saul Landau, and a young intellectual, Manuel E. Yepe, drove from Havana to the town of Viñales in Pinar del Río, the island's westernmost province. They arrived late at night at the La Ermita Hotel, and Mills went to his room. Early the following morning, Yepe brought Mills to Castro's room, where they found him still in bed, holding a machine gun. Vallejo, who was fluent in English, came by to interpret. They shut the door and talked for the next eighteen hours. The following day they traveled around the province, where it is likely that Mills accompanied Castro, with Castro as guide, on an inspection tour of several "people's farms" (*granjas del pueblo*), agricultural establishments that were breeding chickens, hogs, cattle, ducks, and goats. That night, Arcocha, Castro, and Mills had dinner at the hotel, and afterward the conversation continued for many hours; Fidel and Mills passionately discussed the Cuban Revolution. "A solid friendship," Arcocha noted, "was forming between those two very different men."[24]

Whatever differences Arcocha may have had in mind, it is clearly the case that Castro and Mills had in common several constitutional and biographical influences. At forty-four, Mills was almost exactly ten years older than Castro. But both possessed an indomitable dedication to everything they did and believed in, coupled by seemingly boundless energy. Both looked to youth, in the emerging New Left and in the Cuban leadership, respectively, to create a better society. Both inherited, and subsequently abandoned, the Roman Catholicism of their mothers. Both were considered outlanders: Mills because of his "backwoods" origins in Texas, Castro because he was from rural Oriente, the "Texas of Cuba." Both had a penchant for firearms—pistols, rifles, shotguns—which they owned and delighted in shooting. Both men were fiercely ambitious, wanting—needing—to make a mark in their lives, which they believed would soon be cut short: Mills because of his worsening heart problems and the threats made on his life by Cuban exiles, Castro because of assassination attempts by exiles, defectors, mercenaries, the Mafia, and the CIA.

Commonalities and differences between the two men notwithstanding, Mills appears to have assiduously maintained his relationships with Castro and Vallejo long after departing the island. Indeed, he would again see Castro a few weeks later, this time in New York City, where the prime

Fellow-Traveling with Fidel

minister went to address the Fifteenth General Assembly of the United Nations and deliver a four-hour speech in which he inveighed against the imperialist policies of the United States toward the Cuban nation. A few days prior to that historical speech, Mills met Castro at the Hotel Theresa, a residential hotel in the heart of Harlem, where they discussed plans for Mills to conduct a six-to-eight-week seminar in Havana that would cover the ideological differences between China, Yugoslavia, and the Soviet Union. The seminar was to be attended by Castro and several other revolutionary leaders.[25]

A few months after that, and shortly after suffering a major heart attack, Mills wrote to Ralph Miliband, telling him that: "Fidel keeps cabling me to come on down and convalesce in Cuba, and my friend Vallejo . . . a medical man of real ability, as well as head of INRA in the Oriente, says that just one step on the island will cure me! And that he has some things to talk over anyway!"[26] Vallejo was indeed a good friend to Mills. The leftist European journalist K. S. Karol tells of how, years after Mills's death, whenever he and Vallejo met, they would exchange reminiscences about Mills.[27]

If Mills shared some characterological similarities with Castro, he could not have been more different from Vallejo, a diffident, almost frail-looking man and the one Cuban official with whom Mills had the closest association. The forty-year-old *comandante*, Vallejo, having been educated in the United States, spoke flawless English, an ability that doubtless served him well in connecting with the severely monolingual Mills. The ever-smiling and affable bearded physician, who seemed to have had his soldier's cap perpetually glued to his skull, was, by all accounts, an outstanding pulmonary surgeon—and most important for Mills, he was Castro's closest friend and confidant. Aside from perhaps Juan Arcocha, Vallejo was the traveling companion who accompanied Mills to the most locales he visited on the island; several of which were around the Manzanillo district.

Indeed, as Mills and Vallejo traveled southwest from the port city of Manzanillo, they toured the countryside near the town of Media Luna, where Mills encountered scores of the miserable Cuban *bohíos*—the ubiquitous one-room, dirt-floor, palm-thatched hovels—devoid of electricity, running water, and plumbing facilities of any kind. At one point he and Vallejo entered one of these and photographed two women and a young girl in their dirty print dresses along with their meager possessions—a few cooking utensils, two small beds, a hammock. These pictures are reminiscent of those that photographer Walker Evans took, in the 1930s, of Cubans under the Machado dictatorship (*The Crime of Cuba*), but are perhaps even more like Evans's photos of tenant families in the U.S. South during the Great Depression (*Let Us Now Praise Famous Men*). With Vallejo as his guide, Mills then headed to Puerto de Belic, where he saw a huge new agricultural cooperative that was being established in the area—and also visited the historic spot on the seashore where the *Granma* expeditionaries coming from Mexico had disembarked four years earlier. As they drove through the countryside, Vallejo proudly pointed to vast fields that had previously been neglected but were now brimming with crops. He also told of the spectacular success INRA was having in rice cultivation, where Japanese methods of transplantation were being introduced.[28]

All these traveling experiences raise the obvious question: How well did Mills feel that he *knew* Fidel Castro, René Vallejo, and the other Fidelistas? In *Listen, Yankee* he had proclaimed emphatically of Castro and his regime that, "The Cuban Government, as of mid-1960, is *not* 'Communist' in any of the sense legitimately given to this word.... The leading men of Cuba's Government are not 'Communist,' or even Communist-type as I have experienced communism in Latin America and in research work in the Soviet Union."[29] He wrote this, even after Manuel Urrutia and José Miró Cardona, the first president and the first prime minister, respectively, of the Revolutionary government, had resigned in early 1959, and after Comandante Huber Matos had been imprisoned—all because of their protests of Communist influence in the government. These events marked Castro's open espousal of the policy of equating anticommunism with counterrevolution, and thus, with treason. Mills believed that Castro's ideology was Marxist, though of a different type than the Soviet Union's "vulgar" variety, and that U.S. policies were forcing the Cuban political regime to identify anticommunism with counterrevolution. For Mills, Cuba represented the possibility of a third way between U.S. liberalism and Soviet totalitarianism; the Revolution, in his eyes, provided for a humanistic socialism, a Marxism with heart.

It is always a difficult task to attempt a simple summing up of any personality, especially one as intricate as that of Fidel Castro. As Meyer and Szulc, who were both acquainted with the Cuban leader, put it in their understated way, "[Castro] presents an orchestration of dissonant themes."[30] But in reference to his personage, perhaps the question should really be: How much did Mills *identify* with Castro? Irving Louis Horowitz suggests that whatever esteem Mills had for the Cuban prime minister stemmed from Mills's opposition to, first, Dwight D. Eisenhower and then John F. Kennedy.[31] Indeed, Mills continuously dismissed Eisenhower as a silly, arrogant crackpot who was resolute in doing all he could to destroy the Revolution. As for Kennedy, he was nothing more than an impetuous young man whose ambition exceeded his intellectual capabilities and moral qualities. Castro and his revolution thus represented for Mills, and for that matter, for many Latin Americans, a sort of reaction formation to Yankee imperialism.

It is important to note, however, that Mills's approbation of Castro and his revolution was not unbridled. Although Castro enjoyed the enthusiastic and affectionate support of a great majority of Cubans, Mills nonetheless had serious personal concerns that Castro could potentially subvert freedom and democracy in Cuba. "I do not like," Mills wrote in his own voice in the afterword to *Listen, Yankee*, "such dependence upon one man as exists in Cuba today, nor the virtually absolute power that this one man possesses."[32] And it was precisely Castro's charismatic authority—his cult of personality, in the messianic tradition—that Mills feared the most.[33]

In *Character and Social Structure*, Hans Gerth and Mills identify three psychological aspects experienced by the charismatic leader and his or her disciples following a revolution. Doubtless Mills had these in mind in expressing his unease about Castro's absolute power.

First, charismatic leaders experience time as a crisis, a turning point. They see their time as the beginning of all time. Sartre captures this sense of a new time, different from the past, in revolutionary Cuba when he writes: "All that was said, written, done before the first day of the Year (1959) will remain a dead letter."[34]

Second, Gerth and Mills contend that charismatics and their followers experience social life as a new reality, one that is optimistic and seemingly infinite. "With eyes fixed on the distant yet foreshortened goal, they move ahead with the certainty of the sleepwalker, often immunized against the costs of blood, self-sacrifice, and terror which the deliberate destruction of the old entails."[35] But as Franz Stettmeier noted, Cuba's new optimistic reality was an *uneasy* one, tempered, as it was, by foreign military and economic aggression.

Third, the charismatic leader and followers feel that freedom has increased for all. This liberation produces an expanded generalized "other," in the sense of the symbolic interactionists, which inspires the charismatic group's mission. This sense of newfound freedom against tyranny was excitedly expressed by Elvira Escobar in her interview with Mills: "I feel so free for the first time in my entire life. And I see a lot of people who talk and say things and they forgive each other. I have never in my entire life seen so much freedom. True freedom."[36]

Mills knew well that if left unchecked these aspects of revolutionary mentality could potentially subvert the Revolution. He also knew, from Max Weber, that charismatic authority was inherently fleeting and unstable and that the leader had to prove his charismatic quality by constantly performing deeds that contribute to "the welfare of the governed."[37] As Mills indecorously put it in his interview with Franz Stettmeier, "In other words, it could all go to hell"—particularly in light of the fact that Castro was living precariously. But also implied in that remark is the eminently reasonable inquiry concerning the succession of power. At the time, no clearly defined political structures had yet emerged through which the charismatic authority vested in Fidel Castro could be transmitted to others. But as Robert Taber made clear, such political structures—the "routinization of charisma," in the sense of Weber—could not be artificially or arbitrarily imposed: "they must arise from the needs of the country and develop naturally in a manner consistent with their social and economic base."[38]

Not only is charismatic authority unstable, disposition or personality can also be highly volatile, particularly in powerful public figures. Though Stettmeier, a psychiatrist, maintained of Castro that, "I think he is mentally a very healthy man," Mills, at the end of that interview, inferred that power has a dialectical and mutable quality to it: it can corrupt as well as ennoble.

For all this, Mills had previously formulated a sociology of leadership around four sets of questions—in reference to social context, role, the person, and images—that he no doubt considered in his effort to understand the leader that was Fidel Castro.[39]

1. In what context does the leader arise? How is it structured? Did this particular man "create" it by modifications of existing contexts, or did he simply become a leader in it as it existed?
2. What are the salient traits of his role as a leader? In what social orders and spheres does he lead others?—only in opinion, or in activity as well? Did he invent this role? What modifications, if any, has he made in it, and how? Has he elaborated it as he received it, constricted its scope, amalgamated other roles with it?
3. How did this man come to be in this role? How was he recruited for it? What character traits were relevant to his assuming or inventing this role? What traits are relevant to his continuing to enact this role?

4. What images do those he leads have of him as man and as leader? Why do they obey him? What techniques does he use to diffuse this image, these legitimations?[40]

But a leader's biography and character are difficult to pin down—especially in a person as protean as Fidel Castro. In his highly critical profile of the Cuban leader, published some thirteen years after interpreting for Mills in Cuba, Juan Arcocha maintains that Castro's character is one of metamorphosis. He makes this assessment after having personally witnessed Castro's long-term transition as a bourgeois youth, a supposed gangster in his university days, and then, successively, as a politician, a prisoner, a guerrilla fighter, and a political leader. "Once in power," writes Arcocha of Castro, "he has recreated himself in the image of Jesus Christ, of Simon Bolivar, of Lenin—and as of the moment that I am writing these lines—of Stalin."[41]

Yet another way of posing the question concerning Mills's relationship with Castro is: Did Castro, given his extraordinary powers of persuasion, telegraph his own vision of the Revolution via Mills and *Listen, Yankee?*[42] Cleary, Arcocha believed this had happened in the case of Jean-Paul Sartre: "Many intellectually responsible European journalists and writers, who have in all good faith written about Cuba ... arrived in Cuba completely ignorant of the language and, as such, their main fount of information was ... Fidel Castro. They literally drank up his words and when they returned to their countries, they wrote what he so convincingly expounded to them. Indeed, one of the most brilliant minds of this century was taken in by it. I'm referring to Jean-Paul Sartre, whom Fidel Castro charmed completely."[43] If Sartre had indeed succumbed to Castro's blandishments, why not also Mills?

Arcocha further contends that having been "seduced" by Castro, Sartre also, in turn, seduced the French people by telling them that he had assisted in the "honeymoon" of a revolution and that in Cuba there existed what he called "direct democracy."[44] He was convinced that this was surely the Athenian-type of democracy that had sprouted in ancient Greece. Sartre, according to Arcocha, romanticized the Cuban Revolution and was captivated by the very concepts that he himself had invented for it. Could this have also been the case with Mills?

And yet neither the perspicacious philosopher nor the sapient sociologist were dupes who could be easily entranced. They were both keenly aware of the internal dangers that could threaten Cuban culture and its humanistic revolution—and that one of these internal threats could potentially be the Maximum Leader himself.

An Improbable Revolutionary

The same month that Mills submitted the manuscript of *Listen, Yankee* to the publisher, September 1960, Castro and Soviet Premier Nikita Khrushchev publically embraced each other in a Russian bear hug on the floor of the UN General Assembly. This, however, did not change Mills's opinion about Castro's noncommunist stance, and in April 1961, just days before the Bay of Pigs invasion, he felt that he could confidently write: "*Listen, Yankee* is still right on the ball. . . . It does help now and then to have a little bit of historical reality on your side, doesn't it now?"[45] Three months later, even after the May Day festivities in Havana that included a visit by Soviet cosmonaut Yuri Gagarin, who made the first space flight in history, and depictions of Karl Marx in effigy, Mills would continue to flatly proclaim of Castro: "In principle, I do not believe that Fidel Castro has 'adopted' any system or series of ideas. Naturally, he has modified some of his ideas, or, let us say, history has taught him much in the last three years. Above all, it has taught him that Cuba's enemy has been and is the government of the United States of America. Additionally, he has discovered—for now, at least—that the Soviet bloc is willing to help Cuba economically and militarily, *without asking for anything in return*."[46] He acknowledged, however, that the belligerent course of U.S. policy toward the Cuban island could indeed force Castro to align himself with Moscow and transform Cuba into a hardened police state.

By the end of the year, in a televised address to the Cuban people, Castro proclaimed being a Marxist-Leninist and that the Revolution was communist after all. Daniel Geary states that Mills felt personally betrayed by Castro after Castro's famous self-declaration.[47] Indeed, an FBI report indicated that, upon returning from Europe on January 1962, Mills appeared to be "disillusioned with the Castro regime because of the actions and statements of Prime Minister Fidel Castro of Cuba concerning his Communist sympathy and Communist Party membership."[48]

If *Listen Yankee* contained errors of prediction (e.g., "It seems to us, the Russians want to carry on their great contest with [the United States] by *non*-military means"[49]), it also allowed for self-correction, giving, as Mills did, an apprehensive warning, in his own voice this time: "It is possible to entertain about Cuba several nightmare hypotheses." But did Mills in the end believe that his friend and traveling companion, Fidel, created those nightmares?

When Mills died about a year and a half after visiting Cuba, Castro had a wreath sent to the funeral. The Cuban Youth Union of Writers and Artists sent a message of sympathy to his widow. The Cuban newspaper, *El Mundo*, called Mills "a mentor and distinguished representative."[50]

But for all the support and his many friendships with the Cubans, including Fidel Castro, Mills was at bottom an ambivalent spokesman for the Revolution—and, in the end, an improbable revolutionary. Juan Arcocha gives the impression of Mills's uncertainty in a story he tells of how, one evening around midnight, after a long and tiring day traveling and speaking with the Cuban leader, Mills, in a moment of self-doubt, confided to Arcocha: "What the hell am I doing here? I was very quietly writing a book in New York and thinking about the next one. All of a sudden I decided to leave everything and come here to write the truth about Cuba. Now I have to confront myself with a lot of problems I didn't have before. Isn't that foolish? What do you think? Can you explain to me why I came here?"

Arcocha told Mills that he, Mills, was stirred by the temptation to change himself into a man of action. "All your life," Arcocha said to him as they were lying on their cots with the lights out, "you wrote books about revolutions and now you suddenly see yourself put right in the middle of a real revolution. You are a revolutionary who ignores yourself." After a moment of silence, Mills asked in an insecure voice: "Do you *really* think so?"[51]

CHAPTER SEVEN

The Book That Sold Half a Million Copies

The historian Van Gosse has stated that "*Listen, Yankee* exists only as a passing reference to a dying man's folly, cloaked in mystery or embarrassment."[1] Irving Louis Horowitz places the book's misfortunes more directly at Mills's doorstep, contending that the book "ended up as his poorest effort in social analysis, a tract placed at the disposal of political forces he knew little of but cared much for."[2] Half a century after its publication, both assessments are shown to be untrue. First, Mills was certainly not aware that he was dying when he wrote *Listen, Yankee*; his first major heart attack would not occur until four months after he left Cuba. Thus, whatever folly, mystery, or embarrassment may or may not characterize the book, it clearly did not stem from existential issues related to Mills's health or mortality. Second, Mills never intended for *Listen, Yankee* to be a work of social analysis, rather it was meant as a message, a pamphlet, more along the lines of a journalistic exposé. Thus, a deeper and more expansive consideration of this 60,000-word provocation requires judging it against the backdrop of Cold War national security concerns.

Listen, Yankee was Mills's tenth book, the last one published during his lifetime, and the one that sold more than any of his other books. The impetus for writing it likely came from Robert Taber, who had arranged for Mills to visit Cuba. And even before leaving for the island, Mills had produced a first draft based on what he regarded as the best recent material on Latin America, the Cuban Revolution, and the history of U.S.–Cuba relations.[3] Upon returning to New York he rewrote the manuscript completely and in a frenzy. Working sixteen-hour days, from notes and the taped interviews, he had, by mid-September, completed a preliminary draft that was reviewed by Carleton Beals, who praised it "as a magnificent book and a very necessary one."[4] Advance copies were dispatched to Ernest Hemingway, who had lived in Cuba for many years and had a personal interest in the Revolution, and K. S. Karol, a friend of Mills who wrote a two-page review of *Listen, Yankee* in the French newsmagazine *L'Express*. Democratic presidential candidate Adlai Stevenson was forwarded a mimeographed copy of the manuscript to request an endorsement. The book was also sent to the newly elected U.S. president, "Jack Kennedy, not for a quote but for his edification, with a polite note" from the publisher.[5]

Listen, Yankee was released for mass distribution, both in hardcover and paperback, on November 28. It was rushed into print so quickly, there was no time to make it available to many booksellers and librarians when it first appeared. Thus, it is hardly surprising that, given the haste in which it was produced, the book does have an urgently imperative quality to it, sounding rather like a cross between a newsreel voiceover and one of Fidel Castro's marathon disquisitions—but this may just have been the effect that Mills intended.

Peter Hulme regards *Listen, Yankee* as "the most significant piece of travel writing" on early Revolutionary Cuba and identifies three characteristics typical of such travel writing—characteristics that fittingly describe Mills's "Cubalogue" method of exposition.[6] The first is that political travel writing at the outset of the Revolution was based on firsthand knowledge of what was happening on the island and, as such, possessed the authority of eyewitness testimony. Here, the writer was on the scene to convey what was actually happening on the ground. Additionally, the predominant tone of this travel writing was a mixture of euphoria and urgency. It had a "breaking news" quality to it. "The overwhelming impression," writes Hulme, "is of a reality that is changing so rapidly that writing struggles to keep up: it needs to become journalistic because tomorrow's Cuba will be different from today's."[7] Finally, political travel writers in Cuba endeavored to describe what Revolutionary Cuba was *like* by comparing it to other places and events about which they were knowledgeable, whether that was pre-Revolutionary Cuba, the Spanish Civil War, the colonial struggles of Algeria, the 1830 Revolution in France, or the U.S. South. For Mills, the contrasting social and cultural structure was the overdeveloped society, based as it was on the postwar United States, marked by hypercapitalism, excessive consumerism, and overconformity. In any event, Mills's juxtapositioning of overdeveloped U.S. society against Cuba's developing society rendered a momentary—but most perceptive—social view of its unfolding Revolution.

> Travel texts offer not eternal truths about other cultures but rather snapshots that bring together—as it were—camera and subject for a single moment before both metamorphose into something completely different. However, though change is constant, rate of change varies. This was obviously Revolutionary Cuba, at a moment of

dramatic change; but it was also—less obviously—U.S. culture at a moment of transition toward the 1960s and the New Left. The forms of writing—the journals and the notes—capture the essential ephemerality of the moment. Perhaps only C. Wright Mills developed a new form of travel writing for this moment, but so far he has had little or no recognition for his achievement.[8]

Cuba's Revolutionary Voice

Written in a sardonic, accusatory tone, *Listen, Yankee* consists of eight "letters" in which Mills uses direct speech, the first-person plural, in addressing the U.S. citizenry.[9] This epistolary account is meant to convey a synoptic viewpoint of how the Cuban revolutionaries see their Revolution as well as how they define their aspirations and relationship to the United States. It is instructive to note Mills's social-psychological use of several literary devices in communicating his anonymous composite revolutionary's point of view.

To begin with, there is the ostensibly depersonalized "we" that he employs as part of his ongoing effort to reach a wide U.S. readership, and which is really a generalized "I."[10] Mills's disclaimer notwithstanding—"insofar as I have been able, I have refrained from expressing a personal opinion"—he does seem to be speaking for his partisan self.[11] And *Listen, Yankee* does have the feel of having been written by someone who has internalized and converted to the idea of Cuba's Revolution; indeed, as Mills well knew, for the propagandist, absolute belief justifies and motivates his actions in converting others and thus spreading his faith.[12] However, K. S. Karol, who was well acquainted with Mills during this period, contends that, "above all, Mills had nothing of the hidebound propagandist about him, was not given to letting his enthusiasm run away with him, to seeing everything through rose-tinted glasses."[13]

Moreover, speaking to U.S. readers specifically, Mills doggedly addresses them by the moniker, "Yankee." This appellation presents Americans with the idea that *others* hold views of *them*. Thus, in employing this politically charged epithet, Mills intends to dislodge North Americans from their provincialism and civic apathy and make them conscious and self-aware of the fact that a hatred had been building up of what the U.S. government and American corporations were doing in the hungry nations: "What is done and what is not done In Your Name about Cuba, is being watched by people all over the world. In it, these peoples see 'the Yankee' revealing himself;

when they read about Cuba and about the United States, they are reading about what 'Yankee' means today.... Nobody ever sees himself as others see him, and we've tried to explain ... why you and we have not really known each other."[14]

In the final letter, Mills tells his North American readers that "Yankee" has practically meant one thing to Cubans: insane hurtfulness. The appellation Yankee, being synonymous with arrogant imperialism, is not a favorable one, and Mills presses its significance to great advantage by peppering the book with the revolutionary cry of defiance, *Cuba sí, Yanqui no*. Furthermore, the designation Yankee—as a symbol—confronts North Americans with an image of their national character, an image dramatically different from that which they hold of Latin Americans. Accordingly, Mills not only makes it clear that Yankees are not Cubans and Cubans are not Yankees, but that there are "two Americas," a rich northern half and an impoverished southern half. Speaking in the voice of the Cuban revolutionary, Mills exhorts that "perhaps we Latin Americans had better realize that the people of whom we are a part is not part of whatever civilization you North Americans belong to. Once and for all, let us get it straight: we belong to the peoples of the hungry nations."[15]

But why, one might ask, didn't Mills utilize the Spanish designation, Yanqui, instead? Perhaps because it would sound too unfamiliar and confusing to U.S. readers who would likely have pronounced it as *Yan-kwē* and not understood its significance in the way Mills intended.[16] Yankee, to be sure, is a complicated word, and it has different meanings to different people. Civil rights activist Stokely Carmichael tells of when he went south to participate in the Freedom Rides in 1961 and was jailed in Mississippi, where he read *Listen, Yankee*: "You know how dumb them crackers are? In jail they took away all my books—stuff by DuBois, King, Camus. But they let me keep Mills's book about Castro, *Listen, Yankee*, because they thought it was against Northern agitators."[17] Sartre states that in Cuba, U.S. citizens were either called Americans or Yankees.[18] Theodore Draper disagrees ("No one ever said, 'Listen, Yankee!' or 'Yankee this' and 'Yankee that' to me")[19] and considers Mills's use of the word merely a touch of artistic license. And specifically in reference to the people that Mills met in Cuba, Robert Taber explains that what they referred to as Yankee was not the citizens of the United States, but rather "Yanqui *imperialismo*."[20]

However all this may be, the fact is that Mills uses the term "Yankee" as a vocative expression no less than forty-five times—eight times alone in the book's climax: the last two pages of the last section of the last letter titled

"What Does 'Yankee' Mean?" Correlatively, he employs, with intonation, the word "listen"—as in "listen to us" and "listen, Yankee"—and more frequently, the entreaty "please"—imploringly, but also sarcastically—as in "please remember," "please note," and "please understand." Mills adroitly uses *please... listen... Yankee* to convey a sense of imperativeness and urgency about the situation in Cuba.[21]

But perhaps the most effective rhetorical technique that Mills utilizes is that of speaking in the vernacular of an imaginary and anonymous Cuban revolutionary. This "voice" is a synthesis of the various comments his Cuban informants communicated to him. In attempting to make the Cuban voice sound *authentic*, Mills endeavors to imitate the idiomatic inflection of translated everyday Spanish: "[Your U.S. officials] would have really to 'associate' with us, even if our skins were dark, and—Mother of God!—that would never do!"[22]

However, in order to give *legitimacy* to this collective voice, Mills positions himself not as an observer, but as an actor in the revolutionary process; in effect, he internalizes the role of the Cuban revolutionary. The upshot is that he introduces North Americans to the vocabulary of motive of the generalized other that was emerging in revolutionary Cuba. What is more, Mills considers Cuba's voice as the voice of the hungry-nation bloc, and the archetypal revolutionary, he believes, was speaking (mainly through Mills's book) in the name of many people in that bloc. For him it was imperative that Cuba's voice be heard in the United States because this country was too powerful, its responsibilities to the world and to itself too great, for its citizens not to listen to every entreaty from the hungry world. Up to that point the U.S. public had largely ignored the Cuban island, and Mills pleads with them to hear well the message of its Revolution. For only by dealing with the perils of ignorance could the perils of disastrous mistakes be avoided.

It is, however, one thing to construe Cuba's voice through composite interviews with Cuban revolutionaries, but quite a different matter to claim that it also represents a chorus emanating from all the impoverished areas of the developing world—from all the exploited peoples of Africa, Asia, and Latin America—particularly since Mills does not seem to have spoken with many *campesinos*. Just as Ché's strategy to spread revolution was not practically *exportable* to the Congo and Bolivia, so too Mills's rendition of Cuba's voice was not practically *extrapolatable* to, say, Burundi and Haiti. However, *symbolically* at least, the Cuban Revolution did and does continue to represent the archetypical case of defiance against monopoly capitalism and, more specifically, against the manipulations and machinations of U.S. imperialism, in much the same way that Korda's iconic image of Ché became a political and (ironically) commercial "global brand," a potent symbol of resistance.[23] And it is the symbol, the message, and the image of Cuba's Revolution as exemplar to underdeveloped agricultural nations, especially those in Latin America, that both Mills and Sartre understood well. Indeed, in an interview Sartre had with a group of Cuban writers during his visit to the island in 1960, he told them that the Revolution had become of the utmost importance to the developing countries of Latin America—and it was this that basically accounted for the tenor of the conflict between their country and the United States. Further, perilous conditions were arising from a dialectical choice between danger and benefit. On the one hand, the United States could not possibly allow Cuba to become an exemplary light to the mass of people in Latin America—particularly since they could follow the Castro pattern of nationalizing all U.S.-owned property. On the other hand, given the transnational character of corporations, Latin American countries were compelled to take an increasingly favorable attitude toward the Cuban republic. It was between this danger and this benefit, Sartre told his audience, that U.S. policy toward Latin America would be played out.[24]

The question of the universality of Cuba's voice aside, Mills does, on the whole, depict quite accurately the thoughts and actions of the Cuban revolutionary (an endeavor at which, as Appendix 1 in this volume demonstrates, he succeeded quite admirably). But does he correctly express their *sentiments*: their joy and confusion, their frustrations, their ranting, their worries? In the foreword to *Listen, Yankee*, Mills describes the voice of the Cubans he met as being tinged primarily by two powerful emotions: euphoria and anger.

In letter six, titled "Revolutionary Euphoria," the voice conveys the great enthusiasm that typically accompanies the creation of something original and different—of building a completely new and better society, from top to bottom, in all spheres of life, for everyone. That national élan that was sweeping over Cuba was clearly expressed by several interviewees, for example, in Isabel Rielo's excitement of and devotion to the school cities project: "I love the cause so much. I believe I'm being useful enough in that sense. If they are going to build ten more school cities I'd like to have the privilege of being in all of them—helping the children of the *campesinos*." It is also evident in the commitment of Elvira Escobar's son, who was serving as a physician to the peasants in the Sierra Maestra: "Don't you understand? I love Cuba."

But the optimistic atmosphere that Mills encountered and that many Cubans still experienced in the summer of 1960 was not only a product of constructing a new society, it also stemmed from the existential need to defend it from its enemies. The clinical psychologist Franz Stettmeier described it as an uneasy optimism, one that compelled the Cuban revolutionary to sacrifice his life if need be: "They mean it as the Russian soldier might on the front. 'Here I am, you have to kill me.'" That sentiment was echoed by Elvira Escobar: "If someone imposes himself on us we will fight. Even if I'm in a wheelchair."

The Revolution's civic spirit and patriotic fervor was thus coupled with what Juan Arcocha described as "a palpable and pervasive sense of danger." In mid-1960 Havana, with the *La Coubre* explosion still fresh in the minds of most habaneros, "one could almost feel, in the very air that was breathed, the threat that would materialize a few months later, on April 1961, with the invasion at Playa Girón," the Bay of Pigs.[25]

To be sure, the revolutionary euphoria was correlated with "the only real worry, the real fear we have," the counterrevolutionary threat to all their efforts. That worry and fear, particularly of direct, armed intervention by the "Colossus of the North"—a country with almost literally infinitely greater firepower—was articulated time and again by Mills's respondents. It was expressed by Juan Arcocha, who wondered how long Russia's missiles would keep the U.S. Marines in Florida; by Captain 2, concerning the recent bombings of Cuba and his expectations of future aggressions by mercenaries; and by the Cuban soldier stationed on the Isle of Pines, that Mills recorded telling Castro that should the Isle of Pines be taken, he, Castro, should know that all the soldiers there had sacrificed their lives. This then was a euphoria mixed with worry, an enthusiasm mingled with fear. Indeed, Mills predicted that the revolutionary enthusiasm would run high and continue for some time, precisely *because* of the U.S. threat.

But was the Cuban revolutionary's voice the *angry* voice that Mills depicts in *Listen, Yankee?* The fact is that neither the interviewees' words nor their tone in the recordings convey much anger. And when anger or a similar emotion *is* expressed, it is directed at more immediate and tangible matters and events rather than at the Yankees—and certainly never toward Mills, himself the epitome of a Yankee. So we hear of Elba Luisa Batista Benitez's fury at Batista's soldiers, who were "idiots": "Remember, because of them I had such a terrific fall at the airport that I had a buttock like this!" They were intolerable, rude, and disagreeable to her directly. Arcocha expresses acrimony toward the venerable North American institution *Time* magazine and sees it as horrible, dangerous, and distorting the truth. But if the term Yankee meant "insane hurtfulness" to the Cuban revolutionaries Mills interviewed, they did not respond to it through enmity.

Where, then, does the popular moral indignation depicted in *Listen, Yankee* come from? Perhaps it was conveyed by the Cubans Mills spoke with but did not audiotape—notably, the top leaders in the Revolutionary government like Castro, Guevara, Vallejo, and others. Perhaps Mills experienced it as a collective representation, in the sense of Durkheim, which derived from the numerous interactions and discussions he had with many people during the two or so weeks he spent on the island. Perhaps there was the fury that, five months after the explosion of the munitions ship *La Coubre*, lingered when Mills was in Havana.[26] Or perhaps it stemmed from Mills himself. At various points in the book there is an overlapping of voices between the Cuban leaders and Mills that makes it difficult to distinguish between them as speakers. Draper contends that, with Mills's Cubans, "one never knows where they end and he begins."[27] Indeed, the major points of acrimonious attack in *Listen, Yankee*, specifically those directed at the military and economic power elites, are the very same that Mills makes in his other books.[28] However all that may be, Mills did write *Listen, Yankee* in an angry voice; but it is a voice delivered in a modulated tone of mockery and sarcasm, not of spit-flying rage. And as that voice became louder and shriller, it would compel, not only Yankees, but hundreds of thousands of readers throughout the world, to do what he wanted them to do: listen.

A Book Intended to Be Heard

Sometime between late May and early August 1960, before Mills left for Cuba, he met with Ian Ballantine, cofounder, along with his wife, Betty, of Ballantine Books. Ballantine and Mills had known each other for many years. They had first met at Columbia University while Mills was at work on *White Collar*, perhaps in the late 1940s. Some ten years later, when Mills attempted to get a book about the drive and thrust toward nuclear war to a broad audience, he approached Ballantine, and out of that partnership came the highly influential *The Causes of World War Three*.

For some reason Mills audio-recorded the meeting with Ballantine, which likely took place at Mills's home in West Nyack, New York. Several people were present.[29] At this point Mills was in the early stages of writing *Listen, Yankee*—a title he had already settled on—but was still working out its style and structure. He proposes to Ballantine a couple of ideas he has about the book.

To begin with, Mills pressed to have *Listen, Yankee* printed in an unusually short time. He was writing specifically to North Americans and needed to tell them what their government was doing and failing to do *in their name*. He wanted them to know that the U.S. government had an urgent duty to act responsibly and avoid "the perils of disastrous mistakes" in its relations toward Cuba, toward Latin America, and indeed toward all of the countries of the hungry-nation bloc; even if this duty amounted to ensuring that their government did not use violence, directly or indirectly, in any form, against Cuba's Revolution. In essence, the critical message from the Cuban revolutionary to U.S. readers was, "Hands off Cuba!" No doubt the book's publication took on a greater sense of urgency after Franz Stettmeier told Mills that, "In two months all you think and tell about the Cuban Revolution can be terribly antiquated," much as Stettmeier had found that Sartre's articles on Cuba had been quickly outrun by events.

Listen, Yankee required immediate release; Mills did not expect it to be, like *White Collar*, a book that would "stand a long time."[30] He was under pressure to get out the message of "what it's really like in Cuba now," as soon as possible. He thus treated *Listen, Yankee* rather like a journalistic piece that he was writing under deadline—events were unfolding rapidly and it needed to be released immediately, because "perhaps it is not too late for us to listen—and to act."[31]

Most surprising of all, and seemingly in contradiction to a quick publication, is that Mills intended *Listen, Yankee* to be heavily illustrated with photographs to be taken by himself. Indeed, he was something of an accomplished photographer, as demonstrated by the extraordinary snapshot that he took and subsequently used in the black-and-white dust jacket to *White Collar*. In this photo, there is, toward the bottom, a solitary white-collar man in his long overcoat and fedora, dwarfed by the big city landscape as he scurries past the National City Bank on Wall Street. The image is arguably one of the most iconic in all of sociology.[32]

Mills tells Ballantine that he wants to include a number of photos, likely the ones he was expecting to take in Cuba, giving the book a layout reminiscent of James Agee and Walker Evans's *Let Us Now Praise Famous Men*. Mills had long admired the Agee/Evans volume and regarded it as a true feat of "sociological poetry," one that allowed readers to "hear" the voice of the voiceless. This sociological poetry is a type of style-as-orientation that was needed for writing about the human condition; it is "a style of experience and expression that reports social facts and at the same time reveals their human meanings." Particularly significant for Mills was Agee's imaginative writing and painstaking reporting on his observations and experiences with southern sharecroppers. But for him the book's greatest appeal came from Agee's capacity for great moral indignation: "This fury is what makes him take it big."[33] There is, however, one major problem in Agee's prose, as Mills saw it: Agee inserted too much of himself into the experience and thus obscured the very subjects and scenes he wanted to communicate to his readers. Mills would avoid Agee's tendency for self-indulgence by writing *Listen, Yankee*, not in his own words, not from his own perspective, but from that of the composite Cuban revolutionary. But at this point he informs Ballantine that he is writing *Listen, Yankee* in a different style, as a script; one written, as he puts it, "by ear, for ear" and that includes voice tone. It is a book intended to be *heard*.

Additionally, Mills believed that providing full-page photos—as many as one hundred—similar to those taken by Walker Evans, would allow readers to also *see* the daily lives of Cubans. Contrary to Agee's writing, Evan's photographs never intrude in the slightest upon the scene being shown. For Mills, the people depicted in those photographs "are just there, in a completely barefaced manner, in all their dignity of being, and with their very nature shining through."[34]

So, at this stage, prior to his experience in Cuba, Mills imagined *Listen, Yankee* as a hardbound album-like volume—an odd admixture that was to be part investigation, part pictorial, part script—but clearly not yet as an inexpensive trade book written as a series of letters from the knowledgeable Cuban revolutionary's point of view. However all that may be, it is doubtless the case that *Listen, Yankee* would have been much different had Mills included his Cuba photographs. In this respect it may have perhaps turned out more like *Castro's Cuba, Cuba's Fidel*, the volume produced by photojournalist Lee Lockwood, which contains over one hundred black-and-white pictures depicting everyday life on the island and various images of the bearded Cuban prime minister circulating among the common people.

Mills also expressed to Ballantine that he was strategically looking for the right publishing house and considering Oxford University Press, publisher of *White Collar*, *The Power Elite*, and *The Sociological Imagination*.

The transcribed conversation between Mills and Ballantine follows (unidentified male and female voices are also on the recording):

MILLS: ... I don't know how. But I know I can do it like this. And that's the way Agee and Evans did it in on this *Let Us Now Praise Famous Men*. Do you remember how that book was set up by Little, Brown? You just opened it and there were photographs.

BALLANTINE: Uh-huh, yeah.

MILLS: Nothing messed around with. No captions. Then in the back, little notes and acknowledgments where you would credit purposes and also you will give what they were and where they were taken and things like that. But that's three-fourths done, you know.

BALLANTINE: Wonderful.

MILLS: I've done everything I can in terms of the research here. Now I've got to go down and, you know, ... [35]

BALLANTINE: What's your comfort-zone position on that?

MILLS: I've got a wonderful title here, if you like: *Listen, Yankee*.

BALLANTINE: [Laughter] Fine. That's fine.

MALE VOICE: It's spelled Y-A-N-Q-U-I?

MILLS: No. I'm not sure about that yet.

[Several people speaking at the same time]

MILLS: One can, of course, in the body of the letters, I guess.

FEMALE VOICE: Yeah.

MALE VOICE: *Oye, Yanqui*.

MILLS: The thing has terrific radio possibilities, my God. And I'm writing it as a script.[36]

BALLANTINE: Uh-huh.

MILLS: That is to say, I'm actually putting in before certain things the voice tone and, you know. It's the first thing I've ever written Ian, by ear, for ear, you know? Actually it's in force when I get through. So it's a different style then I've ever had.

BALLANTINE: This is happening all over the world.

MILLS: Is it? You mean guys are starting to write dramas?

BALLANTINE: Herb Gardner just completed a play called *A Thousand Clowns*.[37]

MILLS: That's a good title.

BALLANTINE: ... and, ah. ... He still draws *The Nebbishes*, you know. ...

[Several people speaking at the same time]

MILLS: Who are the thousand clowns?

BALLANTINE: I know nothing about what's in the play. We're having dinner with him tomorrow night and I'll hear all about it. He didn't make a single Nebbish for the last three months. He's kept this comic strip going because it would be just a crime to let this...

MILLS: Who is this guy?

BALLANTINE: A guy named Herb Gardner.

[Several people speaking at the same time]

MILLS: Oh, that's a marvelous thing. Yeah, sure. I didn't mean to dodge your question.

BALLANTINE: No, no.

MILLS: The publishing position? It'd probably be Oxford [University Press]. And I've been fooling around, quite frankly. Confidentially, I've kinda been shopping around because of all of these things coming up. But Brown,[38] whom I simply must trust on some of this stuff, thinks that, particularly for this book, because of its really quite daring content, given the stuff that's been appearing, well it would be foolish not to have the authority and the stooginess...

BALLANTINE: Of Oxford.

MILLS: Precisely, the stooginess of Oxford. So I put it to Oxford and I said, "I'm not going to crap around. If you do it, I want it published by November 17th. Don't tell me you can't, because I know it can be done."

BALLANTINE: Good.

MALE VOICE: This year?

BALLANTINE: Let me give you a little information there. Mockery's gone. A book called *The Political Zoo*, which is a piece of pictures of animals.[39]

MILLS: Wasn't that a very long time ago?

BALLANTINE: No, no, you're thinking of *Office Zoo*.[40]

MILLS: Oh, yeah, yeah.

BALLANTINE: This is a book that was done really for the Democrats. And they wanted to have it for the convention.[41] I produced the book in fifteen days. Flew it out to the convention and published it nationally in another fifteen days. So you can do it if you wanna to do it.

MILLS: Sure. Well, you pay a bit for it but not terribly much more so.

[Several people speaking at the same time]

BALLANTINE: Cash projects? Well,....

MILLS: ... You still have about 100 full-page photographs and about 150...

MALE VOICE: A hundred pages of photographs?

MILLS: Yeah.

[Several people speaking at the same time]

BALLANTINE: ... a scintillating production process which is expensive. But rather it is that there is an economical selling technique for a hardbound book. It divides the year into two seasons and you find that you can list a number of books in *Read* and *Publisher's Weekly* and you've got the catalogue. And the salesmen have all been out and they've already been to some of the places and they're not going back. So that if you throw a fall book into the schedule now, you've got to write everybody ...

[The recording ends here.]

Mills realized that a short publication time was not likely with Oxford University Press. As he had previously told Oxford's trade editor, in regard to *The Causes of World War Three* that Ballantine Books had issued in 1958, "Oxford, as far as I know, is not set up to do this quickie sort of thing, which is rather like the old 'Penguin specials,' with which Ian [Ballantine] has had experience. He has got the kind of distribution apparatus that makes it feasible, and he is interested in it."[42] Mills could have said the same about *Listen, Yankee*, which Oxford did not publish. Ballantine Books released it in paperback in late November 1960, within weeks of receiving the final manuscript, doing a first printing of 160,000 copies at fifty cents each. At the same time, McGraw-Hill put out the hardcover at $3.95. It appears that Ian Ballantine was confident that it was "destined to be a bestseller."[43] As with *The Causes of World War Three*, Mills wanted the same for *Listen, Yankee*: "to get it out fast, to distribute the hell out of it all at once, and so maybe raise a little impolite hell."[44]

A Reception at the Theresa Hotel

According to Juan Arcocha, Mills arrived in Cuba pondering a moral problem and thought about writing *Listen, Yankee* in the first person. He wanted to speak through the mouth of a fictitious Cuban who would expound before the world his arguments and grievances—the reasons for his fight—and the ideals that inspired him. As Arcocha dramatically put it, "The Cuban Revolution had been placed in the defendant's seat, and Mills wanted to change that by being its defense attorney."[45] But by writing *Listen, Yankee* in the first person, by positioning himself as the Revolution's champion and advocate, had Mills undermined his own arguments before the court of public opinion? Even a staunch supporter of the Revolution and trusted friend of Mills, such as E. P. Thompson, was led to inquire:

> If what is under consideration is an ideological phenomenon, arising from multiple convergent experiences of imperialism, national struggle, and hunger (in situations where agrarian problems are primary), then should we not distinguish between the roles of interpreter and analyst, and that of apologists? I was uneasy at the confusion between the two in Mills's *Listen, Yankee*. It is one thing to respond with deep sympathy to the writings of Fanon, Touré, Sengher, or Ché Guevara.... It is another thing to ape these views, or to propagate them uncritically because they are moving and authentic in their own context.[46]

Several weeks after Mills's return from the Caribbean island, on the evening of Thursday, September 22, a reception, sponsored by the Fair Play for Cuba Committee (FPCC), was held in honor of Castro at Harlem's Theresa Hotel, where the Cuban prime minister had been staying during his visit to the UN General Assembly. Among the 250 guests in attendance were such luminaries of the North American Left as the poets Langston Hughes and Allen Ginsberg; FPCC cofounder Robert Taber, who was working in Havana for *Revolución*; the journalist I. F. Stone, who had frequently criticized U.S. policy toward Cuba—and, of course, C. Wright Mills, who told everyone there that he was writing a book on Cuba.[47] The atmosphere in the Theresa's ballroom was fraternal and free-and-easy as "the proletarian staff of the hotel, the olive-green uniforms of the *guerrilleros*, the general lack of formality, all helped to emphasize the gaiety and the stimulating, if not revolutionary, character of the meeting."[48]

At the reception Mills was interviewed by Michael B. Conant, managing editor of the *Columbia Owl* (one of Columbia University's student newspapers), who had himself just recently spent a month in Havana. Conant queried Mills about his own Cuba trip and about his forthcoming book, *Listen, Yankee*. Mills explained that the book was already partially printed but that he was giving the typesetters "a hell of a time." He told Conant that the book dealt with the "stupidity" of U.S. foreign policy in relation to Latin America, with Cuba as a typical example; that he had interviewed Cuban revolutionaries and written the book from their point of view; that the Revolutionary regime was not communist and that its pattern of economic development was a non-Stalinist pattern; and, finally, that North American journalistic reporting on the Revolution had been a combination of deliberate vilification and fear and thus provided a distorted picture of what was really happening on the island. Asked if he thought that a Democrat would have handled the Cuban situation differently from a Republican, Mills replied—just weeks before JFK's election—that "the administration does not make that much difference. The present campaign is an advertisement to the world of U.S. silliness."[49] Mills's mission was to counteract that campaign by telling North American readers the truth about Cuba.

Criticism

The initial run of 170,000 copies of *Listen, Yankee* was quickly bought up, with Ballantine reporting "lots of rush telephone orders." A few weeks later, another 100,000 were printed. By the spring of 1961, well over 450,000 paperback copies had been sold.[50] Curiously, Herbert J. Gans does not include it (or any of Mills's other books) in his list of book sales of bestsellers written by North American sociologists. But if we assume that *Listen, Yankee* sold about half a million copies, then only three books on Gans's list—David Riesman et al., *The Lonely Crowd*; Elliot Liebow, *Tally's Corner*; and Philip Slater, *The Pursuit of Loneliness*—with much longer print runs, have outsold it.[51]

But the success of any book can't be captured by bibliometric surveys—or by the number of printings, or even by sales figures. It is, instead, a matter of *impact*, and *Listen, Yankee* was nothing less than a worldwide literary sensation. Van Gosse considers it one of the key radicalizing texts of the Sixties generation, along with Allen Ginsberg's *Howl!*, Martin Luther King's "Letter from a Birmingham Jail," and *The Port Huron Statement*.[52] Richard E. Welch Jr. states quite accurately that "with a single exception, one cannot point to a speech, article, book, or open letter by an American academic and say with confidence that it influenced either public opinion or government policy. The exception was C. Wright Mills and his book, *Listen, Yankee*," which had a significant influence on the origins and credo of the New Left, and on countless readers throughout the world.[53] Indeed, the book was eventually translated into Greek, Italian, Japanese, Polish, Portuguese, and Spanish—and read in such far-flung places as Angola, Ethiopia, Haiti, and Laos.[54] However, its message was addressed directly to a North American audience, and that's where its real impact was intended to be felt. In his assessment of *Listen, Yankee* over half a century after it was published, Raúl Roa Kourí has this to say: "On reading it, it seemed to me the best of what had been written on Cuba after Huberman and Sweezy's book [*Cuba: Anatomy of a Revolution*]. Moreover, Mills's work had an additional importance: it was directed at the middle-of-the-road American, who, in general, did not know much about the history and culture of our people. It was a direct appeal, much like *The Ugly American* had been, to confront the disagreeable truths not previously published in the mainstream press."[55]

A lengthy extract from the book, reprinted with slight modifications under the title "Listen Yankee: The Cuban Case against the United States," appeared as the cover story in the December 1960 issue of *Harper's Magazine*, which had a circulation at that time of close to half a million.[56] Both the magazine's 5,000-word excerpt and the book were extensively reviewed in various newspapers and periodicals, and Mills received more than his share of criticism. And while both positive and negative reviews of *Listen, Yankee* quickly poured in, on balance the negative ones seem to have prevailed in quantity—or perhaps just in their viciousness.[57]

The rural sociologist Lowry Nelson undercuts Mills's claim concerning the lack of adequate and unbiased news about Cuba in the U.S. press, writing that "this irritating book," *Listen, Yankee*, covered "nothing particularly new to any reader of the most reliable newspapers in the United States."[58] Another review, this one favorable, partly counteracted Nelson's assertion: "The reader who does not read Spanish, or cannot obtain the Cuban material, can form a good idea of the Cuban position from this valuable book."[59] Latin Americanist Fredrick B. Pike praised Mills for giving the best available insight into the attitudes of the Cuban revolutionaries—and, for that matter, of a growing number of people throughout Latin America. As for North Americans: "If enough Yankees listen," writes Pike, "the Mills book could represent the most substantial contribution to hemisphere relations that has been published in the last twenty years."[60]

One of the harshest and most relentless critics of Mills, *Listen, Yankee*, and Castro's revolution was the Latin America correspondent for the *Chicago Tribune*, Jules Dubois, who only the previous year had written a book largely sympathetic of Castro and his populist insurrection. In an apparent about-face, Dubois was now writing poison-pen reviews of *Listen, Yankee* and the Cuban Revolution. In his syndicated newspaper column, "Report from Latin America," he casts Mills as a "left wing professor of sociology" and predicts that *Listen, Yankee* will "be hailed in Havana, Moscow, and Peking as an accurate portrayal of the Cuban situation." Dubois offers that the book "reads like translated tape recordings of Castro's interminable and repetitious tirades against the United States—and it is just as tiring and tedious." In an apparent non sequitur, perhaps as an attempt to shut Mills down, Dubois concludes: "In 1951 the Russian censor banned an article by Mills from the magazine *Amerika*, a Russian language publication circulated in the Soviet Union by the state department."[61]

Dubois's criticisms became more strident a few weeks later in another stinging invective against *Listen, Yankee* that appeared in the *Saturday Review*. Now Castro's tirades were not just "interminable and repetitious," they had become, for Dubois, "interminable and paranoiac brainwashing" outbursts. Whereas in Dubois's syndicated column Mills's book had been "replete with errors of fact," in this new review it now "bulged with half-truths, complete distortions, and outright untruths." The agrarian reform of which Mills approved is for Dubois "a dismal failure"; Mills's insistence that it was U.S. policy that was pushing Castro into the Soviet bloc "is utterly false"; Mills's claim that Castro enjoyed overwhelming support from the Cuban people "avoids reality and distorts the facts." In closing the piece, rather than evoking Russian censorship as he had in the previous review, this time Dubois chooses to go in the opposite direction and anticipates Russian mass dissemination of *Listen, Yankee*: "Nor would it be surprising if Moscow should announce plans to publish Mills's book in Russian and other Soviet bloc languages."[62]

But Dubois's comments would not go unchallenged. In the next issue of the *Saturday Review*, no fewer than eight intellectuals of the Mexican Left—novelists, publishers, and professors (the four who had previously interviewed Mills in Mexico City in 1960, Carlos Fuentes, Víctor Flores Olea, Enrique González Pedrero, and Jamie García Terrés, in addition to four others, Fernando Benítez, Arnaldo Orfila Reynal, Francisco López Cámara, and Pablo González Casanova)—sent a signed letter to the magazine's editor decrying the bad faith and cynicism of Dubois's arguments against Mills and the Cuban Revolution. The letter ended: "We, the friends of C. Wright Mills in Mexico, vigorously protest against Jules Dubois's fallacious criticism, and with equal vigor back C. Wright Mills, whom we consider the true voice of the North American people, for his honesty, his courage, and his awareness of the new forces in the underdeveloped world."[63] It may have been this very public rejoinder from the leading luminaries of Mexico's intelligentsia that finally put an end to Dubois's denigration of Mills and his book.

But with the matter of *Listen, Yankee* Mills seemed to have more foes than friends. And one of the more clamorous of the former was a Cuban exile named Fermím Peinado, who self-published a forty-six-page booklet titled

Beware, Yankee: The Revolution in Cuba.⁶⁴ In this unremarkable piece of unadorned anti-Castro propaganda intended "for the greater enlightenment of American university students," Peinado proposes to correct mistakes about the Cuban Revolution made in several articles that had recently appeared in U.S. periodicals—one of which was Mills's essay in *Harper's*.⁶⁵ Peinado criticizes Mills on a number of negligible and significant points: for not doing sufficient research for his "very intense study" of Cuba's Revolution, for being duped by the Cuban Communist minority, for lacking sociological perceptiveness, for portraying the voice of Castro as the voice of Cuba, for his ignorance of the Spanish language, for claiming that the voice of the Cuban Revolution had not been heard in the United States, for denying that the only variety of leftist thought and action in Cuba was that of communist totalitarianism, for denying that there was a serviceable information agency for foreign journalists in Cuba.⁶⁶ Peinado ends by issuing a warning to his readers in the tone of McCarthyite paranoia: "the most dangerous foes of this great nation [the United States] are to be found from within. It is necessary to be alert." Perhaps of greater socio-historical significance than its alarmist message is that *Beware, Yankee* mimics *Listen, Yankee* in every particular in regard to its presentation. Not only did the booklet possess a similar title and the same subtitle, it used the identical front-cover design—from the white background, to the typeface, to the black-orange-pink color scheme; it even had the same dimension trim size. In an attempt at maximum mimicry, even the pamphlet's back cover was done in the same yellow color as Mills's book.

A couple of other commentators on the *Harper's* article also deserve mention, if only for their historic affiliations with Castro and Mills. Two of several opinion pieces, printed in the Letters to the Editor section in the magazine's February 1961 issue, were submitted by the Cuban historian of U.S.-Cuba relations Herminio Portell Vilá and by congressional representative from Oregon Charles O. Porter. Portell Vilá had been Fidel Castro's tutor at the University of Havana in 1947. In the early summer of 1953, while the distinguished professor was sitting at a bar in Havana, the twenty-seven-year-old Castro revealed to him that he was planning an attack on the Moncada barracks. Portell Vilá tried to dissuade his former student, but Castro was adamant, explaining that he was prepared for the assault and that it would be a great moral blow to the Batista tyranny.⁶⁷ On the success of the Revolution, Portell Vilá moved to the United States, where he composed press releases critical of Castro's government and began broadcasting for the Voice of America. Portell Vilá wrote *Harper's* to protest Mills's "much biased and mendacious article" and challenged him for not disclosing that he was a member of the Fair Play for Cuba Committee, which Portell Vilá charges with "playing in the U.S. the game of the dictatorship of Fidel Castro in Cuba."[68] By contrast, Porter's letter to the editor was laudatory, congratulating the magazine on the "emphasis and space" that it had given Mills's essay. "We norteamericanos," Porter proposed, "are going to have to listen and understand this point of view if we are going to make our way effectively in the world today."[69] The congressman wrote these lines very near the time when he served as Mills's surrogate on a nationally televised debate in which he took the "pro-Castro" position (see Chapter 8).

Some six months after releasing *Listen, Yankee*, Ballantine Books brought out another inexpensive paperback on the Cuban revolutionary project, *Sartre on Cuba*. It was a compilation of essays Jean-Paul Sartre had written for the French newspaper *France-Soir*, and was touted by its publisher as "a valuable complement" to *Listen, Yankee*. Indeed, the two books are similar in several ways: they both take a journalistic approach in providing historical accounts of the Revolution, they both give penetrating insights into Castro's thinking and eyewitness descriptions of events. Mills thought highly of Sartre's effort and crafted a strong endorsement:

> The obvious truth of *Sartre on Cuba* once again reveals to the world the Yankee school of falsification—about Cuba and about the United States. No matter what now happens, this fascinating book will not become "dated." It reads like a dramatic novel, and it conveys the moral meaning of Castro's Cuba for our time. That meaning is this: Whether or not they know it, for the generation just coming to maturity, the revolution in Cuba is their "Spanish Civil War." More than that: it is foremost among those several events that are signaling the beginnings of a new left in the world. That so many older U.S. intellectuals do not understand this is a sign of their own moral cowardice and cultivated provinciality. But Jean Paul-Sartre knows it—and in this book he tells The Cuban Story as only Sartre could.[70]

The main difference between Mills's and Sartre's books is that the Frenchman's prose is formal and stilted, it possesses none of the Texan's verve and fiery rhetoric.

Listen, Yankee was also reviewed by none other than Eleanor Roosevelt in her "My Day" syndicated newspaper column. Just a few weeks before, on November 19, Mills had delivered the address "How to Improve Relations with Cuba and South America" before a meeting of Americans for

Democratic Action (ADA), a liberal political organization Mrs. Roosevelt had cofounded.[71] No doubt he conveyed to the ADA audience much of the information in the recently completed *Listen, Yankee*, including urging the U.S. government to accept Castro as the legitimate leader of Cuba. And much to the delight of influential legal scholar Louis B. Schwartz, who was in attendance, Mills also raised the issue of the role of the big corporation in U.S. foreign policy.[72] But according to Saul Landau, the ADA audience was furious with Mills and practically accused him of being a communist. Mills answered their questions for hours on the platform. The audience baited and cursed him, but Mills stood there with the most compelling arguments, with facts and statistics and documentation of all kinds—still, he didn't convince anyone. After it was over, Mills expressed his frustration brusquely and passionately: "Goddamn liberals!," he complained to Landau, "They are political idiots. Liberal obfuscators! Obfuscators!"[73]

Mrs. Roosevelt was much more sympathetic to Mills's message than the ADA audience had been. By December 14 she had read part way through *Listen, Yankee* and wrote in her "My Day" column: "Up to this point, while I would disagree with certain of the things [the Cuban revolutionaries] have told Mr. Mills, a preponderance of their complaints against us seems valid to me. And though we may not like these expressions from the Cuban revolutionaries I think we should read them and weigh them with care, because they do affect our whole Latin-American policy." She goes on to note that the United States had long exhibited an irresponsible complacency toward Cuba and Latin America in ignoring their economic and social problems. As long as Americans got the sugar, tobacco, coffee, or whatever commodities they wanted, the United States never protested if a country developed a one-crop economy and never demanded that North American business leaders—who were only interested in profit making—raise the living standards of the people in those countries. She acknowledged that Cuba was building a socialist economy, but this was out of necessity, and it did not necessarily signal their acceptance of Soviet Communism. "If you read the letters in Mr. Mills's book carefully, however, I think you will realize that in spite of the fact that you want to deny many of their statements and explain many of our acts in a different way from the way they do, still you will have to acknowledge that there is some reason why they should believe as they do. And you would perhaps have to agree that it would be well for us to think with a little humility about our own mistakes in understanding, in exploitation, and in sheer laziness."[74]

Eleanor Roosevelt was one Yankee who did listen to the message in Mills's book and commented that Americans "had better begin ... to study what is being done in Cuba and to try to allay the Cuban fear" of an invasion by the United States. Such an invasion, she wrote, "would be counter to all our commitments to the U.N. and unthinkable for us as a nation and the leader of the non-Communist area of the world."

But the former First Lady was severely mistaken—when at the beginning of her column she praised the incoming president-elect's transition-team appointments of Dean Rusk as secretary of state, Chester Bowles as undersecretary, and Adlai Stevenson as U.S. ambassador to the United Nations—in thinking that such a team would implement new ideas and better approaches in world affairs. In fact, these men, along with their chief executive, JFK— all members of the ruling elite—would soon be embroiled in the covert operations program for the CIA invasion of Cuba and the attempted overthrow of yet another Latin American leader, this time, Fidel Castro.[75]

But the lame-duck Eisenhower, who had instigated the invasion, was still in the Oval Office in December 1960. There is no evidence that he or his officials took any account of *Listen, Yankee*—and if they had, they certainly would not have heeded its warnings. There is, however, some indication that Kennedy may have read the advance copy that Ballantine Books sent him "for his edification." Only a few weeks before Kennedy's assassination, the French journalist Jean Daniel, who was on his way to interview Castro, met briefly with the president in the White House. Kennedy surprised Daniel by telling him that he had, from the outset, followed developments in Cuba with painstaking attention; that the Batista regime had been the result of a number of misdeeds by the United States, a matter with which Kennedy was in agreement with the first Cuban revolutionaries; that he had approved of Castro's Sierra Maestra proclamation for justice; that U.S. policies toward Cuba had unwittingly created the Castro movement. But the situation was no longer only a Cuban problem, Kennedy told Daniel; it had become an *international* problem, and it was important to realize that, as president of the United States, he was subject to the constraints of office. "I am the President of the United States and not a sociologist."[76]

Escucha Yanqui

After three English-language printings, a Spanish translation, *Escucha, yanqui*, was released in April 1961 by Arnaldo Orfila Reynal, director of Mexico's leading publishing house, Fondo de Cultura Económica.[77] In its first run it had a remarkable printing of 20,000 copies, sold exceptionally well, and several pirated copies were distributed by unknown parties. Orfila was effusive in his praise of the book and wrote to Mills, telling him that, "In reading aloud your *Listen, Yankee!* with my wife, we were deeply touched with the greatness you show in your sheer understanding of the root of the problems of our Continent. It is the exact essence of the Cuban Revolution. I want to express to you the profound satisfaction I feel to be able to diffuse your beautiful message to the Spanish-speaking world."[78]

Fondo, however, was a semipublic institution, and Orfila was fired in 1965, allegedly as a result of releasing the second edition of *Escucha, yanqui*, to which the conservative Mexican president Gustavo Díaz Ordaz had supposedly objected because it had been supported by funds provided by a foreign government.[79] It is not known which foreign government is referred to, but if the presumption was that it was the Cuban government, this was certainly not the case. In fact, in a letter Mills wrote to Mexican novelist Carlos Fuentes,[80] who had helped him publish the Spanish translation with Fondo, he bluntly tells Fuentes that Fondo "must realize that I do not know the Cuban government's attitude towards the book, especially my candid handling of Communism."[81] So even though the Cuban political regime had financed the Fair Play for Cuba Committee, and the FPCC had organized Mills's trip to Cuba, *Escucha, yanqui* was not, strictly speaking, a politically commissioned book.

However that may be, *Esucha, yanqui*—and Mills—had their share of detractors in Latin America, not the least of whom was Fondo's founder, Daniel Cosío Villegas, who deemed it a "stupid" book that should never have been published, not because of its ideological bent, given that Cosío Villegas believed it was neither pro- nor anti-Castro, but chiefly because of Mills's linguistic deficiencies: "That is to say, when you know that this gentleman [Mills] has produced this book on the basis of taped recordings of Cubans' opinions, that this gentleman did not know one word of Spanish, and therefore could not have posed questions, could not have known the responses, that gives you a sense of the gravity that this book could possibly possess."[82] But Cosío Villegas's criticisms are wide of the mark, given that Mills had much previous experience interviewing respondents in several countries and in languages he did not speak, to say nothing of the fact that he had previously worked out effective rules for interviewing a small and highly selected number of respondents while briefly visiting a country (see Chapter 3). Perhaps just as significant to the interviewing protocol that Mills followed is that his interpreter, Juan Arcocha, provided him with first-rate service in interpretation.

Whatever the critiques, the upshot is that the book became an instant commercial success throughout Latin America. In 1964 Mexican historian and economist Jesús Silva Herzog estimated that *Escucha, yanqui* had sold between 70,000 and 80,000 copies and believed that it was the most successful of Fondo's books up to that point.[83] Twenty years later, *Escucha, yanqui* was listed as one of Fondo's fifty most reprinted books, with over 100,000 copies sold.[84]

Escucha Otra Vez, Yanqui

In April 1961, while vacationing in Switzerland with his family, Mills and Saul Landau, who was now his confidant and personal secretary, worked on an update to *Listen, Yankee*. Mills instructed Landau to type what he had dictated as follows:

> In his campaign President Kennedy convinced many that there would really be a New Frontier. (Capitalize that.) The New Frontiersmen who took up the cry were many of the best known liberal academicians. In Kennedy's cabinet and in the advisory positions, they have shown themselves to be nothing more or less than moral schlemiels. (You know how to spell that? O.K.) With his decision to send the group of United States financed, trained, equipped and blessed thugs to their just rewards in the well-named Bay of Pigs, Mr. Kennedy has clearly demonstrated before the world that he has neither the brilliance of mind nor the quality of heart to qualify him for greatness, no less for destiny. And the men around him, the Schlesingers and Berles, have proven themselves to be no more than mouthpieces for immorality, spokesmen for thugs and hoodlums.[85]

Pursuing this theme further, Mills and Landau wrote a satire in the May 19, 1961, issue of the *Tribune*, London's democratic socialist newspaper. It is in the form of an open letter to President Kennedy, in which, four months into his presidency, they offer a few modest proposals that they believe will prevent the United States from falling into disaster. They also warn Kennedy of the many perils he faces, not only abroad but also in his own cabinet, given that he has been the victim of the "cowardly suggestions," the failed policies, of his own advisors, his liberal obfuscators. One of these cowardly suggestions was the "feeble attack" at the Bay of Pigs of the previous month, which simply did not go far enough in eliminating the Communist Conspiracy in Cuba, write Mills and Landau mockingly. They suggest that Kennedy purchase the French Foreign Legion, recruit patriotic Americans into it, and turn it into the American Foreign Legion. Its goal would be to protect, by whatever means necessary, U.S. private investment in Latin America from becoming nationalized. They urge Kennedy to repudiate any support by all radicals at home and abroad. Domestically, they recommend a return to the McCarthyite practices of carefully screening all employees in all industries and ruthlessly weeding out all Communists and Russian agents. Universities must be cleansed of the ideology of Collectivism, which has become the dominant trend on all campuses. "All Professors should, of course, be given loyalty oaths and lie detector tests regularly, and if necessary at gun point," write Mills and Landau facetiously. "But more than that—they must be constantly watched, in and out of the classrooms, by Loyal Students some of whom are working loyally for our own FBI. More should be." Here is Mills at his sarcastic best. He and his collaborator end the letter, dripping with contemptuous irony, stating, "There are countless other suggestions that we might make to you, Mister President, but in this brief letter we are seeking merely to congratulate you on so courageously completely your first one hundred days in office. It has indeed been a Profile in Courage."[86]

That same month, Arnaldo Orfila Reynal contacted Mills to tell him that since all copies of the first and second editions of *Escucha, yanqui* had sold out, it was necessary, in light of the Bay of Pigs invasion and other happenings, that Mills prepare an update for a third edition: "This led us to prepare a third edition, which we deemed should be ready for the end of June, but in view of the dynamics of the Cuban Revolution, we have thought that it would be most interesting to add a foreword or appendix, with reference to the fundamental events of the last months, particularly the recent aggression."[87]

The update, ultimately published as "Escucha otra vez, yanqui," served as the afterword to the third Spanish edition and was presented in interview format. It consists of fifty questions posed to Mills during July 1961. The afterword is particularly significant given that the major event that had transpired within a year of Mills's visit to Cuba, and that outraged him to no end, was the U.S.-engineered armed invasion at the Bay of Pigs.

"Escucha otra vez, yanqui" was the last piece written by Mills to be published during the remaining eight months of his life. It is important because, of all his controversial writings, it represents the furthest political limb on which he went out and the greatest risk to his scholarly authority. It is, in fact, his most candid—and angry—statement in which he resolutely opposes the U.S. neocolonial foreign policy toward Cuba and the military invasion. Here Mills names names and exposes the complicity—and hypocrisy—of U.S. government officials and the North American press. It may also provide a type of preview of some of the issues Mills may have covered in the television debate he was to have with Kennedy advisor Adolph A. Berle Jr. later that year (see Chapter 8).[88]

The inquiry begins with Mills being asked if anything had happened since August 1960 that would have changed his viewpoints in *Listen, Yankee* concerning the Cuban Revolution. Mills replies with an emphatic "no"; to the contrary, the opinions he had stated, particularly in the second Note to the Reader, were being confirmed day by day. Mills insists that he had no reason whatsoever to alter any essential aspect of what he had written since mid-1960.

He then spends the first part of the piece giving a chronological account of the April 1961 assault by the CIA-armed mercenaries and the events leading up to it. The Cuban victory at the Bay of Pigs, he insists, was a direct result, a product, of Cuba's Revolution. It made the Revolution a reality. The CIA organized—illegally—a counterrevolution on U.S. soil. At the same time, it allowed, probably encouraged, and possibly organized—again, illegally—aerial bombings on sugarcane fields as well as various acts of sabotage on the island. In the spring of 1961, the CIA reunited all of the exile groups and instructed them to accept as their chief José Miró Cardona.[89] The CIA was in charge of the training, planning, and management of the invasion. Miró Cardona and the other Cuban counterrevolutionaries were, in fact, mere puppets of the United States. The Chiefs of Staff at the Pentagon assumed the final military planning and the Defense Department and Army provided the CIA with military advisors. The Marines made available landing craft and engaged in deceptive maneuvers to cover for the real military disembarkation.

It is now clear and obvious, Mills continues, that the anti-Castro forces were nothing more than fronts and puppets, and that without the U.S. there is, in fact, no real counterrevolution in Cuba. This signifies to Mills that Yankee government officials, "with or without their little plastic explosives," did not know how to listen. No truly impartial observer of revolutionary Cuba could, as far as Mills is concerned, fail to listen to the people and their leaders.

After the invasion, Mills maintains that neutral diplomats residing in Cuba had, as of May 1961, calculated that around 5 percent of the Cuban population harbored counterrevolutionary sentiments, but that at least 70 percent enthusiastically supported the Revolution. What is more, before the invasion, around 25 percent of the population was "passive and undecided." But after the invasion, this 25 percent came closer to 70 percent in fully supporting the Revolution.[90]

The invading exiles, deceived by the illusion that the Cuban people were going to support them, found that the Cuban militias proved to be a superior military force, but more importantly they discovered that the militias were a superior *moral* force. The vast majority of the mercenaries, more than 1,200 them, surrendered within seventy-two hours of their landing on the Bay of Pigs—a site badly selected but one well-named, considering the circumstances.

Mills then turns his attention to the media and charges that after the military intervention, when it was no longer possible to cover up the defeat, U.S. newspapers continued printing lies, likely disseminated by the CIA. Indeed, North American newspapers, magazines, and television are as censored, or better yet, as *self-censored*, as any in the world. But at this point, Mills continues, not only are the media to blame, so is the president of the United States, who had pressed them to censure themselves. Among notable exceptions to this self-censorship—many on the staff of the *New York Times*—Mills singles out James Reston, Tad Szulc, and Herbert Matthews, as well as independent journalists I. F. Stone and Joseph Hansen. Their reporting prior to the invasion (and Mills may have included his own reporting in *Listen, Yankee*) made it possible for at least some readers to follow events intelligently *during* the invasion.

Mills admits that it is possible to maintain that, concerning the Bay of Pigs debacle, Kennedy was misadvised by CIA director Allen Dulles; Chairman of the Joint Chiefs of Staff General Lyman Lemnitzer; former U.S. Ambassador to Cuba Earl E.T. Smith—and, of course, by the always-available advisor on all things Latin American, Adolph A. Berle Jr., as well as the new presidential advisor, the Harvard professor of U.S. history who was ignorant of everything concerning Latin America, Arthur M. Schlesinger Jr. Mills refers to them as first-class obfuscators and dogmatic anticommunists of historical, and hysterical, proportions. These Cold War liberals, under the banner of liberalism, have gradually become obfuscators, and, like the conservatives, they also partake of a doctrinaire anticommunism more suitable to the Stalinist era. Given the events of the Bay of Pigs—and what occurred before and after—these buttoned-up liberals have fashioned themselves as "defenders of a New Frontier of thieves and assassins." What is more, the U.S. naval base on the island—at Guantánamo Bay—is considered by the Cuban people and government, and indeed by all Latin Americans, to be a threat to Cuba's sovereignty and a symbol of U.S. imperialism.

Because of their subversive aggression toward Cuba, the liberal obfuscators had squandered the moral prestige of the United States before the world and had lost all influence in Latin America—except that which is based on intimidation, violence, and the economics of hunger. Above all, states Mills, it is now evident that concerning the "Cuba situation," the United States is not a government of laws. All these errors in their various expressions, says Mills, can be read in the writings of anticommunist and anti-Cuba liberals such as Schlesinger's *White Paper on Cuba* and freelance journalist Theodore Draper's *Castro's Cuba: A Revolution Betrayed*.[91]

Asked if he still believed, after all that had transpired, if there existed the possibility that Cuba could become truly neutral again, Mills replies that the actions taken by the United States and the USSR since Castro's triumph had worked against that possibility. "It may be much too late," he opines, "but I continue to hold out hope." Still, he did not believe that Cuba would be left alone. Its Revolution represented too much of a crucial fact in the political emotion of Latin America, too much of an ideal concerning the economic livelihood to which Latin America aspired, and too much of a symbol of national liberty and true independence for the hungry nations for the United States to simply leave it alone. In the end, Mills contends, everything depends on whether or not the Yankees can listen.[92]

A Good and Honest Book

Dan Wakefield describes Mills's buoyant spirit while convalescing at the Good Samaritan Hospital in Suffern, New York, during January 1961, after having suffered a serious heart attack a few weeks earlier:

> It was incredible to see Mills in a sickbed, and yet his old fire and enthusiasm hadn't left him. He was pleased and proud about the sales—if not the U.S. reception—of *Listen, Yankee*, and above his bed was an advertising poster proclaiming there were four hundred thousand copies of the paperback edition in print. Mills delightedly explained that such posters were carried on the sides of news delivery trucks in Philadelphia. He was reaching a greater public now than he ever had—'mass circulation stuff,' he proudly called it. He lectured us on publishing, emphasizing that paperbacks were now the important thing.[93]

In the end, according to Harvey Swados's unflattering memoir of him, Mills was betrayed by the Revolution. Indeed, Mills had hoped to achieve the properly developing society, the humanist revolution, in the context of democracy. But democracy in Cuba had begun to slip away, and this caused in Mills an immense mental strain. "In his last months," writes Swados, "Mills was torn between defending *Listen, Yankee*, as a good and honest book, and acknowledging publicly for the first time in his life that he had been terribly wrong."[94] Rafael Rojas explains the Columbia sociologist's cognitive dissonance as follows: "Mills's book was published in the midst of the revolutionary government's communist evolution, which forced the author to confront reality in the face of his insistence that the Cuban leaders were not communists."[95]

But as Rojas also points out, Mills's main argument in *Listen, Yankee*—one not taken as seriously at the time as it should have been—is that the New Left should not delay supporting the Cuban Revolution until it took a clear ideological stance, because by supporting it now, the American Left could prevent Cuba from being swallowed up by the Soviet orbit of influence.[96] Further, it could avert on the island the formation of a socialist power elite, which Mills had warned about in *The Causes of World War Three*. But, by year's end 1961, it was too late for anyone north of the Rio Grande to listen—and much too late to act, responsibly.

CHAPTER EIGHT

Confronting the Enemy

C. Wright Mills was no stranger to controversy, inside or outside of American academic sociology. Throughout the 1950s—in books such as *White Collar*, *The Power Elite*, *The Causes of World War Three*, and *The Sociological Imagination*—he had distinguished himself as one of the foremost dissident intellectuals of postwar America, and an outspoken critic of big business and mass society, of U.S. foreign policy and national security strategy.

Although he remained the quintessential North American throughout his life, Mills had an ostentatious disdain of everything "Made in America." He was especially indignant toward academic social scientists who were uncritically accepting of what he called the "Great Celebration" of U.S. society without addressing its cultural deficiencies. But his was no simple-minded negativism; indeed, he was always critically concerned with the preservation of the democratic tradition in the United States.

It is significant that Mills wrote the aforementioned books at a particular time in U.S. history: "in the age of the atom bomb and Eisenhower, the Cold War and McCarthy, at the twilight of Stalinism and the zenith of 'The American Century.'"[1] This was an era marked by mass political apathy and widespread conformity, by rabid anticommunism and a stalwart belief in American exceptionalism—all symptoms of a social neurosis expressed audaciously, and sanctimoniously, as national arrogance, particularly toward the United States' self-proclaimed "backyard," Latin America. And the Cuban Revolution, as Robert Taber put it starkly, *"was and is, above all, a Cuban declaration of independence from the United States."*[2]

At the dawn of the new decade, Mills was becoming increasingly interested, not in the overdeveloped society but in the hungry-nation bloc; not in the other-directed organizational men in their gray flannel suits, but in the revolutionary *barbudos* in their olive-green military fatigues. And as he journeyed to countries and focused his researches on issues that, at first glance, appeared to counter U.S. interests, he was increasingly coming to be seen as a security threat by federal authorities, perhaps even as someone who could be gathering intelligence for foreign governments. This, in a pre-Watergate world, when governmental institutions were still largely free from scandal and most North Americans had unwavering faith and trust in those institutions and their representatives. "In the United States," Jules Dubois underscored to his fellow U.S. citizens in 1959, "we accept the honest official statements issued by the White House, by the Pentagon, or by the FBI."[3]

It was against this backdrop that in early 1960 Mills gave a seminar on Marxism at the National University of Mexico, but more suspicious to the security agencies was his visit to the Soviet Union later in the spring, and even more questionable still was his journey to Cuba that summer, a country very much in the throes of revolutionary, and therefore of troubling, zeal. It was to be expected that Mills, like many other U.S. citizens at the time, would come under the close scrutiny of the Federal Bureau of Investigation when a confidential informant—identified only as "T-1" in the FBI files—apprised the New York field office of Mills's upcoming trip to the USSR. The informant's identity is not known, but Mike Forrest Keen is perhaps correct in thinking that it was a friend, or more likely a colleague, of Mills at Columbia University.[4] In any event, T-1 had detailed information of Mills's travels plans and other comings and goings. In September, while Mills was intensely working on *Listen, Yankee*, the same T-1 told the FBI that Mills had visited Cuba the previous month and carried out interviews with Cuban officials, which he intended to publish. T-1 also said that Mills was planning a series of five programs to be broadcast on a U.S. or British radio broadcasting station to be called "Dear Yankee" or "Listen Yankee."[5]

"Mr. Hadley"

In this context of close monitoring of his movements and inspection of his writings, of confidential informants and FBI surveillance, Mills taped a telephone conversation sometime in the autumn of 1960, while he was still working on *Listen, Yankee*. Mills's chat is with a "Mr. Hadley," doubtless one of the security analysts who had been assigned to his case. Hadley had phoned Mills at this home in West Nyack, a suburb of New York, wanting to arrange a meeting with him in the city. The reasons Hadley gives for requesting the meeting are vague and questionable. Mills is reticent to speak, his responses are short and measured. The recording of that telephonic exchange follows:

> MILLS: ... Well, that doesn't matter. Who the hell's gonna pick that up? Well, anyway, I'm sorry.
> HADLEY: Yeah, I [inaudible] that. And you say there's no way of getting there [West Nyack] by train.

MILLS: Well, you can come by bus to Nyack and get a cab from there. It's not very far. You take a . . .

HADLEY: Well, that seems like a rather slow and arduous journey. You don't expect to be in New York, I take it.

MILLS: No, I couldn't possibly do that. I'm tied down with this manuscript [*Listen, Yankee*].

HADLEY: Uh-huh. Well, what if we try to make it next time in New York, which I'll be back, oh, in about three or four weeks.

MILLS: Well, that's alright with me. I wish you'd tell me what you wish to see me about though. I haven't got it clear at all.

HADLEY: Well, the [inaudible] now. I'm talking on another phone from work. I've worked for the last three and a half years in the executive decision-making branches of the government. Essentially my background is in psychology and mathematics and I've been working very precatory in psychological warfare and so forth. I'm a member on a number of committees of the government which is technically responsible for policy and in the capacity as one of the members [inaudible]. I've met and I have sat in committee meetings. I've been involved with a sufficient number of the agencies. I know in general how they work and how decisions are created and generated. I have thought for a while that I would like to write a book about it. However, I've given long consideration and decided that it would be rather risky for me to do it. I feel that there are certain things which are worth saying about the issue of power relationships and how decisions are formulated and how they're made.

MILLS: Well, your interest in this and in seeing me is then academic only.

HADLEY: Yes, only.

MILLS: Uh-huh.

HADLEY: I'd like to pass some information on to someone.

MILLS: What information?

HADLEY: Information concerning the way these things are done.

MILLS: Yeah.

HADLEY: Which I think is essentially your interest.

MILLS: Well, that's one of them, yeah.

HADLEY: Seeing as some of these things are said, which I feel that I cannot personally say.

MILLS: Yeah.

HADLEY: With the understanding, of course, that [inaudible] you would not divulge any of this information.

MILLS: Well, I never have when I've talked to the United States government or any other government, and I've done a lot of that in the kind of work I've done for my publications.

HADLEY: In terms of your interest in Cuba, I might add that I was present at policy formulating sessions concerning Cuba.

MILLS: Uh-huh.

HADLEY: So let me correct this. If there is anything that I would pass on to you, it would be of a nonclassified nature.

MILLS: Yeah, sure.

HADLEY: But I believe there's a great deal to be said that does not involve security information.

MILLS: Well, I don't need or want any security information, Mr. Hadley.

HADLEY: I'll tell you, of course, I do not provide anyone with that.

MILLS: Yeah. What is your position now with the federal government?

HADLEY: I am the staff assistant in the executive branch of government.

MILLS: Well, what branch of government?

HADLEY: This, I'm sorry [chuckles], is classified information.

MILLS: Well, are you speaking to me with the knowledge of your superiors?

HADLEY: No, I'm not.

MILLS: Uh-huh.

HADLEY: No, I'm not.

At this point Mills invites Hadley to visit him in West Nyack and gives him several options for taking public transportation from New York City and instructions on getting to his house. They agree to meet the following afternoon. Hadley ends the conversation by saying, "I would like to speak with you about some of these things, with, of course, the clear understanding that you've never heard of me, you see."

At whatever point Hadley made contact, by November 8 the FBI office in New York was instructed not to initiate an active investigation of Mills or of *Listen, Yankee* because "investigation of Mills, an author and college professor, under these circumstances would appear undesirable and might result in embarrassment to the Bureau."[6]

FBI Surveillance

A few weeks earlier, the FBI had obtained a mimeographed copy of the manuscript to *Listen, Yankee* from publisher Ian Ballantine. The special agent in the New York office, perhaps the enigmatic "Mr. Hadley," described the document as "an artfully written piece of pro-Castro and pro-communist propaganda, handled in a competent manner and easily readable style, it is highly likely to become a factor in disarming and confusing public opinion in this country and persuading unwary elements of the reading public to a viewpoint contrary to what he understands as the established outlook of the United States regarding the current Cuban regime."[7] Special Agents in Philadelphia and Washington, D.C., also obtained mimeos and submitted their assessment.

Also around this time, someone from the Bureau approached Ian Ballantine in order to convince him to solicit proposals from other writers who would refute the arguments in *Listen, Yankee*. Ballantine adroitly handled the matter by telling the FBI that it would be able to pursue such a project in a more effective and sophisticated manner than he could himself.[8]

Mills knew full well that *Listen, Yankee* would be provocative—indeed, the book's front cover posted, and boasted, that it was "The Outspoken, Controversial Book about what is Really Happening in Cuba"—and Mills knew that it was "in for much clobbering."[9] Nevertheless, he was compelled to put it out and take the consequences. But had he allowed himself to become so captivated by the revolutionary fervor of the Cubans he interviewed that he lost all sense of perspective and overly identified with their cause? It was reported that in the Social Stratification course he was teaching at Columbia University during the 1960 fall term, he told his students: "I don't know what you guys are waiting for. You've got a beautiful set of mountains in those Rockies. I'll show you how to use those pistols. Why don't you get going?"[10] By the following spring he was indeed issuing a call to arms. Several days after the Bay of Pigs, Mills wired a telegram from London to a Fair Play for Cuba prorevolutionary demonstration in San Francisco, where 2,000 demonstrators marched from Union Square to the Federal Building. Mills requested that his statement be read at the rally and told the crowd that: "Kennedy and company have returned us to barbarism. Schlesinger and company have disgraced us intellectually and morally. I feel a desperate shame for my country. Sorry I cannot be with you. Were I physically able to do so, I would at this moment be fighting alongside Fidel Castro."[11]

The same month that *Listen, Yankee* was issued, Mills received his first death threat in the form of an anonymous letter informing him that an operative disguised as a South American would assassinate him on his next visit to Cuba, to which he expected to return in early 1961.[12] "I received an anonymous letter," Mills confided to Carlos Fuentes, "it says that if I continue to defend Cuba, I should take care that my daughter does not meet with an accident."[13] He also got threatening phone calls at his home from Los Tigres, a paramilitary group founded by Rolando Masferrer, and from other counterrevolutionary organizations of Cuban exiles in the United States.[14] Given the increasing dangers that confronted him and his family, Mills purchased a gun for their protection.[15]

Another menacing letter from a self-described "ordinary private American citizen," addressed to Mills with the salutation of "Listen, Communist," quotes a passage from *Listen, Yankee* (189) in which Mills cautions against the genteel mannerisms of U.S. spokesmen concerning Cuban grievances about the United States. The writer informs Mills that he can see "through your masterly deceitful arguments in favor of a peaceful coexistence by the U.S. in the Cuban situation." Copies of the letter, mailed from Miami, were sent to President Eisenhower, FBI director J. Edgar Hoover, CIA director Allen Dulles, U.S. senator John F. Kennedy (D-MA), and U.S. senator George Smathers (D-FL), a persistent critic of Castro. The writer accuses Mills of wanting to overthrow the United States by force and violence and asks if *Listen, Yankee* is "legal."[16]

Similar letters addressed to Hoover about Mills and *Listen, Yankee* were quite common. One such missive from Plainview, Nebraska, was apparently written by a local teacher distressed about books and magazines in libraries that posed a "great danger in spreading communism from the shelves." Of particular concern in this regard were Norman Cousins's *Dr. Schweitzer of Lambaréné* and the *Saturday Review* magazine, of which Cousins was editor. The troubled teacher implied that the good citizens of Plainview were questioning Cousins's lenient attitude toward communism. The letter also included a newspaper clipping from the *Omaha World-Herald* that contained another of Jules Dubois's excoriating assessments of Mills and *Listen, Yankee*.[17] The teacher ends by stating, in obvious reference to the Columbia professor of sociology: "It is too bad that American people cannot look to the educators in our universities as leaders."[18]

Upon the publication of *Listen, Yankee* in November, the previous directive not to actively investigate Mills was lifted, as J. Edgar Hoover ordered a discreet preliminary investigation with a complete background check. The

New York field office was to look into whether Mills was being directed or financed by Cuban officials and was engaged in intelligence activity. After an exhaustive investigation, no evidence was found to support any of the allegations. FBI surveillance of Mills's residence was nevertheless initiated. His movements in the United States and abroad continued to be monitored by both the FBI and the Immigration and Naturalization Service. Mills's name was ultimately removed from the FBI's Security Index, the database used to track individuals considered dangerous to national security—but only after his death had been verified by a special agent.

The Debate That Almost Was

After the enormous effort to get out *Listen, Yankee*, instead of relaxing Mills shifted himself back into high gear to prepare for the nationwide NBC television program *The Nation's Future*, in which he was slated to appear.[19] The one-hour live show, which had a studio audience and was broadcast from New York City, was moderated by popular talk-show host John McCaffery. The show's format pitted two internationally recognized public figures against one another as they expressed their different opinions on a specific issue of the day. Wanting to air an episode on U.S. foreign policy in Latin America, NBC contacted the Fair Play for Cuba Committee seeking a speaker, and FPCC convinced Mills, who had become the most sought-after keynoter at their rallies, to take the "pro-Castro" position in the debate. The "anti-Castro" position was to be represented by Mills's colleague at Columbia Adolf A. Berle Jr., the Kennedy administration's expert on Latin American affairs.[20] The sixty-five-year-old Berle had served as FDR's ambassador to Brazil and as assistant secretary of state for Inter-American Affairs. But now as a New Frontiersman, Berle was, as journalists Karl Meyer and Tad Szulc put it, "handicapped by his tendency to see current developments through the spectacles of the past."[21] Mills accepted, and the show was scheduled for December 10 at 9:30 p.m., Saturday night, with a viewing audience of about 20 million. A preview summary of the upcoming program read as follows: "9:30–10:30 P.M. (4)—The Nation's Future. 'What Should U.S. Policy Be toward Cuba and Latin America?' Adolf A. Berle Jr., former Assistant Secretary of State and a former U.S. Ambassador to Brazil, has a challenging opponent in tonight's debate. He's Professor C. Wright Mills of Columbia, who has recently returned from a tour of Cuba, and uses words like 'self-defeating' and 'self-deceiving' in his analysis of the course we've taken so far."[22]

Four general questions were to be addressed: How should we deal with Castro? Have we neglected Latin America? How can we identify with Latin American aspirations? What economic policies will promote Latin America's development and freedom?[23]

For an hour before the NBC program was to air, a Miami audience of about one hundred invited representatives of local civic and professional groups would discuss the debate topic at the broadcast studio of a local television station. Featured speakers included a former U.S. attorney for south Florida, a spokesman for an anti-Castro movement, and the seemingly omnipresent Jules Dubois. During the second half of the NBC program, the Miami audience, which was overwhelmingly critical of the Castro regime, was to pose questions to Mills and Berle in New York.[24]

According to Dan Wakefield, Mills immersed himself in preparation for the debate and alternated between being terribly worried and unsure of himself and being brashly confident. "He seemed to take it as some crucial test that he would either pass or flunk with profound results."[25] Whatever his doubts and trepidations, Mills, at least in public, downplayed the upcoming event, depicting it as just a lot of "program format nonsense" and postured himself as a gutsy and self-assured spokesman for the Cuban Revolution. "All I need," he told *Columbia Daily Spectator* news editor Arnold Abrams about his scheduled television appearance, "is twenty minutes by myself in front of the camera. I wouldn't need any help in that situation. That stage fright business is a lot of nonsense."[26]

Bravado aside, Mills was clearly concerned, privately admitting that he had limited knowledge of hemispheric affairs, and spent the month prior to the scheduled debate soliciting information from such Latin Americanists as Fredrick B. Pike, Donald Bray, Ray Higgins, Waldo Frank, and Ronald Hilton. He requested exact information on the hemisphere, on U.S. military supports, and on Berle himself.[27] One of those experts who responded to Mills's appeal was Samuel Shapiro, an assistant professor of history at Michigan State University's Oakland campus. Shapiro sent Mills sundry materials, including several articles highly critical of U.S. policy toward Cuba that he had written for the *New Republic* and *The Economist*. In preparation for Mills's bout with Berle, Shapiro recommended that the Columbia sociologist put to the diplomat several concrete questions. He was to ask him what specific good he thought the current get-tough U.S. policy on Cuba had accomplished, how he thought he could get rid of Castro, and to name a Latin American regime that was undertaking the land reform program that everybody (including Berle) agreed was necessary. Shapiro listed anticipated rebuttals with which Berle could counter and also recommended several U.S. policy proposals that Mills could advance: send an ambassador back to Havana; avoid menacing military moves in the Caribbean; agree to have Mexico, Brazil, or a committee of the Organization of American States mediate between the United States and Cuba; and in dealing with the Castro government's expropriation of U.S. investments on the island, use as the model the noninterventionist Good Neighbor policy employed by FDR during the Mexican oil expropriation of 1938. Perhaps just as beneficial to Mills was the moral support Shapiro offered, encouraging him to "keep cool" during the debate; he depicted Berle as a relic—a frustrated would-be politician—who "has no good answers."[28]

Mills also had assistance from Saul Landau, who collected for Mills everything he could find on Cuba and Latin America. But Mills was not unschooled on the issues; he had already conducted a vast amount of research and was quite current on the Cuba situation. By October he had a mine of information, which was the result of years of clipping articles from newspapers and magazines and the widest variety of reading. By November he had even more material, as he prepared for his Americans for Democratic Action (ADA) speech, "How to Improve Relations with Cuba and South America." By early December he had finally completed his preparations, and Mills had about 400 pages of detailed notes with key facts on every South American country; enough, in fact, to write a definitive work on modern Latin America.[29]

Just as he had in "Escucha otra vez, yanqui" and in the ADA talk, Mills was ready to criticize the clandestine U.S. sponsorship of the Bay of Pigs fiasco; condemn the Kennedy administration, including Berle, for violating the United States' own laws and treaties in its aggression toward the Cuban nation; excoriate the American press for its collusion in covering up the affair; and offer a pointed critique of past U.S. policy vis-à-vis Latin America. But Berle, who dismissed Mills as no more than "a ranting propagandist," would have made a most formidable opponent—one not lacking in bluster, and who, as he pugnaciously put it, "was ready to plaster" Mills.[30]

Despite being on the edge of exhaustion, Mills felt compelled to participate in the broadcast. "It's my goddamned duty," he wrote E. P. Thompson, "because nobody else will stand up and say shit outloud, but . . . I have to. Then the pressure on me because of Cuba, official and unofficial, is mounting. It is very subtle and very fascinating. But also worrisome and harassing."[31] Clearly, the most worrisome and interesting thing for Mills was the unknown, the unforeseen consequences of what could happen to him, personally and professionally, but also, and perhaps more importantly, what would happen to the Revolution he so admired. He told Carlos Fuentes that "what started out as a little 60,000-word pamphlet is becoming a big thing, or at any rate we hope so. God knows what will happen given the monolithic anti-Castro press and opinion in the USA. It is going to be fascinating to see."[32]

The much-anticipated televised match between Mills and Berle did not take place, at least not with Mills. He suffered a massive heart attack the evening before the program was to air and had to cancel the engagement. It was a terrible disappointment to him. He was convinced that the debate would have shown Berle's position to be suicide: "It would present to all the New Frontiersmen a reasonable and logical approach to Cuba and Latin America, a way out of a terrible situation."[33] For his part, rather than show sympathy for a stricken colleague, the self-aggrandizing Adolf Augustus Berle Jr. attributed Mills's heart attack to Mills being frightened of having to debate him.

At the last minute, Congressman Charles O. Porter, whom Berle regarded as being "on the wooly-headed side," was called in as a substitute for Mills. Saul Landau curtly describes the result: "Berle waltzed through the debate with Congressman Porter. It was a farce."[34]

A Rough Time

Mills knew only all too well that with the publication of *Listen, Yankee* he was "going to be in for it." In a letter to Ralph Miliband in early 1961, Mills tells him that, "I'm afraid there is going to come about a very bad time in my country for people who think as I do; and there is some reason to expect that I personally am in for quite a time."[35] But Mills could hardly have anticipated the backlash that was to come. Just a few days before writing to Miliband, and while he was convalescing from his heart attack, the FBI conducted a surveillance of Mills's house in West Nyack and reported that Igor G. Aleksandrov, head of the Union of Soviet Societies for Friendship and Cultural Relations, had visited him for one hour. Mills had met Aleksandrov on his visit to Moscow the year before.

Around the same time, a defamation lawsuit was filed against Mills and the publishers of *Listen, Yankee*—Ballantine Books and McGraw-Hill—for a total of $25 million in damages on behalf of Amadeo Barletta, Barletta's son, and three Cuban corporations in which they owned controlling shares: Ambar Motors (a General Motors car dealership in Havana), the El Mundo

Corp (a daily Cuban newspaper), and Telemundo (a television station). The Barlettas' complaint cited two paragraphs in *Listen, Yankee* (139-40) in which Mills describes an unnamed Cuban businessman, "a friend of Mussolini," owner of *El Mundo* newspaper, radio and television stations, and forty-three other businesses, who had ties "with a general somewhere" and with the Italian Mafia, and who was involved in drug smuggling. Barletta sued on the grounds that he was readily identifiable as the anonymous man and that Mills's allegations of black-market dealings and mobster associations were false.[36]

Barletta, Italian by birth, "had indeed a rather dubious international past."[37] All of the facts that Mills gives about Barletta in *Listen, Yankee* are correct. In 1939 Mussolini had named him as the Italian ambassador to Cuba. The "general somewhere" referred to by Mills was Generalisimo Rafael Trujillo of the Dominican Republic, where Barletta had lived. In 1949 Barletta's Ambar Motors had over thirty auto dealerships in Cuba. He had previously served as sales representative for several major U.S. auto manufacturers on the island. As for his connections with the Italian Mafia, journalist Richard Schweid writes that Barletta, "the man who sold the Italian Mafiosi their Cadillacs ... had close ties to the gangsters."[38] According to T. J. English, "with the backing of Cuban and U.S. financial institutions, he accrued a dizzying array of businesses, many of which served as fronts for various criminal rackets in Havana, including the trafficking of narcotics and precious gems."[39] In 1960 Castro expropriated all of Barletta's businesses, and Barletta was forced into exile with his family.

Saul Landau planned on going to Cuba on behalf of Mills and Ballantine Books to gather facts and documents for defense against the lawsuit. Many of the facts concerning the Cuban government's accusations of corruption against Barletta had been published in articles in the newspapers *Revolución* and *Diario de la Marina*; the documents were kept in the files of the Revolutionary government's Office for the Recuperation of Stolen Property. But Landau never made it to Cuba, as his passport was denied by the U.S. State Department.

And so Mills did indeed come in for a rough time, but he evoked the sympathy of friends like K. S. Karol: "It made one sad to see this Texan—and I have never met anyone more typical of the free and independent pioneer—up against a solid wall of hostility and vilification."[40] But it wasn't all a matter of persecution for Mills; there was also adulation, or at least admiration, from Cuba sympathizers. Indeed, he typically received seven to ten letters a day, from people all over the world, thanking him for having written *Listen, Yankee* (which had now been translated into all major languages). Many of these people inquired: "How can you help me to get to Cuba so I can help Fidel?"[41]

Mills was now beginning to realize the significance of *Listen, Yankee* and was increasingly coming "to see [it] as a pivotal book for me, and not merely a pamphlet."[42] But by late April it was time to escape the lawsuits, the criticisms, the surveillance, and the country that he believed was preparing another attack on Cuba. And so Mills and his family departed for the Soviet Union and Europe. That summer, while in Switzerland, he wrote the sixty-page update of *Escucha, yanqui* that appeared in the third Mexican printing as the appendix titled "Escucha otra vez, yanqui." In the United States, sales of the book were approaching the half million mark.

That same month, Mills traveled from Switzerland to Paris to meet Jean-Paul Sartre and Simone de Beauvoir for dinner at the *La Coupole* restaurant on the left bank. All three had visited Cuba the previous year—Sartre and Beauvoir in the spring, and then again in the autumn, and Mills during the summer—and speculated about what was happening there at the moment. They acknowledged that the Communist Party members had stepped in to fill the administrative vacuum that existed in the Revolutionary government and about which Mills had so assiduously inquired in his Cuba interviews (see Interviews 1, 6, and 7). Unfortunately, the party contained a clique led by Aníbal Escalante, whom Sartre and Beauvoir had considered "a pompous imbecile" when they met him in 1960 and whose "sectarianism and opportunism," they believed, were threatening the Castro regime.[43] Sartre expressed disenchantment with the direction the Revolution was taking.[44] "But don't you think Fidel will keep it straight and honest?" inquired Mills. The French philosopher stated that Castro was a great and honest man, but as the Revolution was forced into an ideological rigidity he would lose some of his power, and the sectarians and the United States would then drive Cuba into the Soviet orbit.[45] Mills remained optimistic or, perhaps more likely, hopeful, that the Cuban leader's originality would be strong enough to allow the Revolution to retain its many good elements. The conversation then turned to the Kennedy administration, which Mills described as a "liberal obfuscation." Sartre wanted to know how Mills explained the Kennedy administration in terms of the power-elite thesis. Mills stated that the Cold War liberals who dominated the cabinet demonstrated the triumph of the political elite over the businessmen and generals. However, he predicted that, despite a few minor disagreements on domestic issues, there would be no fundamental falling out between the three circles of power, and "on foreign policy the intellectuals are, if anything, more fanatical and doctrinaire anti-Communists than the businessmen and generals."

K. S. Karol, who was at the meeting to translate for Mills and Sartre, adds that Mills wished to go to Havana to plead with Castro. He hoped to take several nonaligned European intellectuals who were respected in Cuba (whom Karol does not name). Mills expressed that Castro should not be attacked or questioned in regard to his choice of socialism; rather Mills and the European intellectuals would warn Castro about identifying too closely with the Soviet system. As it turned out, the intellectuals either told Mills that the trip to see Castro was too premature, since nothing serious had happened, or that it was much too late for appeals, since Castro had already made up his mind and would act accordingly, no matter what. Not wanting to travel alone to Cuba, Mills gave up on the whole idea. "Meanwhile," Karol wrote, "what scraps of news reached us from Cuba during the latter half of 1961 served merely to confirm our worst fears"—that it was rapidly being turned into Stalinist quagmire.[46]

Ironically, just a few days after Mills, Sartre, and Beauvoir met in Paris, Fidel Castro gave his historic address "Words to Intellectuals" in the auditorium of Havana's National Library to a group of artists and writers of the Cuban cultural apparatus. In it he articulated his famous dictum intended to define the cultural revolution in Cuba and that pertained to freedom of artistic expression: "Within the Revolution, everything; against the Revolution, nothing." Castro told his audience, which included members of the National Council of Culture and representatives of the government, that politically progressive writers from abroad who had previously visited Cuba—and in this context he specifically names Sartre and Mills—had persistently raised to him the fundamental question of cultural freedom. But he had been at a loss as to how to answer them given that a national artistic policy concerning the cultural revolution had, at that time, not yet assumed a clear-cut political form, had not yet become institutionalized.[47] Indeed, Mills captured this undetermined position on revolutionary culture in *Listen, Yankee* as follows: "We want our new cultural establishments to be part of our revolution, and so, like the revolution itself, we want them to be free and useful and beautiful and fluent. So we are thinking about it now, debating quietly among ourselves this great social problem of culture, of art, of literature, of the cinema."[48] After 1961, however, that ambiguity and inchoate ideology had crystallized, as it became increasingly apparent that all aesthetic and intellectual creations were to be adjudged as being within or outside the interests and boundaries of the Revolution by none other than the Maximum Leader himself.

Some four years after that Paris luncheon, Sartre too presumably gave up the idea of appealing to Castro. According to Juan Arcocha, in 1965 Arcocha described to the French thinker the desperate circumstances of censorship in which Cuban writers found themselves. Arcocha requested that Sartre travel to Cuba as, to his thinking, Sartre was the only one capable of explaining to Castro, with the likelihood that he would listen, that his cultural policies were having disastrous consequences. "He will pay me no heed," Sartre replied, uninterestedly. At which point, Simone de Beauvoir added, presumably speaking for both of them: "In reality we have no desire to return to Cuba. We know that things are not going well there. Another trip there would surely bring us face to face with a great disappointment, and we want to keep the marvelous impression we had of Cuba the first time.... In other words, we want to maintain the vivid memories of the Revolution's honeymoon period."[49] Arcocha was devastated; he found Beauvoir's comments horribly "touristic." What he had proposed to them was not a pleasure trip, and he was deeply disappointed. "I came to the conclusion," states Arcocha acidly, "that those intellectuals that I had put up on a pedestal were nothing more than distinguished tourists. I burned my idols and never saw them again."[50]

But, in August 1961, Arcocha did see Mills again, when Mills and his family arrived in Moscow, where Arcocha was now stationed as correspondent for *Revolución*.[51] Arcocha interviewed Mills about the significance for the United States of the abortive CIA invasion at the Bay of Pigs. His reply was a scathing indictment of Kennedy and the liberal theorists and apologists—Schlesinger and Berle, in particular—who made up his brain trust: "First, ... Yankee officials are incapable of listening. They are doctrinaire. They believe what they think they must believe, which means they are often mistaken concerning international questions. But the great consequence of the invasion of Cuba was that it served to unmask Kennedy's 'liberalism.' The liberalism of this ambitious and impetuous young man is not so much a series of moral principles as a mere hollow rhetoric."[52]

After their four-month tour of Europe and the USSR, the Millses returned to New York in January 1962. The following month, Kennedy ordered a total embargo against Cuba (but only after taking personal delivery of 1,200 Cuban cigars), and it was clear that the Revolution had become Sovietized. Castro had, at last, come to embrace orthodox historical materialism—the "vulgar" variety of Marxism that Mills had feared: statist, bureaucratic, and dogmatic. All of this was an enormous weight on Mills; "the decline of the revolution, atop his personal pains, was too much" writes Harvey Swados, who saw Mills for the last time in France just before Mills's departure from Europe.[53]

A Cautious Assessment

It is altogether appropriate, by way of conclusion, to render a cautious assessment of Mills's views on the Revolution that he so admired. In so doing, I address three major concerns. The first pertains to Mills's reading of the Revolution's ideological direction, particularly in regard to Cuba's relationship with the Soviet Union. The second raises the question of whether Mills was veraciously reporting on the situation in Cuba, or was he, in fact, projecting his own hopes onto the Revolution? Third, since this has, in large measure, been an analysis of *Listen, Yankee*, it is important to inquire more closely as to what part of the book reflects the views of the Cuban revolutionaries whom Mills interviewed and what part reflects Mills's own ideas.

Through early 1961 the governments of Havana and the Kremlin continued to make significant gestures for mutual gain that were increasingly bringing their two countries into closer alignment—diplomatically as well as ideologically. For example, between January and April of that year, a parade of Soviet weapons was held in Havana, it was announced that Russia would send 1,000 experts to the island to help organize "people's farms," Cuba's ambassador to Moscow stated that the Cuban people were "Communistic," and Castro was awarded the Lenin Peace Prize. In addition, during that same period, the Castro government took several draconian measures in dealing with counterrevolutionary activities inside the country: 500 armed men who opposed the Revolutionary regime were captured and imprisoned; moreover, two of Castro's former military aides and several counterrevolutionaries were executed in Havana for treason. Despite these and other expressions of Soviet alliance and acts of political repression by the Revolutionary government, as late as the summer of 1961 Mills had expressed to Jean-Paul Sartre his confidence that Castro, and perhaps only Castro, could keep the Revolution "straight and honest"—particularly if he, Mills, personally cautioned Castro against the dangers of Sovietizing the Revolution. Why did Mills continue to hold out hope that the Comandante would not embrace communism? And why, even after Castro's televised address of December

1961 in which he declared that he was a Marxist-Leninist (a euphemism for Communist), was Mills willing to defend him before an American public that until recently had been grievously afflicted by a Cold War nationalistic paranoia? The answer is as simple as it is complex: because Mills so closely identified with Castro, in outlook and disposition, that Mills, who was *never* a communist, could not therefore easily accept that his alter-ego could *truly* be a communist. Only during the last two months of his life would Mills finally be able to allow for the fact that the Pearl of the Antilles had become a dedicated Soviet outpost.

But did Mills's close identification with the personage of Fidel Castro unduly influence his perspective concerning the Revolution that Castro led? In the opening pages of *The Marxists*, Mills famously proclaims, "I have tried to be objective. I do not claim to be detached."[54] This pronouncement became the aphorism for which Mills is best known, given that it was perennially inscribed on his gravestone. But more than an aphorism, it was a research methodology and a life principle that allowed Mills to be both *partisan and objective* in his attempt to ascertain what was happening in Cuba and report it to the U.S. public. For Mills, objective truth, the politics of truth, meant that he was duty bound to reveal the facts of the Revolution through eyewitness, real-time testimony. But as a public intellectual he was also *morally* bound to practice a politics of responsibility, to defend the potential for a true democratic freedom. This was a freedom that was coming into existence in Cuba for the first time in its history and that would presumably allow the Cuban people to determine their own life chances. Cuba under the Revolution, Mills believed, was transforming into a properly developing society where the Cubans would "know where they stand, where they may be going, and what—if anything—they can do about the present as history and the future as responsibility."[55] It may be said, therefore, that Mills both accurately reported the truth about Cuba as he saw it *as well as* bestowed his convictions and values onto its Revolution. In short, he was objective—scholarly and rigorous in his methodology—and also engaged.

Lastly, and related, it must be determined if there is any portion of *Listen, Yankee* that expresses Mills's own beliefs and sentiments independent of those of his interlocutors. Given Mills's personal identification with Castro and his principled engagement with the Revolution, it is inevitable that these would somehow influence his research focus, the questions he asked, the information he opted to include, his interpretation of the facts, and his ultimate analysis of the Cuban situation. But as to whether Mills accurately and faithfully conveyed the collective message of the Cubans he interviewed, the answer is an unqualified yes. This is confirmed in Appendix 1 of this volume, where some passages from the interviews are compared with corresponding passages from *Listen, Yankee*. But it is also the case that Mills's power-elite thesis, which he applied to the situation in Cuba, can be seen as an undercurrent that drives the message of *Listen, Yankee*. This, despite the fact that the thesis was *not* expressly articulated by any of his interviewees. It was, instead, a conceptualization that Mills infused into the contrived letters that he crafted in the words of the Cuban revolutionary. While Mills's interviewees were painfully aware of the immense influence that the U.S. monopolies, the military missions, and the Eisenhower administration had had over their country (and at least one of them—Franz Stettmeier—was familiar with *The Power Elite*), they did not explicitly indicate that this influence was due to the machinations of an interlocking coalition of U.S. decision makers.

In the final analysis, Mills *did* tell the truth about Cuba. Not the whole truth, just the *plain* truth.

He Died Fighting

Mills died of heart failure on March 20, 1962, at his home in West Nyack, New York, at the age of forty-five. On the door of his study was emblazoned the slogan of the Cuban Revolution: *Venceremos* [We shall overcome].

In the end, there is perhaps no epigraph more apt in portraying C. Wright Mills and his convictions to the Cuban Revolution than the one penned by his friend, Carlos Fuentes:

> [Mills] made sure that his ideas mattered in the United States, and for that he was persecuted. He told the truth and he died fighting for it.[56]

Acknowledgments

Many people were most generous in proving assistance to me in researching and writing this book. First and foremost, I am grateful to Kathryn Mills for entrusting me with her father's recorded interviews. The recordings that she made available to me consist of four CDs marked as "Reel 1, Side A"; "Reel 1, Side B"; "End of #2, Part of #3"; "End of #3, Reel #4." They were not dated or labeled with identifying information. I thank Nikolas Mills for allowing me to publish the photos. Lawrence Ferlinghetti was very kind in granting me permission to reprint his poem "A Parade Tirade," with dedication to C. Wright Mills, found in Appendix 2. Javier Auyero rendered uncommon professional courtesy in going out of his way to obtain for me a much-needed and rare article. Skyler Dunfey prepared the "Cuba, 1960" map with professional aplomb, and Emma-Kate Metsker helped get it into its final shape. I am grateful to Norman Birnbaum and Daniel Geary for their endorsement of the project and their recommendations for improvement. Suggestions provided by John Bezis-Selfa on several of the chapters were of great help. I am particularly grateful to Raúl Roa Kourí for reading the entire manuscript and graciously sharing with me his remembrances of Mills from over half a century before. It goes without saying that all errors are my responsibility alone.

APPENDIX 1

Cross-Referencing Interviews and Listen, Yankee

The following cross-referencing scheme is provided so that selected passages from the interviews in Chapters 4 and 5 can be compared with parallel passages from *Listen, Yankee*. This intertext cross-referencing takes some excerpts from the transcribed interviews and corresponding excerpts from the book identified by page number(s). They substantiate Mills's claim that "the facts and the interpretations presented [in *Listen, Yankee*] ... accurately reflect ... the views of the Cuban revolutionary. Most of the words are mine—although not all of them" (8).

Interviews	Listen, Yankee
Interview 1 "ARCOCHA: Very bad. I thought ..."	"Even back then, some who knew him ..." (40)
"ARCOCHA: Exactly. I was convinced ... A change of men."	"The middle class thought ..." (61)
"ARCOCHA: [Laughter]. There's a very popular joke here ..."	"In the meantime, let us tell you a little joke ..." (102)
"MILLS: Do you think the [presidential] election ... won't change anything."	"Will your election of a new President for 1961 ..." (33).
"MILLS: And what is your considered opinion ... of *Time* magazine?"	"Everyone in the world who isn't limited to *Time* Magazine ..." (17)
Interview 3 "The education he received had been of coming home ... further into debt."	"Every year to this rural misery and sloth ..." (45)
"CAPTAIN 2: And anyone else who sells himself ... mercenary."	"Anyway, now that we've got the Russian offer ..." (156)
"Although we now have U.S. citizens who have died ... stopped these attacks."	"Planes have flown from your territory to Cuba, ..." (64–65)
"CAPTAIN 2: Well, we will cooperate in everything ... help can come."	"Our rebel soldiers— ..." (49)
Interview 4 "RIELO: Forty units will form the school city ... 8,000 females."	"But the one thing we are perhaps the proudest of ..." (136)
Interview 6 "STETTMEIER: I think it is just a label ... helping the Revolution."	"The old upper classes have lost ..." (60)
"STETTMEIER: I think it is just ... helping the Revolution."	"There's another thing, too, ..." (60)

(continued)

Interviews	Listen, Yankee
"STETTMEIER: I would say all... destroyed, absolutely."	"Before the revolution there were no examinations..." (141)
"STETTMEIER: It must be destroyed... can't do it in a big country."	"Probably, part of why it works so well..." (124)
Interview 7 "ESCOBAR: Directly, when... after the attack."	"She was in Santiago when Fidel..." (38)
"ESCOBAR: No. Taking those things... I personally did not go."	"Now there was a woman living in a house..." (37)
"ESCOBAR: I can't remember..."	"And then, Fidel landed in 1956..." (38)
"But no one, not even Fidel, expected... to take flight."	"There's one thing about all these defectors..." (55)
"They were afraid because of social laws and of being labeled [communists]."	"As a whole they hadn't the stomach for revolution..." (43)
"Cuba first, party second."	"Cuba first, the party second." (108)
"ESCOBAR: I think that... nobody cares."	"The Communist Party of Cuba..." (108)
"ESCOBAR: I think that... Not here."	"First, if every day in the United States..." (109)
"ESCOBAR: Furthermore, the Communist Party... If it were condemned."	"Second, if the revolutionary Government..." (109)
"They didn't... taken by the revolutionaries."	"They had it down on a little card..." (38)
"That saved my life. That was something else to thank Fidel for."	"How did she get away with it?..." (37)
"ESCOBAR: The people are not apostolic Roman Catholics.... [African] spiritualism." *and* "ESCOBAR: Yes. And perhaps... we were leftist and anticlerical."	"First of all, this religion isn't very deep,..." (62)
"I was Catholic until... nor the other." *and* "ESCOBAR: I was brought up... every day for six years." *and* "ESCOBAR: But my son today is not one thing nor another."	"As far as the more educated people are concerned,..." (62)

APPENDIX 2

A Parade Tirade (for C. Wright Mills)

Good night ladies and good night nuns & priests & monks & ministers who never march in peace parades Protestants shouldn't protest The holy wars are over The only united crusade a fund drive and good night holy ministers who evict peace groups from their premises Onward christian soldiers and good night good grey soldier and good night sweet prince Kennedy your thanksgiving Turkey stuffed with Khrushchev letters Watch out for pumpkin papers We are all good catholics Let us pray Now I lay me down with sheep Good night father of our country Your sons sleep & feed and good night good captains of industry in Bachrach photos with bay windows covered with insignia of various kinds of supremacy People don't know what's good for them We'll show them Harriet Beecher Stowe was wrong The ice ain't breakin' up on the river and good night good night sad cop who turned the hoses on a whole generation and flipped later and good night asinine armistice day parades that nobody under 40 believes in Don't laugh You should take them seriously Those big phoney scenes which have nothing to do with us & the way we want to live The america of the american legion isn't ours This ain't 1919 Let them march off a cliff somewhere with their obscene sidearms & sinister slogans Call out the horse marines & clean up the mess I didn't know they piled it that high You won't get us to run your errands anymore But here comes the band anyway A catch in the throat A lady liberty on a float God save our country's flag she said and god knows Veterans love wars Their eyes have seen the glory When old comrades get together Like the good old days So sweep away the pickets and good day to you Doktor Teller chief steppenwolf who standeth on guard with warheads & strategies of overkill Bomb now pay later United there is nothing we can do So good night blind flight of black avenging angels (bo-marks of death zeroed on infinity) and good night great mute poets & professors who only stand and wait and good night papa Hemingway who also finked out and good night granpa Ezra and good night reverend Eliot who also fabricated & abdicated Hurry up please it's time and good night stream of unconscious novelists & non-objecting painters Thou shalt not kill except by complicity and good day Dylan We shall not go gentle into their good night and good day Neruda and good day Ginsberg and good day Fidel. He doesn't want to marry your sister He just wants to socialize And good night good night sweet dreams crazy Karl Marx I too wish the state would wither away (into a world without countries & their great draggy nationalisms & their great draggy governments which aren't our idea of communities of love) so good night old old comrades The good old days were gone forever so goodbye goodbye death and good morning sun and goodbye senators and good morning

heart that wakes at night & hears itself
and good morning crocus voices and
good morning lovers south of 14th street
about to turn-off the whole evil scene
and turn-on beautiful & great where the
air is green

LAWRENCE FERLINGHETTI

Reprinted with permission by Lawrence Ferlinghetti.

A Note on the Interviews

In the foreword—"Note to the Reader, I"—to *Listen, Yankee*, Mills explains that "for convenience of presentation and for brevity," he does not cite names in the text. Thus, the book as such cannot be consulted to identify the respondents he interviewed. Several clues, however, can be culled from the Note and the interviews themselves to determine the identities of most of his respondents.

Of the nine interviewees audiotaped by Mills, three can be positively identified from the recordings either because Mills explicitly asks them their name or because he addresses them directly by name. These are the journalist Juan Arcocha, Mills's interpreter; the professor and psychiatrist Franz Stettmeier; and the rebel soldier Isabel Rielo.

A fourth, whom Mills describes in the Note simply as "Captain Escalona, Aide to the Prime Minister," is likely the *comandante* who had organized the Pinar del Río Guerrilla Front, Dermidio Escalona. I arrive at this conclusion circuitously, based on the fact that Juan Arcocha, who introduced Mills to Escalona, also introduced K. S. Karol to an "Escalona" (no first name provided in either case) the following year. Karol describes his Escalona as "young, slim, and with an impressive black beard," which closely resembles a photograph of Dermidio Escalona.[1] Of some minor interest may be the fact that Escalona is the only one not named in the acknowledgments in a preliminary draft of *Listen, Yankee*.

The name of another respondent, Stettmeier's wife—Elvira Escobar, also an academic—can be inferred with a very high degree of certainty based on three circumstantial pieces of information. First, her name is listed in the Note right after Stettmeier's; second, Stettmeier, in his interview, recommends to Mills that he speak with his wife, and in the interview Mills asks her how long she had been married to Stettmeier; third, in the Note Escobar is identified as being affiliated with the University of Oriente, a fact she discloses in the interview.

The identities of the other four respondents are more difficult to ascertain, but I feel quite confident that the couple Mills interviewed at the Rousseau ranch are the housekeeper, Elba Luisa Batista Benitez, and her husband, the mechanic Lauro Fiallo Barrero. I infer this from two clues. First, they are the only couple that Mills interviewed jointly, and theirs are the only names he lists together in the Note. Also, in the Note Elba Batista is said to be from the port city of Manzanillo, a fact established during her interview.

As for the two army captains whom Mills interviewed and whom I call Captain 1 and Captain 2, I was unable to find any identifying information. They will have to remain anonymous.

Biographical and other public information on most of Mills's recorded interviewees is sparse or simply nonexistent, in any language, inside or outside of Cuba.

Juan Arcocha, who was a novelist of some prominence, is the most well-known, and material by him and on him can be easily obtained from a number of sources, in English and Spanish, most of which are cited in this book. Isabel Rielo is recognized outside of Cuba—in two English-language sources also cited in this book—mainly for her participation in the all-women's combat platoon in the Sierra Maestra. Dermidio Escalona is occasionally referenced, usually in passing, in histories on the Cuban insurrection and on the trial of Huber Matos.[2] Some limited information can be found on Franz Stettmeier on the Internet and in the Spanish-language journal article cited in Chapter 5, note 3. I have been unable to locate any material on the remaining interviewees.

It is safe to assume that the order of the recordings reflects the sequence in which Mills carried out the interviews. In this book, however, I have presented them in a different order, placing the respondents into two general categories. Though Mills characterized all of his informants as "revolutionaries,"[3] some of them—military officers and government functionaries—could speak in an "official" capacity, whereas those who were private citizens were largely speaking only for themselves. It is for this reason that I separated the responses of those working for the government (in Chapter 4) from private citizens (in Chapter 5).

Two of the interviews were conducted by Mills directly in English, the rest relied on the formidable skills of translation provided by Mills's Cuban interpreter, Juan Arcocha. I have provided my own translations from the Spanish in those parts of the recordings where the interviewee's responses can be heard clearly. In doing so I furnish a more flowing and easier-to-read rendition than Arcocha's more literal interpretation. However, in those cases where the Spanish response is unclear or inaudible, I employed Arcocha's translation exclusively. In addition, I opted to leave untranslated certain Spanish words—e.g., *campesino, cura, latifundista, siquitrillada*—because of their unique flavor in that language and because I feel that no English equivalent quite captures their connotation or colloquial nature. In the more technical of these cases I gave their closest English meaning in the text or else explained them in a footnote.[4]

There are a handful of places where I felt that, for purposes of conversational flow, it was best to summarize those segments of the recorded interview. Also, in a few cases I have omitted short sections—indicated by ellipses—where I deemed that what was being said was not relevant to the larger discussion, or that it would not be of interest to the reader. These brief omissions are based entirely on my editorial judgment, and I hope I have not erred in making them. In addition, I also indicated where there are gaps, due to technological or other reasons, in the audio recordings. My sense is that these gaps are short and they do not adversely affect the discussion.

Biographical Notes

Arcocha, Juan

Born in Santiago de Cuba in 1927. During the 1960s Arcocha served as editorial assistant to Carlos Franqui of *Revolución*. Later he was foreign correspondent in Moscow for *Revolución* and subsequently worked in the press office of the Cuban embassy in France. In 1966, disillusioned by the restrictions imposed on artists by the Cuban government, Arcocha emigrated to France. He made a definitive break with the Castro government over the "Padilla affair" and went into exile in Paris in 1971. In 1973 he published a book highly critical of Castro titled *Fidel Castro en romepecabezas*. Arcocha wrote several novels, all of which have as their central theme the Cuban Revolution: *Los muertos andan solos* (1962), *Por cuenta propia* (1970), *La bala perdida* (1973), *Tatiana y los hombres abundantes* (1982), *La coversacíon* (1983), and *El tiburón vegetariano* (2010). He continued to write until his death in Paris in 2010.

Ballantine, Ian

American publisher known as "the father of the mass-market paperback." He co-founded, with his wife, Betty, Bantam Books and Ballantine Books. They published Ballantine Books from 1952 to 1974, making pocket-sized paperbacks affordable and accessible to the general public. Ballantine titles included C. Wright Mills's *The Causes of World War Three* and *Listen, Yankee*. Ian Ballantine died in 1995.

Batista, Fulgencio

President of Cuba from 1940 to 1944 and dictator from 1952 to 1959. In 1933, in an uprising known as "The Revolt of the Sergeants," Batista seized control of the armed forces and overthrew the government of Gerardo Machado. In 1952 he led a coup against Carlos Prío and suspended constitutional guarantees and the right to strike and also censored the media. Under Batista, Cuba became profitable for American business and organized crime, and the United States supplied Batista with planes, ships, and tanks. He was overthrown by Fidel Castro and the Cuban Revolution and fled the island nation on January 1, 1959. He died in exile in 1973.

Beauvoir, Simone de

French writer, intellectual, political activist, and feminist. She is best known for her 1949 treatise, *The Second Sex*, which is a critique of patriarchy and is considered one of the foundational texts in feminism. Beauvoir had a lifelong partnership with

Jean-Paul Sartre, with whom she visited Cuba in the spring and then again the fall of 1960. She died in Paris in 1986.

Berle, Adolf A., Jr.

U.S. diplomat, economist, and policy maker who was a member of Franklin D. Roosevelt's brain trust and later served as ambassador to Brazil (1945–46). In 1961 Berle was John F. Kennedy's advisor on Latin American affairs, including the Bay of Pigs invasion. Berle was scheduled to debate Mills on the topic of "U.S. Policy towards Latin America" in a television broadcast in December 1960. He is one of the "liberals" explicitly criticized in *Listen, Yankee* for labeling Cuba as communist.

Castro, Fidel

Born in 1926, Castro organized the rebellion against the regime of Fulgencio Batista and founded the 26th of July Movement revolutionary group. He led the Rebel Army in the Sierra Maestra and in 1959 overthrew the Batista dictatorship. He served as prime minister of Cuba from 1959 to 1976 and as president from 1976 to 2008. He died in Havana in 2016.

Escalona, Dermidio

Born in Holguín, Cuba, in 1930. During the insurrection Escalona was arrested and imprisoned for his attempt to participate in the 1956 Santiago uprising. He served as commander of the Guerrilla Front of Pinar del Río. He took an active part in the War against the Bandits rebellion, 1959–65, in the Escambray Mountains. Escalona died in Havana in 2009.

Franqui, Carlos

Born in 1921, Franqui was a writer, poet, and journalist who joined the 26th of July Movement after Batista's coup in 1952 and later joined the Rebel Army in the Sierra Maestra to write for *Revolución*, the guerrilla movement's clandestine newspaper, and for Radio Rebelde, their clandestine radio station. In 1959, he was appointed chief editor of *Revolución*, which was then the official newspaper of the Castro government. Unhappy about the close relationship that Castro formed with the Soviet Union, Franqui became an outspoken critic of Castro and broke with him after he supported the 1968 Soviet invasion of Czechoslovakia. Franqui died in exile in 2010.

Fuentes, Carlos

Mexican novelist and playwright, who was a friend of C. Wright Mills. His works include the novels *Terra Nova* (1975) and *The Old Gringo* (1985) and the play *All Cats Are Gray* (1970). Fuentes wrote pro-Castro articles and essays while briefly living in Havana in 1959 where he began *The Death of Artemio Cruz* (1962), the novel he dedicated to Mills. He broke with Castro when Cuban officials labeled him a traitor in 1965 for attending an international writer's conference in New York. He died in Mexico City in 2012.

Grau, Rámon

Was twice elected president of Cuba. In the 1920s he was involved with the student protests against dictator Gerardo Machado. Grau was elected president in 1933, and Fulgencio Batista, who was then army chief of staff, led a coup against him the following year. In 1944 Grau was again elected president and served until 1948. He died in Havana in 1969.

Guevara, Ernesto "Ché"

Born in Argentina in 1928, Guevara was a revolutionary, physician, and diplomat. He sailed to Cuba aboard the yacht *Granma* along with Fidel Castro and other guerrilla fighters. After the victory of the Revolution, Guevara became a Cuban citizen and served as chief of the Industrial Department of the National Institute of Agrarian Reform, as minister of industry, and, when Mills met with him, he was president of the National Bank of Cuba. In his attempt to export revolution to Bolivia, Guevara was executed in 1967 by the Bolivian army, aided by the CIA.

Hart Dávalos, Armando

Born in 1930, Hart participated in the 1956 uprising in Santiago de Cuba. He served as the first minister of education under the Revolutionary government and directed the Literacy Campaign. He later served as minister of culture.

Karol, K. S.

Born in 1924, Karol was a French journalist of Polish origin who was drafted into the ranks of the Red Army during World War II. After the war he became a freelance writer for the French weekly news magazine *L'Express*. In 1967 Fidel Castro invited him to write a book about Cuba, which resulted in *Guerrillas in Power: The Course of the Cuban Revolution*. Castro was dissatisfied with the book and declared that Karol was a CIA agent. He died in 2014.

Landau, Saul

American journalist, author, and documentary filmmaker who produced over fifty films, including *Fidel* (1968); *Castro, Cuba and the U.S.* (1974); and *The Uncompromising Revolution* (1990). Landau was a research assistant for C. Wright Mills, traveling with him to Europe and the Soviet Union. In the foreword to *Listen, Yankee*, Mills thanked Landau for sharing with him the results of Landau's astute experience in Cuba. Landau died in 2013.

Machado, Gerardo

President of Cuba from 1925 to 1933. In 1930 students from the University of Havana protested Machado's repressive regime. Machado abolished the student organization the Federación Estudiantil Universitaria (FEU) and ordered the expulsion of the leaders of the Directorio Estudiantil Universitario (Student Directory). Those students would later be known as the "generation of the thirties." Machado removed all constitutional guarantees in 1931. He fled Cuba in 1933 and died in Miami Beach, Florida, in 1939.

Oltuski, Enrique

Born in 1930, Oltuski led the urban wing of the 26th of July Movement in central Cuba during the insurrection. After the Revolution he served as minister of communications, director of organization of the Industrialization Department of INRA, and, later, as deputy minister of the Fishing Industry. He died in Cuba in 2012.

País, Frank

Born in 1934, País was urban coordinator of the 26th of July Movement in Oriente province. In November 1956 he organized the armed uprising in Santiago de Cuba in support of the *Granma* landing of Fidel Castro and his guerrilla fighters. País was executed on the streets of Santiago by police of the Batista regime on July 30, 1957.

Prío, Carlos

Succeeded Ramón Grau as president of Cuba in 1948. Prío became involved in politics while a law student at the University of Havana. He led the coup that deposed Gerardo Machado in 1933 and helped organize the Partido Revolucionario Cubano Auténtico. In 1952, Fulgencio Batista, with the support of the armed forces, ousted Prío and took control of the country. Prío became a prominent exile who opposed the Castro government. He committed suicide in Miami Beach, Florida, in 1977.

Rielo, Isabel

Born on October 25, 1925, in Santiago de Cuba. She was commanding officer of the Rebel Army's first all-women's platoon, the Mariana Grajales. She eventually rose to the rank of captain of the Armed Revolutionary Force. Rielo died in Havana in 1989.

Roa Kourí, Raul

Born in 1936 in Havana. Former diplomat, prominent writer, and son of Raúl Roa, Cuba's foreign minister (1959–76). At the age of twenty-three, Roa Kourí was appointed counsel general to the Cuban Embassy in Chile. He served for fourteen years as Cuban ambassador to the United Nations. Afterward he served as ambassador to many countries as well as the Holy See.

Sánchez, Celia

Born on May 9, 1920, in Media Luna in Oriente province. She founded the 26th of July Movement in Manzanillo and in 1957 joined the guerrillas in the Sierra Maestra. After the Revolution she served as secretary to the Presidency of the Council of Ministers. She died in Cuba in 1980.

Santamaría, Haydée

Born in Santa Clara, Cuba, in 1923, she was one of two women who participated on the assault on the Moncada Barracks on July 26, 1953, for which she served seven months in prison. During the insurrection she was a combatant in the Mariana Grajales Women's Platoon. After the success of the Revolution, Santamaría founded the Casa de las Américas, an artistic and literary institution that sponsored the work of Cuban and Latin American intellectuals. She committed suicide in 1980.

Sartre, Jean-Paul

One of the foremost public intellectuals of the twentieth century, Sartre was a French playwright, novelist, political activist, and philosopher of existentialism and phenomenology. His major works are many and include the novel *Nausea* (1938), the major philosophical treatise *Being and Nothingness* (1943), and the play *No Exit* (1944). Sartre and Simone de Beauvoir twice visited Cuba in 1960, first in February–March and then again in October. Soon after his first visit, Sartre wrote a series of newspaper articles that were later reprinted in English as *Sartre in Cuba* (1961). He died in Paris in 1980.

Stettmeier, Franz

Psychiatrist and clinical psychologist of German descent who introduced the Rorschach test to Cuba in the 1940s. He served as professor of psychiatry at the University of Oriente, where he had been teaching since the university's founding in 1947. In 1959, Stettmeier, along with two other professors, developed a plan to bring sociology as an academic discipline to the University of Oriente. Stettmeier was a friend of Ernest Hemingway, and in the summer of 2011 he participated in an international conference held in Havana to honor the American writer on the fiftieth anniversary of his death.

Taber, Robert

Investigative journalist who traveled to Cuba in 1957, with cameraman Wendell Hoffman, to film the CBS News special television report *Rebels of the Sierra Maestra: The*

Story of Cuba's Jungle Fighters. In 1959 Taber was a founding member of the Fair Play for Cuba Committee. He wrote *M-26: Biography of a Revolution*. He was wounded by mortar shells while covering the Bay of Pigs invasion. Taber died in the United States in 1995.

Vallejo, René C.

Born in Manzanillo in 1920, he was a physician and combatant for the Rebel Army. A *comandante*, Vallejo served as director of the Agrarian Reform in Manzanillo and as provincial delegate of INRA, first in Camagüey and then in Oriente, until 1961. He was Fidel Castro's personal physician and confidant and a good friend of C. Wright Mills. Vallejo died in Cuba in 1969.

Notes

Introduction

1. C. Wright Mills, *Listen, Yankee: The Revolution in Cuba* (New York: Ballantine Books, 1960).
2. Saul Landau, "C. Wright Mills: The Last Six Months," *Ramparts*, August 1965, 46.
3. Mills, *Listen, Yankee*, 12.
4. Daniel Geary, *Radical Ambition: C. Wright Mills, the Left, and American Social Thought* (Berkeley: University of California Press, 2009), 181. Geary says the same of Mills's *The Causes of World War Three*.
5. Throughout this book a number of actors involved in the history and politics of Cuba, and in Mills's professional life, are mentioned, some of whom will be generally recognizable, others not. For a fuller description of their identities and roles, the reader is directed to the Biographical Notes located toward the end of this volume.

Chapter 1

1. C. Wright Mills, *Listen, Yankee: The Revolution in Cuba* (New York: Ballantine Books, 1960), 9.
2. C. Wright Mills, Clarence Senior, and Rose Kohn Goldsen, *The Puerto Rican Journey: New York's Newest Migrants* (New York: Harper and Bros., 1950).
3. Rafael Rojas, "El aparato cultural del imperio. C. Wright Mills, la Revolución Cubana y la Nueva Izquierda," *Perfiles Latinoamericanos* 44 (2014): 13.
4. See C. Wright Mills, "The Sailor, Sex Market, and Mexican," *The New Leader* 26 (1943): 5.
5. Preliminary draft, "Listen, Yankee," undated, Box 5S17, Charles Wright Mills Papers, 1934–1965, Dolph Briscoe Center for American History, the University of Texas at Austin.
6. Leo Huberman and Paul W. Sweezy, *Cuba: Anatomy of a Revolution* (New York: Monthly Review Press, 1960), 95. There are some superficial resemblances in terms of personal style between Huberman and Sweezy's book and *Listen, Yankee*. For example, like Mills, they insert themselves into the narrative and address the reader directly: "Please do not misunderstand us" (p. 89), and use similar verbiage: "it is being built—at breakneck speed" (100); "about what is really going on in Cuba" (193).
7. Raúl Roa Kourí, *En el torrente* (Havana: Casa de las Américas, 2004), 130.
8. Ibid., 77.
9. As important as the books Mills consulted in preparation for his research is the book he did not consider or, in any event, does not mention in the Notes and Acknowledgments in *Listen, Yankee*: Ruby Hart Phillips, *Cuba: Island of Paradox* (New

York: McDowell, Obolensk, 1959). The *New York Times* Havana bureau chief, Phillips had lived on the island for decades. She had cordial relations with Fulgencio Batista and Fidel Castro—both of whom found her likeable (indeed, at one point during 1958 Castro sent her a wild mountain orchid, which he had delivered to her office). Compared with the aforementioned books, this one, which covers events up to the spring of 1959, takes a more balanced approach in recounting the insurrection and earliest days of the Revolution. Phillips soon thereafter became highly critical of the Castro government and left the island for good in 1961.

10. Irving Louis Horowitz, *C. Wright Mills: An American Utopian* (New York: The Free Press, 1983), 295.

11. Robert Taber, *M-26: Biography of a Revolution* (New York: Lyle Stuart, 1961), 318.

12. Hans Gerth and C. Wright Mills, *Character and Social Structure: The Psychology of Social Institutions* (New York: Harcourt, Brace, 1953), 445.

13. C. Wright Mills, *The Power Elite* (New York: Oxford University Press, 1956), 198–224.

14. C. Wright Mills, *The Causes of World War Three* (New York: Simon & Schuster, 1958).

15. These events were narrated to me by Raúl Roa Kourí in an e-mail communication on January 27, 2016.

16. David L. Strug, "Witnessing the Revolution: North Americans in Cuba in the 1960s," *International Journal of Cuba Studies* 4 (2012).

17. Rafael Rojas, "Anatomía del entusiasmo: la revolución como espectáculo de ideas," *América Latina Hoy* 47 (2007). See also Paul Hollander, *Political Pilgrims: Travels of Western Intellectuals to the Soviet Union, China, and Cuba, 1928–1978* (New York: Oxford University Press, 1981); Kepa Artaraz, *Cuba and Western Intellectuals since 1959* (New York: Palgrave Macmillan, 2009).

18. Michael B. Conant, "Reception at the Theresa," *Columbia Owl*, October 5, 1960, 1, 4.

19. Fernando Martínez Heredia, "El mundo ideológico Cubano de 1959 a marzo de 1960," in *Sartre-Cuba-Sartre: Huracán, surco, semillas*, ed. Eduardo Torres-Cuevas (Havana: Imagen Contemporánea, 2005), 219.

20. Stephen Fay, "Liminal Visitors to an Island on the Edge: Sartre and Ginsberg in Revolutionary Cuba," *Studies in Travel Writing* 15 (2011): 408.

21. David Caute, *The Fellow-Travelers: Intellectual Friends of Communism* (New Haven, CT: Yale University Press, 1973), 405. And it was Mills's *Listen, Yankee*, in particular, that, at least to some extent, "helped mobilize pro-Cuba and anti-intervention support." Saul Landau, "From the Labor Youth League to the Cuban Revolution," in *History and the New Left: Madison, Wisconsin, 1950–1970*, ed. Paul Buhle (Philadelphia: Temple University Press, 1990), 112. Rojas sees both Mills and Sartre not only as spectators but, more importantly, and dangerously, as *interpreters* of the Cuban Revolution's "theatre of ideas." Rojas, "Anatomía del entusiasmo," 42.

22. Karl E. Meyer and Tad Szulc, *The Cuban Invasion: The Chronicle of a Disaster* (New York: Frederick A. Praeger, 1962), 19.

23. Juan Arcocha, "El viaje de Sartre," in *La Habana, 1952–1961: El final de un mundo, el principio de una ilusión*, ed. Jacobo Machover (Madrid: Alianza Editorial, 1995), 231.

24. Carlos Franqui, *Family Portrait with Fidel: A Memoir*, trans. Alfred MacAdam (New York: Random House, 1984), 68. Sartre and Simone de Beauvoir were in Cuba from February 22 to March 20, 1960. They spent many days with Castro and an evening with Guevara, speaking with him (in French) for several hours. About Guevara, Sartre declared that "he was not only an intellectual, but also the most complete human being of our age." Marianne Sinclair, *Viva Che!: Contributions in Tribute to Ernesto "Che" Guevara* (London: Lorrimer Publishing, 1968), 102.

A few months later, in October, the French couple returned to the island nation and met with workers, civil servants, administrators, and labor leaders, and also with writers and artists. See Jaime Sarusky, "Sartre en Cuba," in *Sartre-Cuba-Sartre: Huracán, surco, semillas*, ed. Eduardo Torres-Cuevas (Havana: Imagen Contemporánea, 2005). They found that Havana had changed; Cuba was toughing up, its atmosphere was tense with the expectation of invasion. By late 1960, Sartre could see that "the honeymoon of the revolution was over." Simone de Beauvoir, *Force of Circumstance*, trans. Richard Howard (New York: G.P. Putnam, 1965), 291.

25. On this point, see Lawrence Ferlinghetti, "Poet's Notes on Cuba," *Liberation* 6 (1961): 11–12.

26. "The Causes of C. Wright Mills," KPFA broadcast, October 1, 1962, Pacifica Radio Archives, no. BB0281b.

27. Built as a hotel-casino in 1957 at a cost of $14 million and originally owned by mobster Meyer Lansky, the Riviera was the largest and most glamorous facility of its kind in Havana; it was Lansky's masterpiece. After the Revolution, as a symbol of mob corruption and unbounded opulence, the Riviera was subjected to great opprobrium: "In an act of revolutionary audacity, *campesinos* brought into the city a truckload of pigs and set them loose in the lobby of the hotel and casino, squealing, tracking mud across the floors, shitting and peeing all over Lansky's pride and joy, one of the most famous mobster gambling emporiums in all the world." T. J. English, *Havana Nocturne: How the Mob Owned Cuba and Then Lost It to the Revolution* (New York: Morrow, 2007), 305.

28. K. S. Karol, *Guerrillas in Power: The Course of the Cuban Revolution*, trans. Arnold Pomerans (New York: Hill & Wang, 1970), 10.

29. Mike Forrest Keen, *Stalking the Sociological Imagination: J. Edgar Hoover's FBI Surveillance of American Sociology* (Westport, CT: Greenwood Press, 1999), 175.

30. Robert Taber, "Cuban Viewpoints: Kennedy and C. Wright Mills," *Fair Play*, September 2, 1960, 2.

31. Ibid., 2–3.

Chapter 2

1. C. Wright Mills, *The Sociological Imagination* (New York: Oxford University Press, 1959), 143–64.

2. There are, quite simply, no unbiased published accounts of the Cuban historical events of insurrection, revolutionary transition, and invasion. Information for the next three sections dealing with these three epochs and occurrences is taken largely from the following conflicting sources: Robert E. Quirk, *Fidel Castro* (New York:

W. W. Norton, 1993); Robert Taber, *M-26: Biography of a Revolution* (New York: Lyle Stuart, 1961); Jules Dubois, *Fidel Castro: Rebel-Liberator or Dictator?* (Indianapolis: The Bobbs-Merrill Co., 1959); Ray Brennan, *Castro, Cuba, and Justice* (New York: Doubleday, 1959); Ruby Hart Phillips, *Cuba: Island of Paradox* (New York: McDowell, Obolensky, 1959); Leo Huberman and Paul W. Sweezy, *Cuba: Anatomy of a Revolution* (New York: Monthly Review Press, 1960); Antonio Rafael de la Cova, *The Moncada Attack: Birth of the Cuban Revolution* (Columbia: University of South Carolina Press, 2007); Karl E. Meyer and Tad Szulc, *The Cuban Invasion: The Chronicle of a Disaster* (New York: Frederick A. Praeger, 1962); Jim Rasenberger, *The Brilliant Disaster: JFK, Castro, and America's Doomed Invasion of Cuba's Bay of Pigs* (New York: Scribner, 2011). The most comprehensive and trusted sources of information are Hugh Thomas, *Cuba, or The Pursuit of Freedom* (New York: Da Capo Press, 1998) and K. S. Karol, *Guerrillas in Power: The Course of the Cuban Revolution*, trans. Arnold Pomerans (New York: Hill & Wang, 1970).

3. Jean-Paul Sartre, *Sartre on Cuba* (New York: Ballantine Books, 1961), 20.

4. C. Wright Mills, *Listen, Yankee: The Revolution in Cuba* (New York: Ballantine Books, 1960), 38.

5. Van Gosse, *Where the Boys Are: Cuba, Cold War America, and the Making of a New Left* (New York: Verso, 1993), 82.

6. The three North American teenagers who joined the rebel fighters and spent several months in the Sierra Maestra were Michael Garvey, fifteen, of Watertown, Massachusetts; Victor J. Buehlman, seventeen, of Coronado, California; and Charles E. Ryan, nineteen, of Monson, Massachusetts. Garvey and Buehlman returned to the U.S. Naval Base at Guantánamo with Taber, while Ryan stayed on, explaining his involvement: "I figure the fight in Cuba is for the kind of ideals on which the U.S. was set up," *Life*, May 27, 1957, 43. Another high-minded U.S. citizen who fought with the rebels was a sailor, Charles W. Barlett Jr., twenty, from Sebastopol, California, who was later court-martialed by the U.S. Navy for going AWOL. But by far the most famous of the North Americans who took up arms against Batista, in the Second National Front in the Escambray Mountains, was the so-called *Yanqui comandante*, William Alexander Morgan, a twenty-nine-year-old former paratrooper from Toledo, Ohio. See Michael Sallah and Mitch Weiss, eds., *The Yankee Comandante: The Untold Story of Courage, Passion, and One American's Fight to Liberate Cuba* (Guilford, CT: Lyons Press, 2015).

7. Dubois, *Fidel Castro*, 313.

8. Hans Gerth and C. Wright Mills, *Character and Social Structure: The Psychology of Social Institutions* (New York: Harcourt, Brace, 1953), 442–43.

9. Walter Lippmann, "U.S. Latin Policy Bigger Than Cuba," *St. Petersburg Times*, January 28, 1960, A1.

10. Gerth and Mills, *Character and Social Structure*, 441–43. Gerth and Mills are silent on the question of the *humanistic* revolution—exactly the kind that Mills, and Sartre, sought in Cuba.

11. Huberman and Sweezy, *Cuba*, 124.

12. Ibid., 77.

13. Phillips, *Cuba*, 406–7.

14. Intervention is the legal term meaning to take over a property provisionally, pending final expropriation. In practice, there was no difference between legal and extralegal seizures.

15. These were the owners of large estates, many of whom were absentee landlords who rented small plots to the peasants under strict supervision.

16. Rasenberger, *The Brilliant Disaster*, 40.

17. Gerth and Mills, *Character and Social Structure*, 444–45.

18. Meyer and Szulc, *The Cuban Invasion*, 146.

19. Ibid., 153.

Chapter 3

1. C. Wright Mills, *The Sociological Imagination* (New York: Oxford University Press, 1959), 132.

2. Robert Taber, *M-26: Biography of a Revolution* (New York: Lyle Stuart, 1961), 338.

3. Kathryn Mills with Pamela Mills, eds., *C Wright Mills: Letters and Autobiographical Writings* (Berkeley: University of California Press, 2000), 331.

4. As he states in *Listen, Yankee*, "I cannot give unconditional loyalties to any institution, man, state, movement, or nation. My loyalties are conditional upon my own convictions and my own values." C. Wright Mills, *Listen, Yankee: The Revolution in Cuba* (New York: Ballantine Books, 1960), 179.

5. Harvey Swados, "C. Wright Mills: A Personal Memoir," *Dissent* 10 (1963): 42.

6. "Try to understand men not as an isolated fragment, not as an intelligible field or system in and of itself. Try to understand men and women as historical and social actors, and the ways in which the variety of men and women are intricately selected and intricately formed by the variety of human societies." Mills, *Sociological Imagination*, 158.

7. Ibid., 174.

8. C. Wright Mills, *The Power Elite* (New York: Oxford University Press, 1956), 304.

9. C. Wright Mills, *White Collar: The American Middle Classes* (New York: Oxford University Press, 1951), xv.

10. Ibid., xvi. Exemplary of the "new little man" is the protagonist in Sloan Wilson's highly popular 1955 novel, *The Man in the Gray Flannel Suit*, that faceless, conforming, lonely everyman of mass society:

> I'm just a man in a gray flannel suit. I must keep my suit pressed like anyone else, for I am a very respectable young man. . . . I will go to my new job, and I will be cheerful, and I will be industrious, and I will be matter-of-fact. I will keep my gray flannel suit spotless. I will have a sense of humor. I will have guts—I'm not the type to start crying now. (98)

11. While Guevara did not publicly propose the notion of the "new man" until 1965 in his brief essay, "Man and Socialism in Cuba," as will be seen below, the ascendancy of the Cuban new man was already being discerned by Mills in 1960.

12. Ché Guevara, *Socialism and Man in Cuba and Other Works* (London: Stage 1, 1968), 10–11.

13. Ibid., 13.

14. Mills, *Listen, Yankee*, 43. Emphasis added.

15. Ibid., 142. Emphasis added.

16. C. Wright Mills, *The New Men of Power: America's Labor Leaders* (New York: Harcourt, Brace, 1948).

17. C. Wright Mills, *The Causes of World War Three* (New York: Simon & Schuster, 1958).

18. While Mills may have expected that revolutionary Cuba could potentially become a properly *developing* society, it was still a long way from being a properly *developed* society. Cuba's transition into a socialist (and later a Soviet-aligned) state was achieved not through any considered, deliberative democratic process, but through the unreflective imitation of its significant leader. As K. S. Karol explains, "A people that says: 'If Fidel is socialist, so are we,' is not really mature enough to build a socialist society; it has only just been admitted to the rank of builder's apprentice," *Guerrillas in Power: The Course of the Cuban Revolution*, trans. Arnold Pomerans (New York: Hill & Wang, 1970), 185.

19. C. Wright Mills, "On Latin America, the Left, and the U.S.," *Evergreen Review* 5 (1961).

20. Mills, *The Causes of World War Three*, 141.

21. Mills, *Listen, Yankee*, 17. Emphasis added.

22. Ibid., 179.

23. Mills, "On Latin America," 120. Here Mills uses the term "intelligentsia" in the Eastern-European sense, to mean all cultural workers, including artists and scientists, as well as "intellectuals" in the Western sense.

24. As quoted in Leo Huberman and Paul M. Sweezy, *Cuba: Anatomy of a Revolution* (New York: Monthly Review Press, 1960), 145.

25. As quoted in Natacha Gómez Velásquez, "La presencia de Sartre en las publicaciones Cubanas de la década del 60," in *Sartre-Cuba-Sartre: Huacán, surco, semillas*, ed. Eduardo Torres-Cuevas (Havana: Imagen Contemporánea, 2005), 243. Emphasis added.

26. Jean-Paul Sartre, *Sartre on Cuba* (New York: Ballantine Books, 1961), 89. The typical age of the rebel youth in 1952, when Batista came to power, was between eighteen and twenty-five years old. See Maurice Zeitlin, "Political Generations in the Cuban Working Class," *American Journal of Sociology* 71 (1966): 496. The average age of the Council of Ministers in 1960 was thirty-three. See Huberman and Sweezy, *Cuba*, 92.

27. Huberman and Sweezy, *Cuba*, 89.

28. C. Wright Mills, "Letter to the New Left," *New Left Review* 5 (September–October 1960). In March 1960 Mills stated that he was "trying to develop" the idea of a New Left, but that he "had not yet gotten [it] straight." Mills, "On Latin America," 122. After witnessing the Cuban Revolution being made, he had indeed gotten it straight.

29. A. Javier Treviño, *The Social Thought of C. Wright Mills* (Thousand Oaks, CA: Sage Publications, 2012), 173.

30. Mills, "Letter," 23.

31. One of Mills's respondents—Elvira Escobar—identified herself as being of the Thirties generation and was later active in the 26th of July Movement. She was forty-eight years old at the time Mills interviewed her (see Chapter 5, Interview 7).

32. Raúl Roa (1907–1982) was a student at the University of Havana and a member of the leftist students' directorate who revolted against Machado. Jorge Mañach (1898–1961), a writer and politician known for his essay "El Pensamiento Cubano: Su trayectoria" (1932), opposed the Machado and Batista governments, and later the Castro government. Rafael Trejo (1910–1930) was a student leader at the University of Havana and member of the Directorio Estudiantil Universitario who was killed for his opposition to the Machado regime.

33. On this point, see Rafael Rojas, "El aparato cultural del imperio. C. Wright Mills, la Revolución Cubana y la Nueva Izquierda," *Perfiles Latinoamericanos* 44 (2014): 13. Ramiro Guerra (1880–1970) was a historian best known for *Azúcar y población de las antillas* (1935) and for editing the ten-volume *Historia de la nación Cubana* (1952). Fernando Ortiz (1881–1969) was an anthropologist and ethnomusicologist who coined the term "transculturation" and wrote *Contrapunteo cubano del tabaco y el azúcar* (1940). *Listen, Yankee* does thrice mention Cuba's foremost national hero of independence, José Martí (1853–1895), but only in passing and without reference to any of his works.

34. Stanley Aronowitz, *Taking It Big: C. Wright Mills and the Making of Political Intellectuals* (New York: Columbia University Press, 2012), 212.

35. At least three of the interviewees that Mills recorded where held to be intellectuals, as he defined them: Juan Arcocha, Franz Stettmeier, and Elvira Escobar.

36. Daniel Geary, *Radical Ambition: C. Wright Mills, the Left, and American Social Thought* (Berkeley: University of California Press, 2009), 112.

37. Mills, *Sociological Imagination*, 205.

38. Saul Landau, "C. Wright Mills: The Last Six Months," *Ramparts*, August 1965, 50.

39. Mills, *Sociological Imagination*, 224.

40. K. Mills with P. Mills, *C. Wright Mills*, 300–301.

41. Theodore Draper, *Castro's Revolution: Myths and Realities* (London: Thames and Hudson, 1962), 8.

42. Mills, *Listen, Yankee*, 8.

43. Robert Taber, "Cuban Viewpoints: Kennedy and C. Wright Mills," *Fair Play*, September 2, 1960, 3.

44. C. Wright Mills, *The Marxists* (New York: Dell, 1962). Ché Guevara is the only Latin American Marxist Mills refers to in the book.

45. Landau, "C. Wright Mills," 46.

46. Mills, *Listen, Yankee*, 11.

47. Mills's mother spoke fluent Spanish.

48. "The Causes of C. Wright Mills," KPFA broadcast, October 1, 1962, Pacifica Radio Archives, no. BB0281b.

49. Lawrence Ferlinghetti, "Poet's Notes on Cuba," *Liberation* 6 (1961): 12. For Ferlinghetti's poem "Parade Tirade," which he dedicated to Mills, see Appendix 2 in this book.

50. Draper, *Castro's Revolution*, 8.

Chapter 4

1. On taking power, Castro dismantled the traditional military apparatus and resolved that there would be no colonels or generals in the Rebel Army; the highest

rank would be *comandante*, roughly equivalent to major. In 1976 this custom was abolished and passed to the conventional ranks under the Soviet designation.

2. Basically, two events, long in coming, compelled Arcocha's defection: Castro's support of the Soviet invasion of Czechoslovakia in 1968, and Castro's censorship and imprisonment, in 1971, of the poet Heberto Padilla, which resulted in the cause célèbre known as the "Padilla affair."

3. Juan Arcocha, *Fidel Castro en rompecabezas* (Madrid: Ediciones R, 1973), 9. Arcocha seems not to have been at a loss of personages against which to compare Castro. In his most recent metamorphosis (in 1973), Castro, Arcocha opines, was beginning to more closely resemble Walter Ulbricht, a German Communist politician and Stalinist bureaucrat, "a man who would open an umbrella in Berlin whenever it rained in Moscow," 31.

4. Ibid., 17–18.

5. On this point, see Tad Szulc, "Cuban Television's One-Man Show," in *The Eighth Art* (New York: Holt, Rinehart and Winston, 1962). In an ironic twist on Gil Scott-Heron's poem that the U.S. civil rights "revolution will not be televised," Castro's Revolution was indeed broadcast into the homes of thousands of Cubans throughout the island. As Ruby Hart Phillips bluntly puts it, "This was a televised revolution." *Cuba: Island of Paradox* (New York: McDowell, Obolensk, 1959), 404.

6. The Federación Estudiantíl Universitaria (FEU) was formed in 1922 as a student organization that had a great deal of influence in Cuban politics. It was created by Julio Antonio Mella, who later founded the Cuban Communist Party. During the insurrection, the FEU was allied with Castro's 26th of July Movement.

7. Arcocha is referring to Castro's first appearance on Cuban television on January 9, 1959, shortly after making his triumphal entry into Havana. Sartre asserts that Castro won the people over from the first time he addressed them: "This nation, satiated with speeches, mistrusted words. Since Fidel has been speaking to them, they haven't heard a single word. They hear facts, demonstrations, analyses." Jean-Paul Sartre, *Sartre on Cuba* (New York: Ballantine Books, 1961), 143.

8. *New York Times* reporter Tad Szulc saw not sincerity, but rather deception, in Castro's propagandistic use of television as a political instrument. See Szulc, "One-Man Show." On the eve of the Revolution, in 1959, there were 400,000 television sets on the Cuban island.

9. After his break with Castro, Arcocha depicted him antithetically to what he had told Mills, writing that "Fidel Castro is, in reality, a cold man. . . . In regard to what is personally important to him—that is to say, the retention of power—he is a calculating machine." *Fidel Castro*, 118.

10. Arcocha would later describe that feeling as follows: "[Castro's] very presence was electrifying and the television screens were not able to filter the almost hypnotic current that emanated from him." *Fidel Castro*, 33.

11. As early as the spring of 1959 Ruby Hart Phillips had noted that the Cuban Communists clearly wielded tremendous influence, not only in the labor unions but also in the Castro government. "In a small country like Cuba," she pointed out, "determined

and dedicated communists can get control of a large number of posts in key positions, thus exerting disproportionate influence." Phillips, *Cuba*, 417. Even as steadfast supporter of the new Cuban regime as Ray Brennan noted that the Communist Party had attempted to infiltrate the government and the labor unions immediately after January 1, 1959. Ray Brennan, *Castro, Cuba, and Justice* (New York: Doubleday, 1959), 275.

12. In this and all others cases reference is made to the Communist Party of Cuba (officially, the Popular Socialist Party, or PSP) that had been founded in 1925 by Julio Antonio Mella. It was not until 1965 that a "new" Communist Party of Cuba, under the leadership of Fidel Castro, was formed.

13. In February 1960 Soviet Deputy Premier Anastas Mikoyan went to Cuba to establish relations with Castro, making him the first Soviet leader to visit the island after the Revolution. The visit resulted in a trade agreement in which the Soviets would purchase Cuban sugar in exchange for Russian oil. In 1962, during the Cuban Missile Crisis, Mikoyan was involved in persuading Castro to allow the removal of the nuclear missiles from the island.

14. The concepts "direct democracy" and "guided democracy" are not synonymous. Arcocha is referring to Sartre's claim that he found in Cuba, and in the actions of Fidel Castro, a "direct democracy" in which the leader addresses the people concretely and directly, without mediations between the government and the masses. For a rather banal description of how direct democracy works in fact, see the "warm lemonade" episode that Sartre recounts in *Sartre on Cuba*, 122. By "guided democracy," Mills may be referring either to the political system set in place in Indonesia in 1957 by President Sukarno or what the American journalist and commentator Walter Lippmann called "the art of persuasion" and "the manufacture of consent." See Walter Lippmann, *Public Opinion* (New York: Free Press, 1997), 158. Given Castro's use of the electronic media to deliver his policy proposals, it is more likely that, in this interview, Mills had in mind Lippmann's notion. According to K. S. Karol, it was Sartre, Mills, and the economist Paul A. Baran "who first spoke of direct democracy in Cuba, at a time when Castro was still too busy practicing it to turn it into theory," *Guerrillas in Power: The Course of the Cuban Revolution*, trans. Arnold Pomerans (New York: Hill & Wang, 1970), 453. Years later, Arcocha would write that the direct democracy that had so impressed Sartre had ceased to exist in Cuba and had been replaced by "paternalistic and incontrovertible directives" that came "from above." *Fidel Castro*, 54.

15. Five months prior to this interview, Eisenhower had approved a secret plan for the CIA to arm and train a force of Cuban exiles to overthrow the Castro government and replace it "with one more devoted to the true interests of the Cuban people and more acceptable to the U.S. in such a manner as to avoid any appearance of U.S. intervention." "A Program of Covert Action against the Castro Regime," *Foreign Relations of the United States, 1958–1960, Vol. 6, Cuba Document* (Washington, DC: U.S. Department of State).

16. On July 9, 1960, Khrushchev had declared that the Soviet Union was prepared to use its intercontinental ballistic missiles to protect Cuba from U.S. military intervention and stated, threateningly, that, "One should not forget that now the United

States is no longer at an unreachable distance from the Soviet Union as it was before." Arcocha's supposition was, according to Huberman and Sweezy, shared by government leaders who were convinced that "Khrushchev's pledge of rocket retaliation in case the United States should directly attack Cuba was wholly serious, and they did not believe that the United States would start World War III over Cuba." Leo Huberman and Paul M. Sweezy, *Cuba: Anatomy of a Revolution* (New York: Monthly Review Press, 1960), 202.

17. The U.S. presidential election was held, three months later, on November 8, with John F. Kennedy winning over Richard M. Nixon.

18. According to Hugh Thomas, the youngest officer in the Rebel Army, Enrique Acevedo, was only sixteen years old (in 1958). *Cuba, or the Pursuit of Freedom* (New York: Da Capo Press, 1998), 1042.

19. In this case, a more apt translation is "conscientiousness."

20. Sartre makes a similar point to that of the captain in noting that only in Cuba does the word "rebel" always precede the words "army" and "soldier"—thus, better to pronounce it as one word, all at once, *rebelsoldier*—because they must always retain their identity of outlaws. *Sartre on Cuba*, 108.

21. C. Wright Mills, *Listen, Yankee: The Revolution in Cuba* (New York: Ballantine, 1960), 64. K. S. Karol, who had served in the Russian Red Army and was an expert on China, appears to contradict the captain when he writes: "The Cuban defense force in no way resembles the Chinese, which is the only truly politicized military force in the world. The Cuban army has a classically hierarchic structure and hence is basically authoritarian, even though it serves the people and is headed by former *guerrilleros* from the Sierra Maestra." Karol, *Guerrillas in Power*, 543.

22. Huberman and Sweezy, *Cuba*, 128.

23. Sartre too was familiar with the situation and describes it thus: The Cuban landowners "are absent; they live in Havana, in New York; they travel in Europe. Their overseers distribute work to day laborers—four months of wages, from December to March. After that, let them go hang themselves elsewhere. They have to live eight months without doing anything. They get into debt, sometimes to the village grocer, sometimes with their boss. Eight months later, when they go back to work, their future salary is consumed in advance by these mercenary loans." *Sartre on Cuba*, 31–32. The *tiempo muerto*, or dead season, was the long period when the field workers and most of the mill hands were idle, and their families hungry.

24. The captain is doubtless referring to, among others, the defecting chief of the Cuban air force, Major Pedro Luis Díaz Lanz, who on July 10 and 14, 1959, testified before the U.S. Senate subcommittee on internal security and gave several "hair-raising" if incoherent and inaccurate accounts of life in Cuba and of communist infiltration at the highest ranks of the Cuban military. See Hugh Thomas, *Cuba*, 1232; and Jim Rasenberger, *The Brilliant Disaster: JFK, Castro, and America's Doomed Invasion of Cuba's Bay of Pigs* (New York: Scribner, 2012), 26. Others who testified before the U.S. Senate against Castro in 1959 and 1960—most of whom had been ardent Batistianos—include Fidel Castro's former brother-in-law, Rafael Díaz-Balart, who served as majority leader of the Cuban House of Representatives and as undersecretary of the interior under Batista; Colonel Manuel Antonio Ugalde Carrillo, who had

been Batista's chief of military intelligence and infantry division commander; and Andres José Rivero-Agüero, who replaced Batista as president of Cuba when the latter fled the island.

25. In early 1960, light aircraft with U.S. markings carried out sabotage and small bombing missions in Cuba. There were several firebomb air raids by North American pilots and Cuban exiles on oil refineries, cane fields, and sugar mills in Cuba. Several were killed in crashes, two were captured. The U.S. State Department acknowledged that one plane, shot down by Cuban troops near Matanzas, carrying two North Americans, had taken off from Florida.

26. These details are taken largely from Mary-Alice Waters, ed., *Marianas in Combat: Teté Puebla and the Mariana Grajales Women's Platoon in Cuba's Revolutionary War, 1956-58* (New York: Pathfinder Press, 2003).

27. Mariana Grajales (1808-1893) was a heroine of Cuba's wars of independence from Spain.

28. A dozen years later, when Margaret Randall interviewed her, Rielo, still a captain in the Revolutionary Armed Forces, was in charge of the 13,000-acre Turibacoa Vegetable Plan at Güira de Melena, about an hour and a half from Havana. Prior to that she had served in the medical corps, in the General Staff, and at the Military Technical School.

29. Margaret Randall, *Cuban Women Now: Interviews with Cuban Women* (Toronto: Women's Press, 1974), 139.

30. Mills, *Listen, Yankee*, 136.

31. In *Listen, Yankee*, Mills states that, during the time he was visiting, there were 250 student-volunteers from various countries in Europe and Latin America working at the school city, digging foundations and constructing the buildings. He quotes Rielo welcoming the volunteers saying, "We are so happy. We feel this is the climax of all our years of effort" (149).

32. In late 1959 Rielo married rebel soldier Rafael Cuadrado, and they had spent their honeymoon in the Sierra Maestra while completing their assigned tasks.

33. Matos, who had been one of the leading rebel chiefs in Oriente province during the war, was charged with treason and conspiring against the Revolutionary government and on December 1959 was sentenced to twenty years in the Presidio Modelo on the Isle of Pines. In *Listen, Yankee*, Mills names him as one of the "defectors"—along with Pedro Luis Díaz Lanz, Raúl Chibás Rivas, Miguel Ángel Quevedo, and Luis Conte Agüero—who deserted the Revolution and Cuba. But in the case of Matos, Mills admits: "That was the biggest blow" (55).

34. This point had previously been made to Mills by Elvira Escobar. See Interview 6 in Chapter 5.

35. Escalona is referring to the Frank País Second Front under the command of Raúl Castro in the Sierra Cristal mountains, about eighty kilometers northeast of Fidel Castro's Sierra Maestra area of operations. This is to be distinguished from the two independent guerrilla groups—also called Second Front—in the Sierra del Escambray of Las Villas province in central Cuba: the Second Front under the direction of the Directorio Revolucionario (Revolutionary Student Directorate, the militant rebel organization of university alumni and students), led by Faure Chomon,

and the Second Front headed by Eloy Gutiérrez Menoyo and the North American William Morgan.

36. I have relied almost exclusively on Arcocha's translation, given that Escalona's comments are largely inaudible on the recording. I have, however, made a few stylistic changes to Arcocha's interpreted syntax in order to make it more comprehensible to Anglophone readers.

37. The counterrevolutionary "aggressions" involved the various bombings and acts of sabotage committed on Cuba by the exiles and defectors.

38. Eusebio Mujal was secretary general of the Cuban Confederation of Workers (CTC), the central labor group, from 1947 to 1959, and engaged in the expulsion of Communist labor leaders.

39. Ordered by Batista under the code name "Christmas Gift," the Bloody Christmas Massacre, as it became known, took place during December 23–26, 1956, in several towns of Oriente province. The bodies of twenty-nine men and boys were left strewn throughout the countryside or left hanging from trees; all were tortured and shot in the back of the neck.

Chapter 5

1. C. Wright Mills, *Listen, Yankee: The Revolution in Cuba* (New York: Ballantine Books, 1960), 37.

2. Robert Taber attributes this phrase, which Taber defines as "the fear of losing status or the advantage that one had hoped to give one's children," to Stettmeier. Robert Taber, *M-26: Biography of a Revolution* (New York: Lyle Stuart, 1961), 330.

3. Stettmeier's insights were doubtless influenced by psychoanalytic theory, given that he taught the courses Psychology of the Normal and Abnormal Personality, Introduction to Psychoanalysis, and Psychological Methods in the Exploration of the Unconscious. See Asel Viguera-Moreno and Yisel González-González, "Acercamiento histórico a las prácticas psicológicas en la Universidad de Oriente durante el período prerrevolucionario (1947–1958)," *Santiago*, Special Issue (2012): 135–51.

4. C. Wright Mills, "On Latin America, the Left and the U.S.," *Evergreen Review* 5 (1961): 112.

5. Mills was requesting Castro's assistance in helping Stettmeier hire British historian E. P. Thompson, whom Mills was recommending for a teaching position at the university. Kathryn Mills with Pamela Mills, eds., *C. Wright Mills: Letters and Autobiographical Writings* (Berkeley: University of California Press, 2000), 315.

6. Literally, "injured ones," those who were hurt—financially, culturally, or politically—by the revolutionary process.

7. *Coup d'état, no! Revolution, yes!* Stettmeier is referring to a declaration made by Fidel Castro through Rebel Radio on January 1, 1959, from General Headquarters on the outskirts of Santiago de Cuba before taking the city. The transmission was made just hours after Batista had fled the country, and Castro was only days away from his triumphal entry into Havana. On taking the city, Castro proclaimed the victory of the Cuban Revolution and again gave the cry, *Golpe de estado, no! Revolucion, sí!*, from the balcony on Santiago de Cuba's city hall.

8. In part, Trotsky's theory of permanent revolution states that, after the revolution is successful and once their narrow self-interests are met, the bourgeoisie will turn to counterrevolutionary measures. It is therefore up to the workers and peasants to continue an uninterrupted process of revolution:

> The dictatorship of the proletariat which has risen to power as the leader of the democratic revolution is inevitably and, very quickly confronted with tasks, the fulfillment of which is bound up with deep inroads into the rights of bourgeois property. The democratic revolution grows over directly into the socialist revolution and thereby becomes a permanent revolution.

Leon Trotsky, *The Permanent Revolution* (Seattle: Red Letter Press, 2010), 312.

9. Stettmeier is referring to the corrupt prerevolutionary practice of appointing massive numbers of teachers, many of whom received full salaries but did not teach. On the "scandal of idle teachers" during the graft-ridden era of Ramon Grau in the 1940s, see Hugh Thomas, *Cuba, or The Pursuit of Freedom* (New York: Da Capo Press, 1998), 1133.

10. K. S. Karol explains this same point as follows: "What was at stake was not simply class privilege, but also old habits of thinking and deeply anchored beliefs and prejudices." *Guerrillas in Power: The Course of the Cuban Revolution*, trans. Arnold Pomerans (New York: Hill & Wang, 1970), 184.

11. Mills uses the terms "intellectual" and "intelligentsia," in this and the following interview, seemingly synonymously. In other writings he had previously used the phrase "cultural workmen" to refer to the intellectuals who influenced "the cultural apparatus," or "all those organizations and milieu in which artistic, intellectual, and scientific work goes on." See Mills, "The Man in the Middle," in *The Politics of Truth: The Selected Writings of C. Wright Mills*, ed. John H. Summers (New York: Oxford University Press, 2008), 175. "Cultural workers"—such as writers, editors, journalists, professors, artists, and scientists—had the power to shape images and ideas of reality and bring about progressive social change. See also Mills, "The Cultural Apparatus," in Summers, *The Politics of Truth*.

12. Mills, *Listen, Yankee*, 111.

13. Ibid., 90.

14. Interestingly, Castro did all of this for a long time—forty-nine years—until his retirement in 2008.

15. Stettmeier is referring to the sixteen articles serialized in the French daily newspaper *France-Soir* in June and July, 1960. The articles were later reprinted in Spanish in a volume titled *Sartre visita a Cuba* (Havana: Ediciones R, 1960) and in English as *Sartre on Cuba* (New York: Ballantine Books, 1961).

16. The Cuban poet Heberto Padilla, writing in *Revolución* in January 1961, stated that the French philosopher, during his visit, had analyzed the history and peculiarities of the Cubans "with more insight and sound judgment than had two generations of Cubans," as quoted in Duanel Díaz, "El fantasma de Sartre en Cuba," *Cuadernos Hispanoamericanos* 679 (2007): 98.

17. Mills titled chapter 6 of *Listen, Yankee*, "Revolutionary Euphoria."

18. Dwight D. Eisenhower, *Crusade in Europe* (New York: Doubleday, 1948).

19. Eisenhower had been president of Columbia University, 1948–1953, during the time Mills was on the faculty there.

20. Stettmeier is referring to the fact that he and his wife, Elvira Escobar, who was a high school teacher during the time in question, were living in a house outside Santiago de Cuba "up the mountain a way, in between the Batista army and the rebel soldiers." Mills, *Listen, Yankee*, 37. Indeed, Stettmeier and Escobar were living as quiet, respectable, middle-class citizens, owners of a medical clinic in Santiago, while also aiding the rebels through the underground support network.

21. Mills, *Listen, Yankee*, 37.

22. Taber, *M-26*, 88.

23. Jules Dubois, *Fidel Castro: Rebel-Liberator or Dictator?* (Indianapolis: The Bobbs-Merrill Company, 1959), 158.

24. The "History Will Absolve Me" speech that Castro made at his trial on October 16, 1953.

25. Perhaps so-called in reference to the Thirty-eighth Parallel, the pre-Korean War political boundary between North Korea and South Korea. In this sense, Escobar's house served as the demarcation between fighting forces: to the north, in the mountains, were the Fidelistas, to the south, the Batistianos.

26. This was the popular uprising in Santiago de Cuba led by Frank País. The uprising was timed to support the landing on Cuba's southeastern coast by Fidel Castro and his expeditionary force that had journeyed from Mexico with him on the *Granma*.

27. Frank País was shot on July 30, 1957, by the Santiago police.

28. The Agrarian Reform Law of 1959 and Decree-Law 135. In pre-Revolutionary Cuba fewer than 3,000 people owned more than 70 percent of the land. The Agrarian Reform Law gave land to the poverty-stricken peasants who worked it. Decree-Law 135, which was part of the urban reforms, introduced price control: it cut rents by 50 percent and sold all apartments to their tenants and reduced telephone and electricity rates.

29. A month before this interview took place, José Miró Cardona resigned his post as Cuban ambassador to Spain, rejecting Castro's government, and went into exile in October. In *Listen, Yankee*, Mills names several defectors, including Miró Cardona (incorrectly listing his previous post as "a former ambassador to the United States"), "with money in the banks all over" who "thought he should have been made the President of Cuba," 55.

30. At the time Roa was foreign minister of Cuba.

31. Raúl Roa Kourí had been instrumental in organizing Mills's stay in Cuba and was familiar with Mills's work, given that he had been a student at Columbia University.

32. The Partido Socialista Popular (PSP).

33. Escobar may here be referring to Paquito Rosales, the first Communist mayor (of Manzanillo) in Cuba in 1940.

34. The first soviets, or organs of popular power, were established in August 1933 by the Communist Party in various provincial sugar centers throughout the island.

35. In April 1959, Fidel Castro accepted an invitation from the American Society of Newspaper Editors to visit the United States. On that trip he also met with Vice

President Richard Nixon. His brother, Raúl, telephoned Fidel and told him that people in Cuba were accusing him of selling out to the Americans. See Robert E. Quirk, *Fidel Castro* (New York: W. W. Norton, 1993), 242. This may have been the reason why Escobar is saying that the immature young man became a communist.

36. The Servicio de Inteligencia Militar, or SIM, was a secretive military intelligence service created in 1934 for the purpose of monitoring the internal movements of the armed forces. After Batista's military coup in 1952 the SIM's function was expanded to include clandestine surveillance of all civilian activities.

37. *Sacerdote*, or priest. *Cura* is a mildly pejorative term. Mills expresses this sentiment in *Listen, Yankee* as follows: "The very word for 'clergy' used so frequently in Cuba is not a very good word" (62). Cuban anticlericalism was not anti-Catholicism, rather it had more to do with the fact that, of the approximately 1,000 priests on the island, about 800 were not Cuban at all; they were from Franco's Spain.

38. At some point during that same summer of 1960, Mills, in a series of autobiographical "letters" that he was preparing for a manuscript to be called *Contacting the Enemy*, wrote the following: "I was an Irish altar boy before I reached the age of consent, . . . I never revolted from it [Catholicism]; I never had to. For some reason, it never took." K. Mills with P. Mills, *C. Wright Mills*, 313. Sartre tells of a similar experience, of revolutionary leader Enrique Oltuski, who was Jewish, joining the 26th of July Movement "as a result of a religious crisis which alienated him from his family and himself." *Sartre on Cuba*, 54.

39. Rafael Trejo was the first student martyred in 1930 as a result of President Machado's repression.

40. Escobar's comments bear out the popular notion that Cubans "speak very highly of the revolutionary generation of the '30s, sadly of the hopeless generation that took over, and enthusiastically of the next, which rediscovered the path of victorious revolution under Castro." Karol, *Guerrillas in Power*, 109.

41. *Latifundista*, owner of a large estate. *Siquitrillada* was a popular term used after the Revolution to refer uniquely to the dispossessed situation of those whose large landholdings had been expropriated by the Castro government. It refers to the landowners having been financially ruined. Here Escobar uses the term as an adjective, "harmed." Arcocha has some difficulty translating the word for Mills but Escobar can be heard in the background explaining it as *rota* (broken) and *afectada* (affected).

42. C. Wright Mills, Clarence Senior, and Rose Kohn Goldsen, *The Puerto Rican Journey: New York's Newest Migrants* (New York: Harper and Bros., 1950).

43. Rose Kohn Goldsen, "Mills and the Profession of Sociology," in *The New Sociology: Essays in Social Science and Social Theory in Honor of C. Wright Mills*, ed. Irving Louis Horowitz (New York: Oxford University Press, 1964), 90.

44. Theodore Draper, *Castro's Revolution: Myths and Realities* (London: Thames and Hudson, 1962), 21.

45. Mills, *Listen, Yankee*, 48.

46. Leo Huberman and Paul M. Sweezy, *Cuba: Anatomy of a Revolution* (New York: Monthly Review Press, 1960), 127.

47. Thomas, *Cuba*, 1108–9.

48. For a description of the ranch, see Robert Taber, "Cuban Viewpoints: Kennedy and C. Wright Mills," *Fair Play*, September 2, 1960.

49. The Rousseau in question may have been the lawyer Enrique Rousseau, who later emigrated to the United States and, in 1969, married American socialite and fashion designer Lilly Pulitzer. Rousseau, who, as an exile, took part in the Bay of Pigs invasion, was so aristocratic that he "reportedly took a tent, cigars, and a houseboy" to the invasion. Barbara Marshall, "How Lilly Became Lilly!," *Palm Beach Post*, April 7, 2013, http://www.palmbeachpost.com/news/news/local/how-lilly-became-lilly/nXFdF/.

50. Sartre, *Sartre on Cuba*, 76.

51. The first answer Elba Batista gave, of being thirty-eight years old, was probably correct: she married at fourteen, was then married for nine years, and had been divorced fourteen years.

52. Arcocha translates this as, "She does not like to sit down."

53. Mills uses a word that is not quite accurate in Spanish. He means to refer to the ranch or farm. And rather than *rancho*, *finca*, or *granja*, he says *ranchera*.

54. Batista uses the slang word *pa'lante*, popular in some Caribbean Spanish-speaking countries. It is a shortened version of *para adelante*, which can be conveyed as "to move forward," "to go ahead," or "onward." At this point Arcocha explains to Mills that it is a difficult word to translate.

55. A distance of about ten kilometers.

56. Though Elba Batista was not a patient of Dr. Vallejo's, it is not surprising that she knew him. After working with the United Nations in 1945, caring for victims of World War II in Germany, Vallejo returned to Cuba and was made director of a hospital in Manzanillo, where he came up against the corrupt politics of the hospital administration. As a result, he opened his own clinic, La Caridad, where he took a social and humanitarian approach in the treatment of all patients, regardless of their ability to pay. At the end of 1956, he converted the clinic into a clandestine aid station where he attended to those wounded in the armed struggle against the dictatorship. The clinic was ransacked by Batista forces, and Vallejo subsequently joined the Rebel Army, providing medical services for the troops.

57. Mills is likely referring to Vallejo, who at the time was head of INRA in the province of Oriente.

58. The practice by INRA was that, when an estate like the Rousseau ranch was appropriated by the government, those who had an established record of employment there would become members of the new cooperative and continue their employment. So it is quite likely that Batista got her wish to remain in the house.

Chapter 6

1. C. Wright Mills, *The Power Elite* (New York: Oxford University Press, 1956), 18.

2. Jules Dubois, "Report on Latin America," *Chicago Sunday Tribune*, November 20, 1960, 16.

3. Though they may not have been able to name specific admirals, generals, and CEOs, the average Cuban was nevertheless much concerned about a military inva-

sion from the "Marines in Florida" and knew well that major U.S.-owned corporations (e.g., The United Fruit Company, the Nickel Processing Corporation, Bell Telephone Company, Chase Manhattan Bank, the Moa Mining Company, Texaco, etc.) had, for decades, exploited Cuban labor and resources. Thus, for most Cubans, the U.S. power elite and Yankee imperialism were one and the same.

4. Tom Hayden, *Listen, Yankee! Why Cuba Matters* (New York: Seven Stories Press, 2015), 35.

5. For journalist Lee Lockwood's detailed, personal account of the many difficulties he experienced in obtaining an interview with Fidel Castro, who was extraordinarily busy and continuously on the move, see *Castro's Cuba, Cuba's Fidel* (New York: Vintage Books, 1969).

6. Michel Foucault, *Discipline and Punish: The Birth of the Prison*, trans. Alan Sheridan (New York: Vintage, 1995), 201.

7. In *Listen, Yankee*, Mills estimates that the soldiers had already planted 600,000 eucalyptus trees, with a total of 5 million expected by the end of the year. *Listen, Yankee: The Revolution in Cuba* (New York: Ballantine Books, 1960).

8. The Isle of Pines was renamed the Isle of Youth in 1978.

9. In *Listen, Yankee*, Mills changes this observation to: "The big ideological fight going on in the Isle of Pines is between eucalyptus trees and pangola grass" (p. 86).

10. In *Listen, Yankee*, Mills reproduces this line as: "If you hear the Isle of Pines is taken, Fidel, know that there is not one of us left alive" (p. 70). The Cubans were in on the well-known secret that the CIA was training an invasion force in Guatemala, and because the Isle of Pines is situated directly in the route of a military operation launched from that country, they believed the Isle would be the first target. The Bay of Pigs invasion occurred eight months later, not on the Isle of Pines, but some 200 kilometers away, at Playa Girón. Just prior to the CIA invasion, however, a Cuban Navy Patrol Escort ship was bombed and destroyed in the Isle of Pines by a U.S. attack aircraft.

11. Lockwood, *Castro's Cuba*, 71–72. Another description of what a conversation with Castro was like is the following by K. S. Karol:

> Fidel finds it difficult to sit still while he speaks. He moves about all the time, gets up, takes a few steps, sits down, stalks back and forth, as if every argument were a kind of hand-to-hand struggle with a wily opponent. His expressive brown eyes remain fixed on his interlocutor and emphasize his words. He uses all the skills of the experienced lawyer—he takes advantage of the slightest weakness, sets traps, interrupts at just the right moment, keeps the initiative all the time. But he does it all so ingenuously, that few people can doubt his sincerity and candor....
>
> Fidel invariably monopolizes conversations, not because he refuses to listen, but simply because he thinks aloud and likes to answer his own questions. In the end, however, he always manages to get to the heart of the problem. His moral integrity, his sense of honor, his attachment to the simple virtues, invariably lead him there. But he makes his point by way of long monologues which, though fascinating to follow, are sometimes rather involved.

Guerrillas in Power: The Course of the Cuban Revolution, trans. Arnold Pomerans (New York: Hill & Wang, 1970), 479–80.

12. See the chapter "A Day in the Country with Fidel" in Jean-Paul Sartre, *Sartre on Cuba* (New York: Ballantine Books, 1961).

13. Sartre recounts the humorous story of a *campesino* throwing himself on the hood of Castro's car, admonishing him for sitting in front: "What are you doing in the front of this car? . . . Go sit in the back with Celia and do me the favor of seating all these people [Sartre and Beauvoir] who are lounging in the rear in the front. . . . Drive around with them as much as you want, but if someone has to die, it might as well be them." *Sartre on Cuba*, 130.

14. Leo Huberman and Paul M. Sweezy, *Cuba: Anatomy of a Revolution* (New York: Monthly Review Press, 1960), 177.

15. Karol, *Guerrillas in Power*, 487.

16. It is not known why Mills did not electronically record the conversation, but a tape recorder would likely have been a distraction, as it was when Lee Lockwood interviewed Castro a few years later. See Lockwood, *Castro's Cuba*, 67.

17. "The Causes of C. Wright Mills," KPFA broadcast, October 1, 1962, Pacifica Radio Archives, Archive number BB0281b.

18. C. Wright Mills, *Escucha, yanqui: La revolución en Cuba*, trans. Julieta Campos and Enrique González Pedrero (Mexico City: Fondo de Cultura Económica, 1961), 240.

19. Indeed, the following year, 1961, saw the second-largest sugar-cane harvest (approximately 7 million tons) in Cuban history.

20. According to Robert Taber, Mills's interviews with revolutionary leaders confirmed that Cuba had passed the point of economic crisis and that the Revolution was "over the hump" economically, due to the trade treaties with China, the USSR, and other countries. Taber, *M-26: Biography of a Revolution* (New York: Lyle Stuart, 1961), 330. The United States, in cutting the Cuban sugar quota, made way for other sugar-producing nations to fill the gap, thus leaving Cuban sugar in control of the world market. What is more, reports Taber, expropriation of U.S.-owned mills restored to Cuba 40 percent of its sugar production, an outcome that more than made up for any losses that resulted from the difference between the U.S. and the world price of sugar. Robert Taber, "Cuban Viewpoints: Kennedy and C. Wright Mills," *Fair Play*, September 2, 1960, 3. "So the Yankee cut in the Cuban sugar quota is going to turn out to be of benefit to us." Mills, *Listen, Yankee*, 75.

21. Enrique Oltuski was at that time director of Organization of the Department of Industrialization of INRA.

22. While the Fidelistas were in the Sierra Maestra they confiscated some herds and distributed them among the *campesinos*. They gave one cow to each *campesino* family, and before long practically all the cows had been eaten rather than kept for milk. This experience of the *campesino*'s preference for the immediate benefit of being able to eat the cow rather than for the longer-range value of having milk, Castro told Lee Lockwood six years after his conversation with Mills, "naturally fortified my conviction that the land of the *latifundistas* should not be divided but should be organized into cooperatives." Lockwood, *Castro's Cuba*, 97.

23. Hans Gerth and C. Wright Mills, *Character and Social Structure: The Psychology of Social Institutions* (New York: Harcourt, Brace, 1953), 404.

24. This scenario is pieced together from accounts given by Yepe and Arcocha in two sources, respectively, Hayden, *Listen, Yankee!*, 37; and "The Causes of C. Wright Mills." The "inspection tour" is speculative, but probable, given that this is how Huberman and Sweezy described their experience with Castro at Pinar del Río just a few weeks after Mills had spent time with him there. See Huberman and Sweezy, *Cuba*, 176, 197.

25. Mike Forrest Keen, *Stalking the Sociological Imagination: J. Edgar Hoover's FBI Surveillance of American Sociology* (Westport, Conn.: Greenwood Press, 1999), 175. The seminar never took place.

26. Kathryn Mills with Pamela Mills, eds., *C. Wright Mills: Letters and Autobiographical Writings* (Berkeley: University of California Press, 2000), 324.

27. Karol, *Guerrillas in Power*, 477. What is more, Mills apparently had sufficient clout in Havana to help Karol gain a personal interview with Ché Guevara. John H. Summers, "The Epigone's Embrace, Part II: C. Wright Mills and the New Left," *Left History* 12 (2008): 114.

28. Mills's experiences at Belic as detailed here are based on inference. It is, however, very likely that something similar to this occurred, based on how Huberman and Sweezy describe the tour of Belic they took several weeks later, with Vallejo as their guide. See Huberman and Sweezy, *Cuba*, 194.

29. Mills, *Listen, Yankee*, 180.

30. Karl E. Meyer and Tad Szulc, *The Cuban Invasion: The Chronicle of a Disaster* (New York: Praeger, 1962), 98.

31. Irving Louis Horowitz, *C. Wright Mills: An American Utopian* (New York: Free Press, 1983), 291.

32. Mills, *Listen, Yankee*, 182.

33. Juan Arcocha gives as the quintessential example of Castro's cult of personality the sixteen-year-old militiaman, mortally wounded in the bombardment of the Bay of Pigs, who, just before dying, wrote on a door the name "FIDEL" with a finger that the teen had dipped in his own blood. Arcocha, *Fidel Castro en rompecabezas* (Madrid: Ediciones R, 1973), 56. Ray Brennan, in *Castro, Cuba, and Justice* (New York: Doubleday, 1959), 264, refers to Castro as "the Rebel messiah."

34. *Sartre on Cuba*, 96.

35. Gerth and Mills, *Character and Social Structure*, 447.

36. C. Wright Mills, Interview 7 (see chapter 5 of this volume).

37. Max Weber, *From Max Weber: Essays in Sociology*, ed. Hans Gerth and C. Wright Mills (New York: Oxford University Press, 1946), 296.

38. Taber, *M-26*, 337.

39. For Gerth and Mills, "person" refers to the human being as a player of roles that involve reference to emotions, perceptions, and purposes. By "images" they refer to "master symbols" that consist of moral figures, sacred emblems, and legal formulae. Gerth and Mills, *Character and Social Structure*, 43, 276–77, 405. According to Huberman and Sweezy, "Like many another social revolution before it, the Cuban Revolution has developed its own symbolism—the beard and long hair of the rebel soldier, the peasant with raised machete, the transformation of fortresses into schools,

such slogans as 'Liberty or Death' and 'Revolution Means to Construct.'" Huberman and Sweezy, *Cuba*, 133. As for the image that the Cuban people created of their leader early in the Revolution, it was that of a redemptive figure, of a "spiritual Fidel." See Robert E. Quirk, *Fidel Castro* (New York: W. W. Norton, 1993), 255.

40. Gerth and Mills, *Character and Social Structure*, 425–26.

41. Arcocha, *Fidel Castro*, 9. Arcocha also compares Castro with Achilles, Robin Hood, and Hitler.

42. Tom Hayden believes this was close to the case: "Fidel was something of a ghost writer for C. Wright Mills's 1960 book." Hayden, *Listen, Yankee!*, 88.

43. Arcocha, *Fidel Castro*, 22.

44. Juan Arcocha, "El viaje de Sartre," in *La Habana, 1952–1961: El final de un mundo, el principio de una ilusión*, ed. Jacobo Machover (Madrid: Alianza Editorial, 1995), 235.

45. K. Mills with P. Mills, *C. Wright Mills*, 330.

46. C. Wright Mills, *Escucha, yanqui*, 241. Emphasis added.

47. Daniel Geary, *Radical Ambition: C. Wright Mills, the Left, and American Social Thought* (Berkeley: University of California Press, 2009), 213.

48. Keen, *Stalking*, 183. This comment was made by an FBI informant and may be of questionable reliability.

49. Mills, *Listen, Yankee*, 95. Emphasis in original. On the topic of wrong predictions, see David Caute, *The Fellow-Travelers: Intellectual Friends of Communism* (New Haven, Conn.: Yale University Press, 1988), 407. The Russians did, of course, resort to military means when, in October 1962, they deployed ballistic missiles on the Caribbean island, thus causing the so-called Cuban Missile Crisis.

50. "Cuba Mourns Professor Mills," *New York Times*, March 24, 1962, 25.

51. "The Causes of C. Wright Mills."

Chapter 7

1. Van Gosse, *Where the Boys Are: Cuba, Cold War America and the Making of the New Left* (New York: Verso, 1993), 176.

2. Irving Louis Horowitz, *C. Wright Mills: An American Utopian* (New York: Free Press, 1983), 300.

3. Saul Landau, "C. Wright Mills: The Last Six Months," *Ramparts*, August 1965, 47. According to Landau, Mills read the first draft to him in Havana.

4. Carleton Beals to Ian Ballantine, September 25, 1960, box 4S17, folder "Listen, Yankee, Letters and Publicity, 1960–1961," Charles Wright Mills Papers, 1934–1965, Dolph Briscoe Center for American History, the University of Texas at Austin.

5. Letter from Barbara B. Collins to C. Wright Mills, November 11, 1960, box 4S17, folder "Listen, Yankee, Letters and Publicity, 1960–1961," Charles Wright Mills Papers.

6. According to Todd F. Tietchen, *Listen, Yankee* might be regarded as a booklength Cubalogue. An explicitly political subgenre of travel narrative, the "Cubalogue" is a politically engaged form of literary reportage of early revolutionary events in Cuba, primarily (but not exclusively) identified with the writers and artists associated with the Beat Generation. See Todd F. Tietchen, *The Cubalogues: Beat Writers in Revolutionary Havana* (Gainesville: University Press of Florida, 2010).

7. Peter Hulme, "Seeing for Themselves: U.S. Travel Writers in Early Revolutionary Cuba," in *Politics, Identity, and Mobility in Travel Writing*, ed. Miguel A. Cabañas et al. (New York: Routledge, 2016), 204.

8. Ibid., 208.

9. *Listen, Yankee* was written during Mills's epistolary-polemical period, when he was using the letter format to sermonize to a mass audience. See, for example, "Pagan Letter to the Christian Clergy," in *The Causes of World War Three* (New York: Simon & Schuster, 1958); "Letter to the New Left," which appeared in *New Left Review* 5 (September–October 1960); and his autobiographical letters written for the unpublished manuscript of *Contacting the Enemy*, which was supposed to be a volume consisting of a set of letters addressed to an imaginary Soviet colleague. Gosse contends that *Listen, Yankee* would have fared better as part of Mills's oeuvre had it been written in the academic third-person with proper scholarly citation. Gosse, *Where the Boys Are*, 179.

10. Horowitz, *C. Wright Mills*, 293.

11. C. Wright Mills, *Listen, Yankee: The Revolution in Cuba* (New York: Ballantine Books, 1960), 12.

12. Hans H. Gerth and C. Wright Mills, *Character and Social Structure: The Psychology of Social Institutions* (New York: Harcourt, Brace, 1953), 292.

13. K. S. Karol, *Guerrillas in Power: The Course of the Cuban Revolution*, trans. Arnold Pomerans (New York: Hill & Wang, 1970), 10.

14. Mills, *Listen, Yankee*, 151–52.

15. Ibid., 30.

16. One concession to both the English and the Spanish spellings of the word is the not uncommon "Yanki." This hybrid rendition, for example, is the title of a documentary about Cuba that aired as an episode, on December 8, 1960, for the ABC network's *Close-Up* series, "Yanki, No!"

17. Quoted in Jack Newfield, *A Prophetic Minority* (New York: New American Library, 1966), 78.

18. Jean-Paul Sartre, *Sartre on Cuba* (New York: Ballantine Books, 1961), 7.

19. Theodore Draper, *Castro's Revolution: Myths and Realities* (London: Thames and Hudson, 1962), 8.

20. Robert Taber, "Cuban Viewpoints: Kennedy and C. Wright Mills," *Fair Play*, September 2, 1960, 4.

21. Tom Hayden contends that the title *Listen, Yankee* was, at bottom, "a complaint that Cuba could not receive a fair hearing as long as the United States officials assumed themselves superior in the relationship, able to bend Cuba to America's will." Hayden, *Listen, Yankee! Why Cuba Matters* (New York: Seven Stories Press, 2015), 224–25.

22. Mills, *Listen, Yankee*, 158.

23. Michael J. Casey, *Che's Afterlife: The Legacy of an Image* (New York: Vintage Books, 2009).

24. Jean-Paul Sartre, *Sartre visita a Cuba* (Havana: Ediciones R, 1960), 25–26.

25. Juan Arcocha, "El viaje de Sartre," in *La Habana, 1952–1961: El final de un mundo, el principio de una ilusión*, ed. Jacobo Machover (Madrid: Alianza Editorial, 1995), 231.

26. Sartre describes the general mood in the aftermath of the *La Coubre* sabotage as anguish, not anger, *Sartre on Cuba*, 145.

27. Draper, *Castro's Revolution*, 8–9.

28. See Rafael Rojas, "El aparato cultural del imperio: C. Wright Mills, la Revolución Cubana y la Nueva Izquierda," *Perfiles Latinoamericanos* 44 (2014): 17. Rojas contends that certain passages in *Listen, Yankee* clearly demonstrate that it is the Cuban leaders who are speaking, not their "New York translator," as in when, for instance, Mills quotes the phrase of the Cuban anthropologist Fernando Ortiz—this "thick broth of civilization which bubbles on the Caribbean fire"—not in reference to the concept of transculturation as Ortiz intended it, but to underscore the nationalist vision of the island as a "major center of world affairs." Mills, *Listen, Yankee*, 160.

29. Kathryn, Mills's five-year-old daughter, can be heard playing in the background, and at times various conversations by several people are also taking place simultaneously.

30. Kathryn Mills with Pamela Mills, eds., *C. Wright Mills: Letters and Autobiographical Writings* (Berkeley: University of California Press, 2000), 101.

31. Mills, *Listen, Yankee*, 8.

32. The photograph, in the style of a sort of social realism, is composed so that it makes the lone white-collar worker, the new little man, look dramatically estranged from community and society—and, in the sense of Marx, alienated from his work. Although he seems to be striding hurriedly, with a sense of purpose, the figure is just a small cog in a vast business machinery. He appears to be bearing the weight of the company, the organization, and the bureaucracy (illustrated by the granite base and massive Ionic columns that form the building's facade) for which he works. The imposing edifice creates a sense of oppression over the human figure. See A. Javier Treviño, "C. Wright Mills As Designer: Personal Practice and Two Public Talks," *American Sociologist* 45 (2015): 342.

33. K. Mills with P. Mills, *C. Wright Mills*, 112.

34. Ibid., 113.

35. Had he finished the sentence, Mills would perhaps have said something like, "Now I've got to go down and, you know, interview the revolutionaries in Cuba and take photos."

36. Mills had entertained the idea of a script—perhaps also in the form of a series of letters—since at least in early 1958, when he was considering writing a "play-novel-movie script" titled "Unmailed Letters to a Fey Tiger" or "The Fey Tiger," with a rather odd theme: going goat hunting in Yugoslavia with Marshal Tito. See K. Mills with P. Mills, *C. Wright Mills*, 262, 330.

37. A cartoonist and playwright, Herb Gardner (1934–2003) was best known for his 1962 play, *A Thousand Clowns*, which was adapted to film in 1965. He was also the creator and illustrator of the syndicated comic strip *The Nebbishes*, which ran in newspapers from 1959 to 1961.

38. Mills may be referring to the publisher Little, Brown.

39. Clare Barnes Jr., *The Political Zoo* (Garden City, NY: Doubleday, 1952).

40. Mills and Ballantine were probably thinking of *White Collar Zoo*, a 1949 book, also by Clare Barnes Jr., that featured animal photos with humorous captions.

41. Ballantine is referring to the Democratic National Convention held in Chicago in July 1952.

42. K. Mills with P. Mills, *C. Wright Mills*, 263.

43. Mike Forrest Keen, *Stalking the Sociological Imagination: J. Edgar Hoover's FBI Surveillance of American Sociology* (Westport, Conn.: Greenwood Press, 1999), 175. The British publisher Secker and Warburg released it in hardback under the title *Castro's Cuba* in March 1961.

44. K. Mills with P. Mills, *C. Wright Mills*, 263–64. It will be recalled from chapter 1 that Dubois's *Fidel Castro* and Huberman and Sweezy's *Cuba* were also written fast and produced fast.

45. "The Causes of C. Wright Mills," KPFA broadcast October 1, 1962, Pacifica Radio Archives, Archive number BB0281b.

46. E. P. Thompson, *E. P. Thompson and the Making of the New Left: Essays and Polemics*, ed. Cal Winslow (New York: Monthly Press Review, 2014), 222.

47. Robert E. Quirk, *Fidel Castro* (New York: W. W. Norton, 1993), 339.

48. Karol, *Guerrillas in Power*, 7. A farcical and flamboyant depiction of the Cuban delegation's stay at the Hotel Theresa is portrayed in Alfred Hitchcock's 1969 film *Topaz*.

49. Michael B. Conant, "C. Wright Mills Talks, Yankee Listens," *Columbia Owl*, October 12, 1960, 1, 4.

50. K. Mills with P. Mills, *C. Wright Mills*, 330.

51. Herbert J. Gans, "Best-Sellers by American Sociologists: An Exploratory Study," in *Required Reading: Sociology's Most Influential Books*, ed. Dan Clawson (Amherst: University of Massachusetts Press, 1998), 19–27. *Listen, Yankee* joins five other titles in Gans's numerical interval of 499,999 to 400,000 book sales: Richard Senett, *The Fall of Public Man* (1976); William Ryan, *Blaming the Victim* (1971); Robert N. Bellah et al., *Habits of the Heart* (1985); Seymour Martin Lipset, *Political Man* (1960); and Lilian B. Rubin, *Worlds of Pain* (1976).

52. Gosse, *Where the Boys Are*, 176.

53. Richard E. Welch, *Response to Revolution: The United States and the Cuban Revolution, 1959–1961* (Chapel Hill: University of North Carolina Press, 1985), 151.

54. John H. Summers, "The Epigone's Embrace, Part II: C. Wright Mills and the New Left," *Left History* 12 (2008): 94. Ironically, as Rafael Rojas notes, *Listen, Yankee* has never been published in Cuba. "Charles Wright Mills y otoros peregrinos," *El País*, April 15, 2007.

55. E-mail communication from Raúl Roa Kourí on January 27, 2016.

56. C. Wright Mills, "'Listen Yankee': The Cuban Case against the United States," *Harper's Magazine*, December 1960, 31–37. The Cuban weekly magazine *Bohemia* published a Spanish translation of the *Harper's* excerpt in its issue of September 11, 1960.

57. *Listen, Yankee* was frequently reviewed in juxtaposition with Nathaniel Weyl's *Red Star over Cuba* (1961), where he argues that Fidel Castro had been a Soviet agent since 1948.

58. Lowry Nelson, "Review of *Listen, Yankee*," *Annals of the American Academy of Political and Social Science* 336 (1961): 191.

59. Henry F. Mins, "A Budget of Books on Cuba," *Science and Society* 25 (1961): 344.

60. Fredrick B. Pike, "United States Military Aid and Policies and Cuba," *Review of Politics* 23 (1961): 417.

61. Jules Dubois, "Report on Latin America," *Chicago Sunday Tribune*, November 20, 1960, 16. The Soviet authorities did prohibit publication of an article by Mills in *Amerika*. It was later published under the title "The Sociology of Mass Media and Public Opinion," in *Power, Politics, and People: The Collected Essays of C. Wright Mills*, ed. Irving Louis Horowitz (New York: Oxford University Press, 1963). Mills was more charitable toward Dubois's *Fidel Castro: Rebel-Liberator or Dictator?*, recommending it, in *Listen, Yankee*, as an informative book on the Cuban Revolution.

62. Jules Dubois, "Apologia for Castro," *Saturday Review*, December 17, 1960, 36. *Listen, Yankee* has yet to be translated into Russian. The only "Soviet bloc language" in which it has appeared is Polish.

63. Fernando Benítez et al., "Letter to the Editor: Aftermath of Revolution," *Saturday Review*, January 21, 1961, 49.

64. Fermín Peinado, *Beware, Yankee: The Revolution in Cuba* (Miami, 1961).

65. Peinado, who had been the dean of the Law School at the University of Oriente, where he taught political theory and philosophy of law, was a conservative Catholic living in Miami. It is not known why he opted to critique the excerpted piece in *Harper's* rather than the full work, *Listen, Yankee*.

66. Peinado was correct on this last point: an official news agency, the Prensa Latina, did exist in Cuba, a fact that Mills ignored.

67. On this encounter, see Hugh Thomas, *Cuba, or The Pursuit of Freedom* (New York: Da Capo Press, 1998), 803.

68. *Harper's Magazine*, February, 1961, 6.

69. Ibid.

70. "Dear Richard: Here is a quote you may use as you wish," letter dated March 16, 1961, Box 4B379, folder "Theory of Cuban Revolution," Charles Wright Mills Papers, 1934–1965.

71. The ADA represented the traditional liberal Democrats; it was "instinctively anticommunist and pro-Kennedy" and "supported the administration's Cuba policy" of regime change. Hayden, *Listen, Yankee!*, 54.

72. Louis B. Schwartz to C. Wright Mills, November 22, 1960, Box 4S17, folder "Listen, Yankee, Letters and Publicity, 1960–1961," Charles Wright Mills Papers, 1934–1965.

73. "The Causes of C. Wright Mills," KPFA broadcast October 1, 1962, Pacifica Radio Archives, Archive number BB0281b.

74. Eleanor Roosevelt, "New Look at Cuba," *New York Post*, December 14, 1960, 43.

75. Mills, the Cubans, and Eleanor Roosevelt were well acquainted with the CIA's engineered coup d'état of the government of Guatemalan President Jacobo Árbenz six years before, in 1954 (and which Ché Guevara, being in Guatemala at the time, experienced directly). Five years later, in 1965, fearing "a second Cuba" in the Dominican Republic, the U.S. Marines invaded that country. U.S. military intervention and CIA involvement, intended to destabilize socialist governments throughout the Western Hemisphere, would continue for the next three decades, in Chile (1973), Nicaragua (1979–1990), and Grenada (1983).

76. Jean Daniel, "Unofficial Envoy: An Historic Report from Two Capitals," *The New Republic*, December 14, 1963, 17.

77. The Fondo had previously issued the Spanish translations of *The Power Elite* in 1957 and, later, *The Sociological Imagination* in 1961.

78. Quoted in Horowitz, *C. Wright Mills*, 297.

79. Gerardo Ochoa Sandy, *80 años, las batallas culturales del fondo*, Kindle ed. (Mexico City: Nieve de Chamoy, 2014), n.p. The Mexican government also took issue with Fondo's publication of Oscar Lewis's *The Children of Sánchez*.

80. Fuentes dedicated his 1962 novel, *The Death of Artemio Cruz*, "To C. Wright Mills. True Voice of the United States of America. Friend and companion in Latin America's struggle." Another book dedicated "To the Memory of C. Wright Mills" was by his friend Ralph Miliband, *The State in Capitalist Society* (1969).

81. K. Mills with P. Mills, *C. Wright Mills*, 318.

82. Quoted in James W. Wilke and Edna Monzón Wilke, *Frente a la revolución Mexicana: 17 protagonistas de la etapa constructiva* (Mexico City: Universidad Autónoma Metropolitana, 1995), 1: 195.

83. Ibid., 389. According to Rojas, Fondo paid Mills more than 10,000 Mexican pesos, or about 800 U.S. dollars in 1961, see Rafael Rojas, *Fighting over Fidel: The New York Intellectuals and the Cuban Revolution* (Princeton, N.J.: Princeton University Press, 2016), 139.

84. Ochoa Sandy, *80 años*, n.p.

85. Landau, "C. Wright Mills," 48.

86. C. Wright Mills and Saul Landau, "The House That Jack Must Build: Modest Proposals for Patriotic Americans," *London Tribune*, May 19, 1961, 5.

87. As quoted in Rojas, *Fighting over Fidel*, 139.

88. Until "Escucha otra vez, yanqui" is translated into English, appraisal of Mills's views on the Bay of Pigs will remain limited to the Spanish-reading public.

89. A week after the invasion, Miró Cardona was featured on the cover of *Time* magazine (April 28, 1961) under the caption "The Cuban Disaster."

90. Mills does not provide a source for these percentages, and pre-invasion figures concerning Cubans' attitudes toward the Revolution vary wildly depending on whether the sources giving them endorse or oppose Castro. For example, Jules Dubois wrote in December of 1960 that "the most reliable estimates" (whose source he does not give) "indicate that the Castro popularity index today does not exceed 30 percent throughout the country and that the decline is steady." Dubois, "Apologia for Castro," 36. In February 1961, Fermín Peinado stated that Castro had "barely 20 percent" of the popular vote. Peinado, *Beware, Yankee*, 29. Perhaps the most reliable, and creditable, account of the Cuban peoples' attitudes toward the Castro regime is from a public opinion survey conducted during the late spring of 1960 by Lloyd A. Free, director of the Institute for International Social Research at Princeton University. Free found that about 10 percent of urban Cubans opposed and 86 percent supported the Castro government. Lloyd A. Free, *Attitudes of the Cuban People toward the Castro Regime* (Princeton, N.J.: Institute for International Social Research, 1960). Mills's figures of revolutionary support are closer to those of Free's. Free's report was sent to the National Security Council, but it was not read by Kennedy's advisors

(who generally believed that the mass of the Cuban people would rise up in deposing Castro) until *after* the Bay of Pigs fiasco.

91. The U.S. State Department *White Paper on Cuba* insists that because Cuba is within "the United States' sphere of influence" it must therefore "sever its links with the international Communist movement" (Department of State Publication 7171, Inter-American Series 66, April 3, 1961). In his volume, republished as *Castro's Revolution*, Draper blasts Mills for having "succeeded brilliantly" as "a front man for the Castro propaganda machine." *Castro's Revolution*, 8.

92. The Yankees were indeed slow to listen. It took over half a century for the U.S. government, under President Barack Obama, to normalize full diplomatic relations with Cuba in 2014.

93. Dan Wakefield, "Introduction," in K. Mills with and P. Mills, *C. Wright Mills*, 13.

94. Harvey Swados, "C. Wright Mills: A Personal Memoir," *Dissent* 10 (1963): 42.

95. Rojas, *Fighting over Fidel*, 11.

96. Rojas, "El aparato cultural del imperio," 27.

Chapter 8

1. James Miller, *Democracy Is in the Streets: From Port Huron to the Siege of Chicago* (New York: Simon & Schuster, 1987), 79.

2. Robert Taber, "Castro's Cuba," *The Nation*, January 23, 1960, 64. Emphasis in original.

3. Jules Dubois, *Fidel Castro: Rebel-Liberator or Dictator?* (Indianapolis: The Bobbs Merrill Company, 1959), 259.

4. Mike Forrest Keen, *Stalking the Sociological Imagination: J. Edgar Hoover's FBI Surveillance of American Sociology* (Westport, Conn.: Greenwood Press, 1999), 174. Mills had come under investigation by the FBI at least as early as 1959, when a confidential informant (perhaps "T-1") told the Washington, D.C., field office that Mills wanted to travel to the Soviet Union. See "C. Wright Mills FBI File," Shamus Khan, accessed December 11, 2014, https://scatter.files.wordpress.com/2012/08/c-wright-mills-fbi-file.pdf.

5. Keen, *Stalking*, 175.

6. Ibid., 177.

7. Ibid., 175–76.

8. Kathryn Mills with Pamela Mills, eds., *C. Wright Mills: Letters and Autobiographical Writings* (Berkeley: University of California Press, 2000), 317.

9. Ibid., 319.

10. Arnold Abrams, "C. Wright Mills: Controversial Figure in Conforming Society," *Columbia Daily Spectator*, November 29, 1960, 3.

11. *The Militant*, May 1, 1961, 4.

12. K. Mills with P. Mills, *C. Wright Mills*, 319.

13. Carlos Fuentes, *Casa con dos puertas* (Mexico: Joaquin Mortiz, 1970), 103.

14. The most notorious of the Batista henchmen, Masferrer had founded Los Tigres, his personal "army" of 2,000 men, to ruthlessly suppress the dictator's critics.

He fled Cuba on the victory of the Revolution and settled in Miami, where, with Mafia members, he plotted several unsuccessful attempts to assassinate Fidel Castro. Masferrer was killed, by Cuban exiles, by a car bomb in Miami in 1975. "It would be an understatement to say that Masferrer was to Oriente what Capone had been to Chicago." Robert Taber, *M-26: Biography of a Revolution* (New York: Lyle Stuart, 1961), 82.

15. Mills owned several firearms, including a 30-30 Winchester, a .22 rifle, and a semiautomatic M1 carbine.

16. Keen, *Stalking*, 179.

17. Jules Dubois, "Leftwing U.S. Prof Plumps for Fidel in Book," *Omaha World-Herald*, November 27, 1960, n.p.

18. "C. Wright Mills FBI File," Shamus Khan.

19. Dan Wakefield, "Introduction," in K. Mills with P. Mills, *C. Wright Mills*, 13.

20. Van Gosse, *Where the Boys Are: Cuba, Cold War America and the Making of the New Left* (New York: Verso, 1993), 181. One episode of *The Nation's Future*, broadcast two weeks before Mills and Berle were scheduled to appear, had featured Martin Luther King Jr. debating segregationist and newspaper editor James J. Kilpatrick.

21. Karl E. Meyer and Tad Szulc, *The Cuban Invasion: The Chronicle of a Disaster* (New York: Praeger, 1962), 101.

22. "TV Key Previews," *New York Journal-American*, December 10, 1960, n.p.

23. Raymond Lowery, "Goings On," *News & Observer* (Raleigh, N.C.), December 10, 1960, n.p.

24. "Miamians to Join TV Debate," *Miami Herald*, December 9, 1960, n.p.

25. Wakefield, "Introduction," 13.

26. Abrams, "C. Wright Mills," 3.

27. Irving Louis Horowitz, *C. Wright Mills: An American Utopian* (New York: Free Press, 1983), 300.

28. "Letter from Shapiro to Mills" dated November 28, 1960. Box 4B379, folder "Kennedy and Latin America, 1961," Charles Wright Mills Papers, 1934–1965, Dolph Briscoe Center for American History, the University of Texas at Austin.

29. "The Causes of C. Wright Mills," KPFA broadcast, October 1, 1962, Pacifica Radio Archives, Archive number BB0281b.

30. Adolf A. Berle, *Navigating the Rapids, 1918–1971*, ed. Beatrice Bishop Berle and Travis Beal Jacobs (New York: Harcourt Brace Jovanovich, 1973), 720–21.

31. K. Mills with P. Mills, *C. Wright Mills*, 320.

32. Ibid., 318.

33. Saul Landau, "C. Wright Mills: The Last Six Months," *Ramparts*, August 1965, 47.

34. Ibid. Representative Porter, a liberal Democrat from Oregon, was likely called in as Mills's replacement because he, along with labor activist Robert J. Alexander, had just completed *The Struggle for Democracy in Latin America*, a book that criticized the United States for supporting dictators like Batista, but that also criticized Castro for his pro-Communist political policies and for not allowing free elections in Cuba. In March 1958 he spoke before Congress against the continued shipment from the United States of lethal weapons to Batista. Porter, a sociology student at Harvard in

the 1940s, had been a teaching assistant to Talcott Parsons. Both Parsons and Porter had been active at Harvard in opposing Nazism in Europe. See Uta Gerhardt, *Talcott Parsons: An Intellectual Biography* (New York: Cambridge University Press, 2002), 110.

35. K. Mills with P. Mills, *C. Wright Mills*, 324.

36. Ira S. Youdovin, "$50 Million Suit is Filed against Mills," *Columbia Daily Spectator*, February 13, 1961, 1.

37. Hugh Thomas, *Cuba, or The Pursuit of Freedom* (New York: Da Capo Press, 1998), 1263.

38. Richard Schweid, *Che's Chevrolet, Fidel's Oldsmobile: On the Road in Cuba* (Chapel Hill: University of North Carolina Press, 2004), 164.

39. T. J. English, *Havana Nocturne: How the Mob Owned Cuba and Then Lost It to the Revolution* (New York: Morrow, 2007), 101.

40. K. S. Karol, *Guerrillas in Power: The Course of the Cuban Revolution*, trans. Arnold Pomerans (New York: Hill and Wang, 1970), 11.

41. K. Mills with P. Mills, *C. Wright Mills*, 326.

42. Ibid., 328.

43. Simone de Beauvoir, *Force of Circumstance*, trans. Richard Howard (New York: G. P. Putnam, 1965), 589–90. Escalante was one of the "old-guard Communists" dating back to the 1930s. He had been editor of *Hoy*, the official newspaper of the Cuban Communist Party. He was national organizer of the Integrated Revolutionary Organizations (ORI) and in 1962 was publicly denounced by Castro for sectarianism and for being unduly loyal to Moscow. In the late 1960s Escalante established the "microfaction," a counterrevolutionary movement of the Cuban Communist Party, for which he was tried for treason and imprisoned. Upon his release he was exiled to Prague. Escalante returned to Cuba, where he died in the 1970s.

44. The rest of the conversation and quoted material are taken from Landau, "C. Wright Mills."

45. In Cuba, in 1960, Sartre had hoped to have at last found what he had been searching for: the synthesis of socialism and freedom, and the perfect coupling of theory and praxis. Yet, he was nonetheless concerned that a reign of terror had the potential to develop. By 1971, when he signed a letter of protest addressed to Fidel Castro on the subject of the Padilla affair, and Castro now looked upon Sartre as an enemy, Sartre "no longer had any illusions about Cuba." Simone de Beauvoir, *Adieux: A Farewell to Sartre*, trans. Patrick O'Brien (New York: Pantheon Books, 1984), 16.

46. Karol, *Guerrillas in Power*, 246.

47. Fidel Castro, "Words to Intellectuals," in *Fidel Castro Reader* (Melbourne, N.Y.: Ocean Press, 2008).

48. C. Wright Mills, *Listen, Yankee: The Revolution in Cuba* (New York: Ballantine Books, 1960), 142.

49. Juan Arcocha, "El viaje de Sartre," in *La Habana, 1952–1961: El final de un mundo, el principio de una ilusión*, ed. Jacobo Machover (Madrid: Alianza Editorial, 1995), 238–39. In January 1968 Sartre was invited as a delegate to the Cultural Congress of Havana, which was convened around the theme of the role of the intellectual and the place of culture in the revolutionary process and in Third World movements of national liberation. Sartre could not attend the congress for reasons of health, but

responded to several questions posed to him in an inquiry. Though Sartre addressed the topic of artistic culture in Cuba, he made reference only to influences *external* (North American) and *traditional* (Spanish) to Cuban culture, but avoided discussing *internal* pressures. He ends the inquiry my stating, "I also want to add that I would be very pleased to return to Cuba, and hope to meet with Fidel Castro, who for me, aside from being a great statesman, is also a friend," as quoted in "Encuesta a Jean-Paul Sartre," in Eduardo Torres-Cuevas, ed., *Sartre-Cuba-Sartre: Huracán, surco, semillas* (Havana: Imagen Contemporánea, 2005), 177. Was Sartre being disingenuous about his relationship with Castro and the issue of cultural freedom, or was Arcocha?

50. Arcocha, "El viaje de Sartre," 238–39. According to Duanel Díaz, Sartre's name, ever-present in literary and political discussions during the 1960s, disappeared almost completely from the Cuban media. For two decades, the philosopher was not published on the island, nor were his works included in the curricula of the universities. "El fantasma de Sartre en Cuba," *Cuadernos Hispanoamericanos* 679 (2007): 102. What is more, not only was Sartre not read in Cuba, he didn't even have the benefit of being earnestly critiqued because his philosophy was seen as an expression of the decadence of Western thought. See Aurelio Alonso, "De algo que Jean-Paul Sartre nos dio filosofando," in *Sartre-Cuba-Sartre: Huracán, surco, semillas*, ed., Eduardo Torres-Cuevas (Havana: Imagen Contemporánea, 2005), 249.

51. After a couple of years in Moscow, Arcocha was recalled to Havana, reassigned to the Cuban Embassy in Paris as a cultural attaché, and was later allowed to go into exile and settled in Paris. See Seymour Menton, *Prose Fiction of the Cuban Revolution* (Austin: University of Texas Press, 1975), 133. Arcocha recounts the details of his removal from his correspondent's position in Moscow: In 1963 when Castro paid his first visit to Russia, Arcocha had written a series of articles for *Revolución* that increasingly departed from the orthodox line. An official with the Soviet diplomatic corps told Castro that he found Arcocha's articles to be anti-Soviet and regarded them as a poor show of gratitude for the hospitality that the Cuban delegation had received in Russia. Later, Castro accused *Revolución* of engaging in bourgeois journalism. Juan Arcocha, *Fidel Castro en rompecabezas* (Madrid: Ediciones R, 1973), 51–54. Karol states that at first people thought that Castro merely had a grudge against Arcocha. "But it became clear soon afterward that it was *Revolución* as a whole that Castro disliked for its independent approach and its continual harking back to the libertarian spirit of the July 26 Movement." Karol, *Guerrillas in Power*, 284n78.

52. Juan Arcocha, "C. Wright Mills on Kennedy," *Fair Play*, August 26, 1961, 2.

53. Harvey Swados, "C. Wright Mills: A Personal Memoir," *Dissent* 10 (1963): 42.

54. C. Wright Mills, *The Marxists* (New York: Dell, 1962), 10.

55. C. Wright Mills, *The Sociological Imagination* (New York: Oxford University Press, 1959), 165.

56. Fuentes, *Casa*, 104.

A Note on the Interviews

1. K. S. Karol, *Guerrillas in Power: The Course of the Cuban Revolution*, trans. Arnold Pomerans (New York: Hill & Wang, 1970), 29. Though Mills refers to Escalona as a

"Captain," he was, in fact a *comandante*, a rank equivalent to major. A photo of Dermidio Escalona may be found at http://www.ecured.cu/index.php/Dermidio_Escalona.

2. The Cuban web-based encyclopedia EcuRed contains short biographies of Isabel Rielo and Dermidio Escalona.

3. This is generally true, since all of the interviewees, to one degree or another, seemed to support the Revolution at the time Mills spoke with them. What is more, most of them, if not in fact all of them, were involved in the resistance, either militarily or politically—as rebel soldiers or in the urban underground movement.

4. In addition, I provided my own English translations of all Spanish-language bibliographic sources referenced in the book.

Bibliography

Abrams, Arnold. "C. Wright Mills: Controversial Figure in Conforming Society." *Columbia Daily Spectator*, November 29, 1960.
Agee, James, and Walker Evans. *Let Us Now Praise Famous Men*. Boston: Houghton, Mifflin, 2001.
Alarcón, Ricardo. "The Return of C. Wright Mills at the Dawn of a New Era." *Critical Inquiry* 34 (2008): 376–84.
———. "Waiting for C. Wright Mills." *The Nation*, April 9, 2007.
Alonso, Aurelio. "De algo que Jean-Paul Sartre nos dio filosofando." In *Sartre-Cuba-Sartre: Huracán, surco, semillas*, edited by Eduardo Torres-Cuevas, 247–57. Havana: Imagen Contemporánea, 2005.
Arcocha, Juan. "C. Wright Mills on Kennedy." *Fair Play*, August 26, 1961.
———. "El viaje de Sartre." In *La Habana, 1952–1961: El final de un mundo, el principio de una ilusión*, edited by Jacobo Machover, 231–39. Madrid: Alianza Editorial, 1995.
———. *Fidel Castro en rompecabezas*. Madrid: Ediciones R, 1973.
Aronowitz, Stanley. *Taking It Big: C. Wright Mills and the Making of Political Intellectuals*. New York: Columbia University Press, 2012.
Artaraz, Kepa. *Cuba and Western Intellectuals since 1959*. New York: Palgrave Macmillan, 2009.
Barnes, Clare, Jr. *The Political Zoo*. Garden City, N.Y.: Doubleday, 1952.
———. *White Collar Zoo*. Garden City, N.Y.: Doubleday, 1949.
Beauvoir, Simone de. *Adieux: A Farewell to Sartre*. Translated by Patrick O'Brien. New York: Pantheon Books, 1984.
———. *Force of Circumstance*. Translated by Richard Howard. New York: G. P. Putnam, 1965.
Benítez, Fernando, Carlos Fuentes, Arnaldo Orfila Reynal, Víctor Flores Olea, Enrique González Pedrero, Jaime García Terrés, Francisco López Cámara, and Pablo González Casanova, "Letter to the Editor: Aftermath of Revolution." *Saturday Review*, January 21, 1961.
Berle, Adolf A. *Navigating the Rapids, 1918–1971*. Edited by Beatrice Bishop Berle and Travis Beal Jacobs. New York: Harcourt Brace Jovanovich, 1973.
Brennan, Ray. *Castro, Cuba, and Justice*. New York: Doubleday, 1959.
Casey, Michael J. *Che's Afterlife: The Legacy of an Image*. New York: Vintage Books, 2009.
Castro, Fidel. "Words to Intellectuals." In *Fidel Castro Reader*, 213–40. Melbourne, N.Y.: Ocean Press, 2008.

"The Causes of C. Wright Mills." North Hollywood, Calif.: Pacifica Radio Archives, No. BB0281b, October 1, 1962. KPFA broadcast. http://www.pacificaradioarchives.org/contact-us.

Caute, David. *The Fellow-Travelers: Intellectual Friends of Communism.* New Haven, Conn.: Yale University Press, 1973.

Conant, Michael B. "C. Wright Mills Talks, Yankee Listens." *Columbia Owl*, October 12, 1960.

———. "Reception at the Theresa." *Columbia Owl*, October 5, 1960.

Daniel, Jean. "Unofficial Envoy: An Historic Report from Two Capitals." *The New Republic*, December 14, 1963, 15–20.

de la Cova, Antonio Rafael. *The Moncada Attack: Birth of the Cuban Revolution.* Columbia: University of South Carolina Press, 2007.

Díaz, Duanel. "El fantasma de Sartre en Cuba." *Cuadernos Hispanoamericanos* 679 (2007): 93–102.

Draper, Theodore. *Castro's Revolution: Myths and Realities.* London: Thames and Hudson, 1962.

Dubois, Jules. "Apologia for Castro." *Saturday Review*, December 17, 1960.

———. *Fidel Castro: Rebel-Liberator or Dictator?* Indianapolis: The Bobbs-Merrill Co., 1959.

———. "Leftwing U.S. Prof Plumps for Fidel in Book." *Omaha World-Herald*, November 27, 1960.

———. "Report on Latin America." *Chicago Sunday Tribune*, November 20, 1960.

Eisenhower, Dwight D. *Crusade in Europe.* New York: Doubleday, 1948.

English, T. J. *Havana Nocturne: How the Mob Owned Cuba and Then Lost It to the Revolution.* New York: Morrow, 2007.

Fay, Stephen. "Liminal Visitors to an Island on the Edge: Sartre and Ginsberg in Revolutionary Cuba." *Studies in Travel Writing* 15 (2011): 407–25.

Ferlinghetti, Lawrence. "Poet's Notes on Cuba." *Liberation* 6 (1961): 10–14.

Foucault, Michel. *Discipline and Punish: The Birth of the Prison.* Translated by Alan Sheridan. New York: Vintage, 1995.

Franqui, Carlos. *Family Portrait with Fidel: A Memoir.* Translated by Alfred MacAdam. New York: Random House, 1984.

Free, Lloyd A. *Attitudes of the Cuban People toward the Castro Regime.* Princeton, N.J.: Institute for International Social Research, 1960.

Fuentes, Carlos. *Casa con dos puertas.* Mexico: Joaquin Mortiz, 1970.

———. *The Death of Artemio Cruz.* New York: Farrar, Straus and Giroux, 2001.

Gans, Herbert J. "Best-Sellers by American Sociologists: An Exploratory Study." In *Required Reading: Sociology's Most Influential Books*, edited by Dan Clawson, 19–27. Amherst: University of Massachusetts Press, 1998.

Gardner, Herb. *A Thousand Clowns.* New York: Random House, 1962.

Geary, Daniel. *Radical Ambition: C. Wright Mills, the Left, and American Social Thought.* Berkeley: University of California Press, 2009.

Gerhardt, Uta. *Talcott Parsons: An Intellectual Biography.* New York: Cambridge University Press, 2002.

Gerth, Hans, and C. Wright Mills. *Character and Social Structure: The Psychology of Social Institutions*. New York: Harcourt, Brace, 1953.

Goldsen, Rose Kohn. "Mills and the Profession of Sociology." In *The New Sociology: Essays in Social Science and Social Theory in Honor of C. Wright Mills*, edited by Irving Louis Horowitz, 88–93. New York: Oxford University Press, 1964.

Gómez Velásquez, Natacha. "La presencia de Sartre en las publicaciones Cubanas de la década del 60." In *Sartre-Cuba-Sartre: Huacán, surco, semillas*, edited by Eduardo Torres-Cuevas, 229–46. Havana: Imagen Contemporánea, 2005.

Gosse, Van. *Where the Boys Are: Cuba, Cold War America, and the Making of a New Left*. New York: Verso, 1993.

Guevara, Ché. *Socialism and Man in Cuba and Other Works*. London: Stage 1, 1968.

Hayden, Tom. *Listen, Yankee! Why Cuba Matters*. New York: Seven Stories Press, 2015.

Hollander, Paul. *Political Pilgrims: Travels of Western Intellectuals to the Soviet Union, China, and Cuba, 1928–1978*. New York: Oxford University Press, 1981.

Horowitz, Irving Louis. *C. Wright Mills: An American Utopian*. New York: Free Press, 1983.

Huberman, Leo, and Paul W. Sweezy. *Cuba: Anatomy of a Revolution*. New York: Monthly Review Press, 1960.

Hulme, Peter. "Seeing for Themselves: U.S. Travel Writers in Early Revolutionary Cuba." In *Politics, Identity, and Mobility in Travel Writing*, edited by Miguel A. Cabañas, Jeanne Dubino, Verónica Salles-Reese, and Gary Totten, 197–211. New York: Routledge, 2016.

Karol, K. S. *Guerrillas in Power: The Course of the Cuban Revolution*. Translated by Arnold Pomerans. New York: Hill & Wang, 1970.

Keen, Mike Forrest. *Stalking the Sociological Imagination: J. Edgar Hoover's FBI Surveillance of American Sociology*. Westport, Conn.: Greenwood Press, 1999.

Landau, Saul. "C. Wright Mills: The Last Six Months." *Ramparts*, August 1965, 46–54.

Lippmann, Walter. "From the Labor Youth League to the Cuban Revolution." In *History and the New Left: Madison, Wisconsin, 1950–1970*, edited by Paul Buhle, 107–12. Philadelphia: Temple University Press, 1990.

———. *Public Opinion*. New York: Free Press, 1997.

———. "U.S. Latin Policy Bigger Than Cuba." *St. Petersburg Times*, January 28, 1960.

Lockwood, Lee. *Castro's Cuba, Cuba's Fidel*. New York: Vintage Books, 1969.

Marshall, Barbara. "How Lilly Became Lilly!," *The Palm Beach Post*, April 7, 2013. Accessed January 8, 2016. http://www.palmbeachpost.com/news/news/local/how-lilly-became-lilly/nXFdF/.

Martínez Heredia, Fernando. "El mundo ideológico Cubano de 1959 a marzo de 1960." In *Sartre-Cuba-Sartre: Huracán, surco, semillas*, edited by Eduardo Torres-Cuevas, 199–220. Havana: Imagen Contemporánea, 2005.

Menton, Seymour. *Prose Fiction of the Cuban Revolution*. Austin: University of Texas Press, 1975.

Meyer, Karl E., and Tad Szulc. *The Cuban Invasion: The Chronicle of a Disaster*. New York: Praeger, 1962.

Miliband, Ralph. *The State in Capitalist Society*. London: Merlin Press, 1969.
Miller, James. *Democracy Is in the Streets: From Port Huron to the Siege of Chicago*. New York: Simon & Schuster, 1987.
Mills, C. Wright. *The Causes of World War Three*. New York: Simon & Schuster, 1958.
———. "The Cultural Apparatus." In *The Politics of Truth: The Selected Writings of C. Wright Mills*, edited by John H. Summers, 203–12. New York: Oxford University Press, 2008. Originally published in *The Listener* 61 (1959): 552–53, 556.
———. *Escucha, yanqui, la revolución en Cuba*. Translated by Julieta Campos and Enrique González Pedrero. Mexico City: Fondo de Cultura Económica, 1961.
———. "Letter to the New Left." *New Left Review* 5 (September–October 1960): 18–23.
———. "'Listen Yankee': The Cuban Case against the United States." *Harper's Magazine*, December 1960, 31–37.
———. *Listen, Yankee: The Revolution in Cuba*. New York: Ballantine Books, 1960.
———. "The Man in the Middle." In *The Politics of Truth: The Selected Writings of C. Wright Mills*, edited by John H. Summers, 173–83. New York: Oxford University Press, 2008. Originally published in *Industrial Design* 5 (1958): 72–76.
———. *The Marxists*. New York: Dell, 1962.
———. *The New Men of Power: America's Labor Leaders*. New York: Harcourt, Brace, 1948.
———. "On Latin America, the Left, and the U.S." *Evergreen Review* 5 (1961): 110–22.
———. *The Power Elite*. New York: Oxford University Press, 1956.
———. "The Sailor, Sex Market, and Mexican." *The New Leader* 26 (1943): 5–7.
———. *The Sociological Imagination*. New York: Oxford University Press, 1959.
———. "The Sociology of Mass Media and Public Opinion." In *Power, Politics, and People: The Collected Essays of C. Wright Mills*, edited by Irving Louis Horowitz, 577–98. New York: Oxford University Press, 1963.
———. *White Collar: The American Middle Classes*. New York: Oxford University Press, 1951.
Mills, C. Wright, and Saul Landau. "The House That Jack Must Build: Modest Proposals for Patriotic Americans." *London Tribune*, May 19, 1961.
Mills, C. Wright, Clarence Senior, and Rose Kohn Goldsen. *The Puerto Rican Journey: New York's Newest Migrants*. New York: Harper and Bros., 1950.
Mills, Charles Wright Papers, 1934–1965. Dolph Briscoe Center for American History. University of Texas at Austin.
Mills, Kathryn, with Pamela Mills, eds. *C. Wright Mills: Letters and Autobiographical Writings*. Berkeley: University of California Press, 2000.
Mins, Henry F. "A Budget of Books on Cuba." *Science and Society* 25 (1961): 338–46.
Nelson, Lowry. "Review of *Listen, Yankee*." *Annals of the American Academy of Political and Social Science* 336 (1961): 190–91.
Newfield, Jack. *A Prophetic Minority*. New York: New American Library, 1966.
Ochoa Sandy, Gerardo. *80 años, las batallas culturales del fondo*. Kindle edition. Mexico City: Nieve de Chamoy, 2014.
Peinado, Fermín. *Beware, Yankee: The Revolution in Cuba*. Miami, Fla.: privately printed, 1961.

Phillips, Ruby Hart. *Cuba: Island of Paradox*. New York: McDowell, Obolensk, 1959.
Pike, Fredrick B. "United States Military Aid and Policies and Cuba." *Review of Politics* 23 (1961): 415–17.
Porter, Charles, O., and Robert J. Alexander. *The Struggle for Democracy in Latin America*. New York: Macmillan, 1961.
"A Program of Covert Action against the Castro Regime." *Foreign Relations of the United States, 1958–1960, vol. 6. Cuba Document* (Washington, D.C.: U.S. Department of State).
Quirk, Robert E. *Fidel Castro*. New York: W. W. Norton, 1993.
Randall, Margaret. *Cuban Women Now: Interviews with Cuban Women*. Toronto: Women's Press, 1974.
Rasenberger, Jim. *The Brilliant Disaster: JFK, Castro, and America's Doomed Invasion of Cuba's Bay of Pigs*. New York: Scribner, 2011.
Roa Kourí, Raúl. *En el torrente*. Havana: Casa de las Américas, 2004.
Rojas, Rafael. "Anatomía del entusiasmo: La revolución como espectáculo de ideas." *América Latina Hoy* 47 (2007): 39–53.
———. "Charles Wright Mills y otoros peregrinos." *El País*, April 15, 2007.
———. "El aparato cultural del imperio: C. Wright Mills, la Revolución Cubana y la Nueva Izquierda." *Perfiles Latinoamericanos* 44 (2014): 7–31.
———. *Fighting over Fidel: The New York Intellectuals and the Cuban Revolution*. Princeton, N.J.: Princeton University Press, 2016.
Roosevelt, Eleanor. "New Look at Cuba." *New York Post*, December 14, 1960.
Sallah, Michael, and Mitch Weiss, eds. *The Yankee Comandante: The Untold Story of Courage, Passion, and One American's Fight to Liberate Cuba*. Guilford, Conn.: Lyons Press, 2015.
Sartre, Jean-Paul. *Sartre on Cuba*. New York: Ballantine Books, 1961.
———. *Sartre visita a Cuba*. Havana: Ediciones R, 1960.
Sarusky, Jaime. "Sartre en Cuba." In *Sartre-Cuba-Sartre: Huracán, surco, semillas*, edited by Eduardo Torres-Cuevas, 221–28. Havana: Imagen Contemporánea, 2005.
Schweid, Richard. *Che's Chevrolet, Fidel's Oldsmobile: On the Road in Cuba*. Chapel Hill: University of North Carolina Press, 2004.
Sinclair, Marianne. *Viva Che!: Contributions in Tribute to Ernesto "Che" Guevara*. London: Lorrimer Publishing, 1968.
Strug, David L. "Witnessing the Revolution: North Americans in Cuba in the 1960s." *International Journal of Cuba Studies* 4 (2012): 68–78.
Summers, John H. "The Epigone's Embrace, Part II: C. Wright Mills and the New Left." *Left History* 12 (2008): 94–127.
Swados, Harvey. "C. Wright Mills: A Personal Memoir." *Dissent* 10 (1963): 35–42.
Szulc, Tad. "Cuban Television's One-Man Show." In *The Eight Art*, edited by Robert Lewis, 197–206. New York: Holt, Rinehart and Winston, 1962.
Taber, Robert. "Castro's Cuba." *The Nation*, January 23, 1960.
———. "Cuban Viewpoints: Kennedy and C. Wright Mills." *Fair Play*, September 2, 1960.
———. *M-26: Biography of a Revolution*. New York: Lyle Stuart, 1961.

Thomas, Hugh. *Cuba, or The Pursuit of Freedom*. New York: Da Capo Press, 1998.
Thompson, E. P. *E. P. Thompson and the Making of the New Left: Essays and Polemics*. Edited by Cal Winslow. New York: Monthly Press Review, 2014.
Tietchen, Todd F. *The Cubalogues: Beat Writers in Revolutionary Havana*. Gainesville: University Press of Florida, 2010.
Treviño, A. Javier. "C. Wright Mills as Designer: Personal Practice and Two Public Talks." *American Sociologist* 45 (2015): 335–60.
———. *The Social Thought of C. Wright Mills*. Thousand Oaks, Calif.: Sage Publications, 2012.
Trotsky, Leon. *The Permanent Revolution*. Seattle, Wash.: Red Letter Press, 2010.
Viguera-Moreno, Asel, and Yisel González-González. "Acercamiento histórico a las prácticas psicológicas en la Universidad de Oriente durante el período prerrevolucionario (1947–1958)." *Santiago*, Special Issue (2012): 135–51.
Wakefield, Dan. "Introduction." In *C. Wright Mills: Letters and Autobiographical Writings*, edited by Kathryn Mills with Pamela Mills, 1–18. Berkeley: University of California Press, 2000.
Waters, Mary-Alice, ed. *Marianas in Combat: Teté Puebla and the Mariana Grajales Women's Platoon in Cuba's Revolutionary War, 1956–58*. New York: Pathfinder Press, 2003.
Weber, Max. *From Max Weber: Essays in Sociology*. Edited by Hans Gerth and C. Wright Mills. New York: Oxford University Press, 1946.
Welch, Richard E. *Response to Revolution: The United States and the Cuban Revolution, 1959–1961*. Chapel Hill: University of North Carolina Press, 1985.
Wilke, James W., and Edna Monzón Wilke. *Frente a la revolución Mexicana: 17 protagonistas de la etapa constructiva*, vol. 1. Mexico City: Universidad Autónoma Metropolitana, 1995.
Wilson, Sloan. *The Man in the Gray Flannel Suit*. New York: Simon & Schuster, 1955.
Youdovin, Ira S. "$50 Million Suit is Filed against Mills." *Columbia Daily Spectator*, February 13, 1961.
Zeitlin, Maurice. "Political Generations in the Cuban Working Class." *American Journal of Sociology* 71 (1966): 493–508.

Index

Agee, James, 139–41
agrarian reform, 27–28, 56, 74, 100, 107, 147
Agrarian Reform Law, 27, 28, 204n28
Americans for Democratic Action (ADA), 149–50, 167, 214n71
anticommunism, 74, 75, 78, 96, 125, 156, 157, 159, 171, 214n71
Árbenz, Jacobo, 31, 214n75
Arcocha, Juan: on Castro, 54–57, 112–13, 123, 128; on Cuban Communist Party, 58–59; as interpreter, 4, 5, 15, 49, 54, 153, 202n36, 205n41, 206n52, 206n54; on Mills, 51, 118, 123, 130, 143; Mills's interview with, 53–62, 198n3, 198n7, 198n10, 199n14, 209n33, 210n41; and *Revolución*, 51, 53, 172, 219n51; on Sartre, 128, 172
Aronowitz, Stanley, 43

Ballantine, Ian, 4, 138–43, 145, 163, 212n40, 213n41
Ballantine Books, 138, 143, 149, 151, 168, 169
Baran, Paul A., 199n14
Barletta, Amadeo, 168–69
Batista, Fulgencio: defeat of, 23, 24, 68, 202n7; tyranny of, 3, 7, 17, 18–19, 20, 22, 23, 74–75, 91, 96, 148, 151
Batista Benitez, Elba Luisa, 17, 51, 99–108, 137, 183
Batistianos, 7, 23, 31, 200, 204n25
Bay of Pigs invasion, 3, 17, 30, 32, 129, 137, 153, 154, 156, 172, 206n49, 207n10
Beals, Carleton, 131
Beauvoir, Simone de, 15, 29, 54, 116, 170–72, 193n24, 208n13

Belic (village), 17, 21, 125, 209n28
Berle, Adolf A., Jr., 34, 41, 110, 153, 155, 156, 165–68, 172, 217n20
Beware, Yankee: The Revolution in Cuba (Peinado), 148
Brennan, Ray, 7, 8, 199n11

Camilo Cienfuegos School City, 9, 17, 26, 53, 69–72, 201n31
campesinos, 16, 22, 52, 72, 88, 93, 99, 100, 116, 135, 136, 193n27, 208n22
Carmichael, Stokely, 134
Castro, Fidel: and Arcocha, 53–55, 57, 198n2, 219n51; and Bay of Pigs invasion, 31–33, 199n15; and communism, 82, 125, 129, 147, 173, 174, 199n12, 217n34; and Eisenhower, 11, 29, 31, 199n15; Mills's meetings with, 1, 4, 15, 16, 110, 115, 118–22, 123–24, 138; personality of, 55, 57, 85, 87, 124, 125, 126–28, 198n3, 198n9, 198n10, 207n11, 209n33, 210n41; popularity of, 215n90; and *The Power Elite*, 109; and Sartre, 42, 170, 193n24, 218n45, 219n49; and Soviet Union, 29, 30, 199n13
Castro, Raúl, 8, 21, 42, 111, 201n35, 205n35
Castro's Cuba, Cuba's Fidel (Lockwood), 140
Catholicism, 54, 94, 98, 123, 205n37, 205n38
Causes of World War Three, The (Mills), 2, 40, 44, 138, 143, 159
Central Intelligence Agency (CIA): attempted assassination of Castro by, 123; and Bay of Pigs invasion, 151,

227

Central Intelligence Agency (cont.) 155, 172, 207n10; and Cuban exiles, 11, 199n15
charisma, 26, 55, 117, 123, 126–27; routinization of, 127
Chicago Tribune, 8, 109, 146
Columbia Daily Spectator (student newspaper), 166
Columbia Owl (student newspaper), 144
Columbia University, 4, 13, 14, 16, 138, 144, 160, 163, 164, 165
Communists, 8, 9, 18, 28, 47, 58, 75, 79, 88, 92, 94, 95, 154, 158, 198n11, 218n43
Conant, Michael B., 144
Contacting the Enemy (Mills), 44, 205n38, 211n9
Cosío Villegas, Daniel, 152
Counterrevolution: and anticommunism, 125; dynamics of, 11; and invasion, 30, 155; as sentiment, 10, 46, 78, 80, 97, 98, 99, 156
Cousins, Norman, 164
Crime of Cuba, The (Beals), 124
Crusade in Europe (Eisenhower), 87
Cuba: Anatomy of a Revolution (Huberman and Sweezy), 8, 146
Cuba: Island of Paradox (Phillips), 191n9
Cubalogue, 132, 210n6
Cuban Communist Party: and Batista's government, 74, 75; infiltration of, 58; influence of, 47, 58, 77, 95, 170; organization of, 47, 79, 94; and Revolution, 79
Cuban exiles, 5, 11, 30, 31, 33, 66, 123, 156, 164, 199n15, 201n25, 202n37, 217n14
Cuban Missile Crisis, 199n13, 210n49

Daniel, Jean, 151
democracy, 40, 55, 60, 64, 74, 126, 128, 158; direct, 37, 55, 60, 128, 199n14; guided, 60, 199n14; participatory, 37

Díaz Lanz, Pedro Luis, 200n24, 201n33
Dorticós, Osvaldo, 28, 51
Draper, Theodore, 46, 52, 99, 134, 138, 157, 216n91
Dubois, Jules, 8, 23, 89, 109, 146–47, 160, 164, 166, 215n90
Dulles, Allen W., 34, 156, 164
Durkheim, Émile, 138

Eisenhower, Dwight D.: administration of, 10, 12, 33, 175; and Bay of Pigs invasion, 31, 151, 199n15; and Castro, 29, 31; farewell address, 12; foreign policy, 12; and Mills, 125, 204n19
El Mundo (newspaper), 130, 169
English, T. J., 169
Escalante, Aníbal, 170, 218n43
Escalona, Dermidio, 16, 51, 53, 73–75, 183, 184, 201n35, 202n36, 219n1, 220n2
Escobar, Elvira: and Catholicism, 98; and Communist Party, 94–95; and freedom, 126–27; and intellectuals, 92–93; Mills's interview with, 88–99; and Moncadistas, 20, 76, 89, 90, 91; and Santiago uprising, 92
Escucha, yanqui: La revolucíon en Cuba (Mills), 151–54, 170
"Escucha otra vez, yanqui" (Mills), 153–54, 167, 170, 215n88
Evans, Walker, 124–25, 139, 140, 141

Fair Play for Cuba Committee (FPCC), 4, 13, 15, 16, 144, 149, 152, 163, 165
Federal Bureau of Investigation (FBI), 129, 154, 160, 162, 163–65, 168, 210n48, 216n4
Ferlinghetti, Lawrence, 14, 51
Fiallo Barrero, Lauro, 17, 51, 99, 100, 105, 107, 108, 183
Fidelistas, 7, 23, 24, 42, 47, 49, 69, 72, 89, 103, 104, 105, 107, 125, 204n25, 208n22
Flores Olea, Víctor, 40, 147

Fondo de Cultura Económica, 152–53, 215n77, 215n79, 215n83
France-Soir (newspaper), 149, 203n15
Franqui, Carlos, 14, 15, 51, 55
Free, Lloyd A., 215n90
freedom, 3, 7, 36, 39, 48, 51, 82, 83, 96–97, 126–27, 166, 171, 174, 218n45, 219n49
From Max Weber: Essays in Sociology (Gerth and Mills), 33
Fuentes, Carlos, 14, 40, 147, 152, 164, 168, 175, 215n80

Gans, Herbert J., 145, 213n51
García Terrés, Jamie, 40, 147
Gardner, Herb, 141, 142, 212n37
Geary, Daniel, 129, 191n4
Gerth, Hans H., 11, 25, 30, 33, 122, 126, 194n10, 209n39
Ginsberg, Allen, 14, 144, 145
González Pedrero, Enrique, 40, 147
Gosse, Van, 22, 131, 145, 211n9
Granma (boat), 17, 21, 68, 76, 90, 125, 204n26
Grau, Ramón, 18–19, 21, 74, 97, 203n9
Guantánamo Bay, 22, 157, 194n6
Guerra, Ramiro, 43, 197n33
Guevara, Ernesto "Ché": as intellectual, 48, 193n24; and Marxism, 48, 197n44; Mills's discussions with, 1, 2, 9; and "new man," 37–38, 195n11; and Sartre, 193n24

Harper's (magazine), 146, 148, 213n56, 214n65
Hart, Armando, 8, 9, 15, 22, 42, 51
Havana: Castro's triumphal entry into, 25, 26, 198n7, 202n7; May Day in, 31, 129; Mills in, 15, 16
Hayden, Tom, 43, 110, 210n42, 211n21
Hemingway, Ernest, 15, 77, 131
History Will Absolve Me (Castro), 20, 111, 204n24
Hoffman, Wendel, 22

Hoover, J. Edgar, 164
Horowitz, Irving Louis, 10, 125, 131
Hotel Riviera, 15, 16, 193n27
Hotel Theresa, 124, 143–44, 213n48
Howl (Ginsberg), 145
"How to Improve Relations with Cuba and South America" (Mills speech), 149, 167
Huberman, Leo, 8–10, 13, 25, 42, 100, 116, 146, 191n6, 200n16, 209n24, 209n28, 209n39
Hulme, Peter, 132

intellectuals: as change agents, 3, 38–40, 43; Cuban, 38, 42, 43, 47, 48, 77, 81–82, 93; as liberal obfuscators, 41; Mexican, 40, 77, 147; Mills's interviews with, 1, 43, 99, 197n35
interviewing, 3, 9, 44–52, 152; questions, 4, 7–8, 9, 44–46, 48, 50, 53, 57, 72, 89; rules for, 45, 51, 115, 152
Isle of Pines, 1, 4, 16, 21, 23, 110–11, 113, 122, 137, 201n33, 207n8, 207n9, 207n10

Karol, K. S.: and Castro, 117, 207; friendship with Mills, 16, 124, 131, 169
Keen, Mike Forrest, 160
Kennedy, John F.: and Bay of Pigs invasion, 33, 167; and Castro, 31; Mills's criticisms of, 126, 153, 156, 163, 167, 170, 172
Kennedy administration, 33, 41, 165, 167, 170
Khrushchev, Nikita, 11, 58, 60, 61, 129, 199n16
King, Martin Luther, Jr., 134, 145, 217n20

La Coubre (ship), 29–30, 137, 138, 212n26
Landau, Saul, 2, 15, 44, 49, 123, 150, 153, 154, 167, 168, 169, 210n3
Lansky, Meyer, 193n27
"Letter to the New Left" (Mills), 43

Index 229

Let Us Now Praise Famous Men
 (Agee and Evans), 125, 139, 141
Lewis, Oscar, 14, 215n79
liberal obfuscators, 41, 150, 153, 156–57, 170
Liebow, Elliot, 145
Lippman, Walter, 25, 199n14
Listen Yankee: The Revolution in Cuba (Mills): criticism of, 5, 8, 52, 131, 132, 145–49, 164; goals of, 41, 43, 46, 131, 158, 173, 211n21; impact of, 145; FBI investigation of, 162–63, 164; production of, 4, 117, 139, 140, 143, 144; publication of, 5, 132, 139, 140, 145, 168; translations of, 118, 170; style, 133, 137, 138, 140, 143
Lockwood, Lee, 115, 140, 207n5, 208n16, 208n22
Lonely Crowd, The (Riesman, et al), 145

Machado, Gerardo, 18–19, 43, 81, 111, 124, 197n32, 205n39
Mafia, 11, 123, 169, 217n14
Mañach, Jorge, 43, 81, 197n32
Manzanillo, 1, 16, 17, 27, 69, 76, 88, 90, 100, 101, 102, 105, 106, 124, 183, 206n56
Mariana Grajales (women's batallion), 68, 72, 201n27
Martí, José, 43, 64, 197n33
Marx, Karl, 37, 48, 129, 212n32
Marxism, 6, 48, 125, 160; plain, 48; sophisticated, 48; vulgar, 48, 173
Marxists, The (Mills), 48, 174
Masferrer, Rolando, 164, 216n14
Matos, Huber, 28, 73, 125, 184, 201n33
Matthews, Herbert, 21, 156
Mella, Julio Antonio, 198n6, 199n12
Mexico, 6, 21, 35, 44, 77, 125, 147, 151, 160, 167, 204n26
Meyer, Karl E., 33, 125, 165
Mikoyan, Anastas, 29, 58, 199n13
Miliband, Ralph, 124, 168, 215n80
Mills, C. Wright: with Castro, 15, 16, 110, 111–22, 123–24; on Eisenhower, 87, 125; in Havana, 15–16; on intellectuals, 38–43, 99–100; on interviewing, 44–52; on Kennedy, 34, 153–54, 156, 163; on leadership, 127–28; photographs, 15, 17, 111, 114, 115, 116, 121, 124, 139, 140, 141, 142; preparations for Cuba, 6–10, 13; on revolution, 25, 122; and Sartre, 149, 170–71, 173; on sociology, 18, 35, 36; and Taber, 13, 16, 47, 51, 54, 131; and Vallejo, 16, 49, 54, 109, 111, 122, 123, 124–25
Miró Cardona, José, 23, 92, 125, 155, 204n29, 215n89
Moncada attack, 19–20, 73, 76, 85, 89, 90, 91, 111, 148
Morgan, William Alexander, 194n6, 202n35
"Mr. Hadley," 4, 160–63
Mujal, Eusebio, 74, 202n38

National Institute of Agrarian Reform (INRA), 28, 49, 51, 63, 77, 112, 120, 124, 125, 206n57, 206n58, 208n21
nationalization, 9, 10
Nebbishes, The (comic strip), 141–42, 212n37
Nelson, Lowry, 146
New Left, 42, 43, 110, 123, 133, 145, 149, 158, 196n28
new man, 37–38, 195n11
New Men of Power, The (Mills), 38
New York Times, 21, 22, 156, 192n9, 198n8
Nietzsche, Friedrich, 82
Nixon, Richard M., 110, 200n17, 205n35

Oltuski, Enrique, 9, 42, 51, 120, 208n21
Orfila Reynal, Arnaldo, 147, 151, 154
Oriente (province), Mills's interviews in, 16, 62
Ortiz, Fernando, 43, 197n33, 212n28
overdeveloped society, 39, 93, 132, 159
Oxford University Press, 140, 142, 143

Padilla, Heberto, 198n2, 203n16, 218n45
País, Frank, 21, 22, 76, 92, 97, 204n26, 204n27
Peinado, Fermín, 147–48, 214n65, 214n66, 215n90
permanent revolution, 79, 203n8
Phillips, Ruby Hart, 26, 192n9, 198n5, 198n11
Pike, Fredrick B., 146, 166
Pinar del Río (province), 16, 53, 73, 110, 123, 183, 209n24
Playa Girón, 32, 137, 207n10
Political Zoo, The (Barnes), 142
Portell Vilá, Herminio, 148–49
Porter, Charles O., 148–49, 168, 217n34
Port Huron Statement, The, 43, 145
power elite, 12, 40, 109, 138, 158, 170–71, 207n3
Power Elite, The (Mills), 1, 34, 49, 87, 109, 140, 159, 175, 192n13, 195n8, 206n1, 215n77
Presidio Modelo (prison), 21, 111, 119, 201n33
Prío, Carlos, 19, 21, 74, 75, 81, 97
properly developing society, 39, 158, 174, 196n18
Puerto Rican Journey, The (Mills, Senior, Goldsen), 7, 44, 99
Pursuit of Loneliness, The (Slater), 145

Randall, Margaret, 201n28
Rebel Army, 17, 22, 23, 24, 62–64, 68, 69–70, 118, 197n1, 200n18, 206n56
Revolución (newspaper), 14, 51, 53, 55, 56, 59, 144, 169, 172, 203n16, 219n51
Rielo, Isabel, 17, 50, 51, 53, 67–73, 136, 183, 184, 201n28, 201n31, 201n32, 220n2
Riesman, David, 145
Roa, Raúl, 32, 43, 76, 81, 93, 197n32, 204n30
Roa Kourí, Raúl, 9, 13, 93, 145, 192n15, 204n31, 213n55

Rojas, Rafael, 7, 13, 158, 192n21, 212n28, 213n54, 215n83
Roosevelt, Eleanor, 149–51, 214n75
Rousseau (ranch owner), 100, 103, 104, 105, 106, 107, 183, 206n49, 206n58

Sánchez, Celia, 68, 76, 87, 93, 107, 116
Santamaría, Haydée, 15, 19, 68
Santiago de Cuba: Mills's interviews in, 76, 77, 88; uprising in, 21, 76, 90, 91, 204n26
Sartre, Jean-Paul: and Arcocha, 172; on Castro, 19, 198n7, 218n45, 218n49; on direct democracy, 55, 60, 199n14; on fieldworkers, 200n23; and Guevara, 192n24; as intellectual, 14; and *La Coubre*, 211n26; on large estates, 100; and Mills, 149, 170–72, 173, 192n21; on Oltuski, 205n38; on revolutionary time, 126
Sartre on Cuba (Sartre), 149, 203n15
Sartre visita a Cuba (Sartre), 203n15
Saturday Review, 147, 164
Schlesinger, Arthur M., Jr., 34, 41, 153, 156, 157, 163, 172
Schwartz, Louis B., 150
Schweid, Richard, 169
Scott-Heron, Gil, 198n5
Servicio de Inteligencia Militar (SIM), 97, 205n36
Shapiro, Samuel, 166–67
Sierra Maestra: Castro in, 23, 109, 201n35, 208n22; Mills's visit to, 17, 26, 67, 69
Silva Herzog, Jesús, 153
Slater, Philip, 145
Smith, Earl E. T., 23, 110, 156
socialism, 9, 38, 42, 125, 150, 171, 196n18, 218n45
Sociological Imagination, The (Mills), 1, 18, 35, 140, 159, 193n29, 193n1, 195n1, 195n6, 197n37, 197n39, 215n77, 219n55
sociological poetry, 139–40
sociology, 1, 5, 18, 36, 127, 139, 146, 159, 164, 217n34

Index 231

Soviet Union (USSR): and Cuba, 11, 30, 125, 173, 199n16; Mills's travel to, 160, 170, 216n4; U.S. relations with, 12
Stalin, Josef, 54, 86, 87, 128
Stalinism, 42, 59, 82, 110, 156, 159, 171
Stettmeier, Franz: and Castro, 77, 81–83, 84–87, 127; and Communists, 79; and Cuban intellectuals, 81, 82; and counterrevolution, 78, 80; Mills's interview with, 16, 49, 50, 51, 76–88, 127, 139; and *The Power Elite*, 49, 175; on Sartre, 84
Stevenson, Adlai, 32, 41, 131, 151
Stone, I. F., 144, 156
Struggle for Democracy in Latin America, The (Porter and Alexander), 217n34
Swados, Harvey, 158, 173
Sweezy, Paul M., 8–10, 13, 25, 42, 100, 116, 146, 191n6, 200n16, 209n24, 209n28, 209n39
Szulc, Tad, 33, 125, 156, 165, 198n8

Taber, Robert: and Castro, 22; and Mills, 13, 16, 17, 47, 51, 131
Tally's Corner (Liebow), 145
Texas, 7, 35, 49, 123
Thomas, Hugh, 200n18
Thompson, E. P., 144, 167, 202n5
A Thousand Clowns (Gardner), 141, 212n37
tiempo muerto, 65, 200n23
Tietchen, Todd F., 210n6
Time magazine, 40, 61, 138, 215n89
Topaz (film), 213n48
Trejo, Rafael, 43, 99, 197n32, 205n39
Trotsky, Leon, 79, 203n8
Trujillo, Rafael, 23, 169

truth, 13, 34, 40, 41, 48, 49, 61, 86, 95, 130, 132, 138, 145, 146, 147, 149, 174, 175; plain, 48, 175; politics of, 41, 174
26th of July Movement: against Batista, 7, 20, 21; and Cuban Communist Party, 58, 95; as political party, 9, 47, 59, 77, 79, 83, 94

United Fruit Company, 32, 207n3
University of Havana, 18, 42, 54–55, 56, 57, 72, 81, 99, 148, 197n32
University of Oriente, 76, 77, 88, 93, 183, 202n5
Urban Reform Law, 27, 204n28
Urrutia, Manuel, 125

Vallejo, René C.: and Castro, 16; and Mills, 16, 27, 49, 109, 122, 123, 124, 125
Viñales Valley, 16, 110, 123

Wakefield, Dan, 157, 166
Weber, Max, 33, 34, 127
Welch, Richard, E., Jr., 145
West Nyack, New York, 138, 160–62, 168, 175
White Collar: The American Middle Classes (Mills), 1, 34, 37, 39, 44, 138, 139, 140, 159, 195n9
White Collar Zoo (Barnes), 212n40
White Paper on Cuba (Schlesinger), 157, 216n91
"Words to Intellectuals" (Castro speech), 171

Yankee, 133–35
Yepe, Manuel E., 123, 209n24

Envisioning Cuba

A. JAVIER TREVIÑO, *C. Wright Mills and the Cuban Revolution: An Exercise in the Art of Sociological Imagination* (2017).

ANTONIA DALIA MULLER, *Cuban Émigrés and Independence in the Nineteenth-Century Gulf World* (2017).

JENNIFER L. LAMBE, *Madhouse: Psychiatry and Politics in Cuban History* (2017).

DEVYN SPENCE BENSON, *Antiracism in Cuba: The Unfinished Revolution* (2016).

MICHELLE CHASE, *Revolution within the Revolution: Women and Gender Politics in Cuba, 1952–1962* (2015).

AISHA K. FINCH, *Rethinking Slave Rebellion in Cuba: La Escalera and the Insurgencies of 1841–1844* (2015).

CHRISTINA D. ABREU, *Rhythms of Race: Cuban Musicians and the Making of Latino New York City and Miami, 1940–1960* (2015).

ANITA CASAVANTES BRADFORD, *The Revolution Is for the Children: The Politics of Childhood in Havana and Miami, 1959–1962* (2014).

TIFFANY A. SIPPIAL, *Prostitution, Modernity, and the Making of the Cuban Republic, 1840–1920* (2013).

KATHLEEN LÓPEZ, *Chinese Cubans: A Transnational History* (2013).

LILLIAN GUERRA, *Visions of Power in Cuba: Revolution, Redemption, and Resistance, 1959–1971* (2012).

CARRIE HAMILTON, *Sexual Revolutions in Cuba: Passion, Politics, and Memory* (2012).

SHERRY JOHNSON, *Climate and Catastrophe in Cuba and the Atlantic World during the Age of Revolution* (2011).

MELINA PAPPADEMOS, *Black Political Activism and the Cuban Republic* (2011).

FRANK ANDRE GURIDY, *Forging Diaspora: Afro-Cubans and African Americans in a World of Empire and Jim Crow* (2010).

ANN MARIE STOCK, *On Location in Cuba: Street Filmmaking during Times of Transition* (2009).

ALEJANDRO DE LA FUENTE, *Havana and the Atlantic in the Sixteenth Century* (2008).

REINALDO FUNES MONZOTE, *From Rainforest to Cane Field in Cuba: An Environmental History since 1492* (2008).

MATT D. CHILDS, *The 1812 Aponte Rebellion in Cuba and the Struggle against Atlantic Slavery* (2006).

EDUARDO GONZÁLEZ, *Cuba and the Tempest: Literature and Cinema in the Time of Diaspora* (2006).

JOHN LAWRENCE TONE, *War and Genocide in Cuba, 1895–1898* (2006).

SAMUEL FARBER, *The Origins of the Cuban Revolution Reconsidered* (2006).

LILLIAN GUERRA, *The Myth of José Martí: Conflicting Nationalisms in Early Twentieth-Century Cuba* (2005).

RODRIGO LAZO, *Writing to Cuba: Filibustering and Cuban Exiles in the United States* (2005).

ALEJANDRA BRONFMAN, *Measures of Equality: Social Science, Citizenship, and Race in Cuba, 1902–1940* (2004).

EDNA M. RODRÍGUEZ-MANGUAL, *Lydia Cabrera and the Construction of an Afro-Cuban Cultural Identity* (2004).

GABINO LA ROSA CORZO, *Runaway Slave Settlements in Cuba: Resistance and Repression* (2003).

PIERO GLEIJESES, *Conflicting Missions: Havana, Washington, and Africa, 1959–1976* (2002).

ROBERT WHITNEY, *State and Revolution in Cuba: Mass Mobilization and Political Change, 1920–1940* (2001).

ALEJANDRO DE LA FUENTE, *A Nation for All: Race, Inequality, and Politics in Twentieth-Century Cuba* (2001).

www.ingramcontent.com/pod-product-compliance
Lightning Source LLC
Chambersburg PA
CBHW030536230426
43665CB00010B/915